The Essential
Robert Burns

Ann Matheson

Text © Ann Matheson, 2014.
First published in the United Kingdom, 2014, by Alloway Publishing,
an imprint of Stenlake Publishing Ltd

54-58 Mill Square,
Catrine, Ayrshire, KA5 6RD
Telephone: 01290 551122
www.stenlake.co.uk

ISBN 9780907526971

**The publishers regret that they cannot supply
copies of any pictures featured in this book.**

Acknowledgements

Thanks to Kate Reilly.

Picture Acknowledgements

7 Margaret Miller.
9 Margaret Miller.
11 Margaret Miller.
13 Victorian etching by E. P. Brandard from a painting by J. Ramage.
16 Margaret Miller.
23 Victorian etching.
28 Victorian etching by E. Scriven from a painting by J. M. Wright.
39 Edwardian postcard.
47 Victorian etching by E. Scriven from a painting by J. M. Wright.
53 Margaret Miller.
61 Victorian etching by F. W. Topham from a painting by J. M. Wright.
67 Irvine Burns Club.
83 Margaret Miller.
93 Victorian etching by E. Scriven from a painting by J. M. Wright.
98 Margaret Miller.
105 Margaret Miller.
112 Margaret Miller.
120 Victorian etching by J. Rogers from a painting by J. M. Wright.
121 (above) Irvine Burns Club.
121 (below) Margaret Miller.
122-128 Irvine Burns Club.

131 Victorian etching.
135 Margaret Miller.
138 Margaret Miller.
143 Victorian etching.
144 Victorian etching by G. J. Stodart from a painting by S. McKenzie.
148 Margaret Miller.
151 Victorian etching.
152 Victorian etching by S. Smith from a painting by J. M. Wright.
153 Margaret Miller.
161 Margaret Miller.
165 Margaret Miller.
168 Margaret Miller.
171 Margaret Miller.
172 Margaret Miller.
174 Margaret Miller.
179 Margaret Miller.
181 Margaret Miller.
183 Margaret Miller.
188-191 Irvine Burns Club.
192 Victorian etching by G. J. Stodart from the statue by G. E. Ewing.

Selected Bibliography

Robert Burns, Donald A. Low
Myths of Robert Burns, Carol McGuirk (*The History of Scottish Literature Volume 2*, ed. Cairns Craig)
Scottish Poetry, A Critical Survey, ed. James Kinsley
Burns in his time, Alan Dent
Scottish Literature, Duncan Glen
The Life of Robert Burns, Catherine Carswell
The Scottish Tradition in Literature, Kurt Wittig
Robert Burns, The Complete Poetical Works, ed. James A. MacKay
The Best Laid Schemes, Robert Crawford and Christopher MacLachlan
Robert Burns and the Sentimental Era, Carol McGuirk
Selected Poems, Carol McGuirk

Contents

Introduction
THE MAN AND THE POET

What is the popular perception of Robert Burns? Was he a poetic genius, a man of the people, sexual predator, tragic figure? There is certainly plenty of evidence to support all of these. What he was not was a 'heaven-taught ploughman'. He was uncommonly well-educated for his day and his poetic genius was honed by craftsmanship and informed by the early education he received from his father and John Murdoch, his teacher and tutor.

As to his status as a 'man of the people', there is no doubt, for he reminds us of his social class, its miserable unrewarded toil, its rich culture, warmth and solidarity, in practically every poem. Nevertheless, he was firmly on the side of the landowners when it came to the Patronage Act of 1711 – 'to restore the Patrons (i.e. the landowners) to their ancient Rights of presenting Ministers to the Churches vacant in that Part of Great Britain called Scotland.' This Act robbed the ordinary people of the congregation of their hard-won right to elect their own ministers. In his poem, *The Holy Tulzie*, he refers to the people as 'brutes'[1] who elected their own 'herds'[2] (ministers). He also seeks and enjoys the company of the sophisticated upper classes whom he denigrates in so many of his poems. And who knows what may have happened if he had emigrated to Jamaica as he intended? Would he have become a slave owner on a plantation – or would he have turned revolutionary and supported the slaves?

His reputation as a vigorously sexual man speaks for itself and, if the lassies were willing, like Annie of the Corn Rigs who needed only 'sma' persuasion to agree to her night of passion, he cannot be labelled as a predator.

There is, however, no doubt that his private life had perhaps more than its fair share of misery. Shortage of money, frequent illness, back-breaking toil on sour farms during several years of incredibly bad weather, rejection and loss were his constant lot – and he died when he was only 37.

Rightly, much has been made of Burns, but the vernacular poets who preceded him have been neglected. Foremost among these was Robert Fergusson, whose life was even shorter and more tragic. Following a head injury, Fergusson was committed to Bedlam, the Edinburgh madhouse, where he died on a filthy bed of straw at the age of 24. Burns freely acknowledges his debt to him, for it was from reading Fergusson's poetry that Burns was fired to write in Scots and several of the themes of Fergusson's poems were the inspiration for his own.

THE POETIC FORMS

Burns uses three traditional types of stanza: his favourite, the Habbie stanza, the Christis Kirk stanza and the Cherrie and Slae stanza.

The Habbie stanza was revived in 1640 when Robert Sempill wrote a humorous epitaph for Habbie Simson, the piper of Kilbarchan in Renfrewshire, but its European origins are from the 12th and 13th centuries.

[1] Brutes – cattle.
[2] Herds – herdsman.

The Elegy for Habbie Simson was printed in Watson's *Choice Collection of Comic and Serious Scots Poems* in 1706 and the poet Allan Ramsay christened the form 'Standart Habby'. This is the final verse:

Alace! for him my heart so sair,	Alas! for him my heart is sore
For of his spryngis I got a skair,	For of his lively tunes I got a share
At everie play, race, feist, and fair,	At every play, race, feast and fair
Bot gyle or greid;	Without guile or greed;
We need not luke for pyping mair	We need not look for piping more
Sen Habbie's deid.	Since Habbie's dead.

Burns made such frequent use of Habbie stanza that many people refer to it as Burns stanza. The Christis Kirk stanza has nine lines with a 'bob' at the end. It dates back to the 15th century poem, *Christis Kirk on the green*:

Was never in Scotland hard nor sene	(There) Was never in Scotland heard nor seen
Sic dansing nor deray	Such dancing and harmless fun
Nouthir at Falkland on the grene	Neither at Falkland on the green
No Pebillis at the play	Nor Peebles at the play
As wes of wowaris as I ween	As the patrons enjoyed, I imagine
A Christis Kirk on ane day:	At Christ's Church on a day
There came out Kitties washen clean	The wenches came out washed clean
In thair new kitillis of gray,	In their new grey frocks
Full gay	Very gay
At Christis Kirk of the grene that day	At Christ's Church of the Green that day

It was printed as a broadside ballad c1701, 'Newly Corrected according to the Original Copy', which merged the two final lines into 'Full gay that day'.

As the original poem celebrated a riotous gathering, this form was an appropriate choice for Burns's 'Holy Fair' and 'Halloween'.

The Cherrie and Slae, by Alexander Montgomerie, first appeared in print in 1597:

The dew as diamondis did hing,	The dew like diamonds did hang,
Upon the tender twistis, and sing,	Upon the tender twigs, and sing,
Ouir-twinkling all the treis:	Over-twinkling all the trees:
And ay quhair flowris flourischit faire,	And always where the flowers flourished fair,
Thair suddainly I saw repaire,	There suddenly I saw repair,
In swarmes, the sownding beis:	In swarms, the sounding bees:
Sum sweitly hes the hony socht,	Some sweetly have the honey sought,
Quhil they war cloggit soir:	Until they were clogged up:
Sum willingly the waxe hes wrocht,	Some willingly have wrought wax,
To heip it up in stoir:	To heap it up in store:
So heiping, with keiping,	So heaping, with keeping,
Into thair hyvis they hyde it:	Into their hives they hide it:
Precyselie, and wyselie,	Precisely and wisely,
For winter they provyde it.	For winter they provide it.

Although Burns uses this stanza rarely, he does so to great effect in '*The Jolly Beggars*', as well as in his '*Epistle to Davie*'.

SCOTTISH LIFE IN BURNS'S DAY

'I dinna ken muckle about the law', answered Mrs Howden: *'but I ken, when we had a king, and a chancellor, and parliament-men o' our ain, we could aye pebble them wi' stanes when they werena gude bairns – But naebody's nails can reach the length o' Lunnon'* [1]

Walter Scott, *The Heart of Midlothian*, ch 4

As this quotation illustrates, many Scots were not in favour of the Union of the Parliaments in 1707, because faraway London became the centre of power and Scotland lost its autonomy. Scotland was, and arguably still is struggling to establish its own identity. It has been suggested that the Jacobite Rebellions of 1715 and 1745 were partly an expression of this struggle and several of Burns's poems echo this nationalistic yearning.

The economic and social conditions of ordinary people were also in a state of flux. Starting in the second half of the 18th century, the Agricultural Revolution brought radical changes to the way people lived. Until then, most people were subsistence farmers, working the land in the runrig system and living in small hamlets called fermtouns. The introduction of new crops, like turnips and sown grasses, meant that cattle could be over-wintered and this led to large-scale enclosing of the fields. New machinery meant that fewer men were needed and the landlords ruthlessly cleared people from the land in both the Lowlands and the Highlands. The country was teeming with beggars who were unable to find work. Ordinary people were very poor, living in hovels, shared with the animals and the stinking tub of urine that was needed to shrink the woollen cloth. Throughout Burns's poetry, there are references to this life, sometimes idealised and always highlighting poverty and inequality.

LANGUAGE

Up to the 18th century, people of all classes spoke Scots. The infamous judge, Lord Braxfield, is quoted as saying, *'Ye're a verra clever chiel, man but ye wad be nane the waur o a hingin'*.[2]

Memoirs of Sir Walter Scott, ch 48

When power shifted to London, ambitious Scots who wanted to 'get on' in the world went to classes in Edinburgh to eradicate the 'Scotticisms' from their speech. This cultural climate was not one that nurtured vernacular poetry. Paradoxically, this was also a period of great intellectual flowering in Scotland: *'Here I stand at what is called the Cross of Edinburgh and can, in a few minutes, take fifty men of genius and learning by the hand'*. (William Smellie 1800, quoting 'Mr Amyat, King's Chemist, a most sensible and agreeable English gentleman').

---

[1] 'I don't know much about the law', answered Mrs Howden: 'but I know, when we had a king and a chancellor and parliament men of our own, we could always pebble them with stones when they weren't good children – but nobody's nails can reach the length of London'.

[2] 'You're a very clever fellow, but you would be none the worse of being hanged'.

These men of genius were part of the great European Enlightenment: philosophers, scientists, lawyers, ministers, academics – and writers, the Literati, who wrote in Augustan English. When Burns attempted this, his poems mostly fell flat because he was an early victim of what G Gregory Smith, developing TS Eliot's original concept, described as 'dissociation of sensibility' – that Scottish writers wrote in English but continued to feel in Scots.

It is often surprising how little of the Scots language can be found in many of the poems. His range of language, however, is astonishing: Scots, Scots-English, English, Biblical, pulpit oratory – all often peppered with Classical allusions, agriculturally technical and legal references.

THE BURNS CULT

Following his death, a Burns cult was quick to emerge. Like the Bible, Burns could be quoted selectively to support divergent points of view and much of his work was admired for superficial reasons and kailyard sentimentality. The poet Robert Garioch was quite vicious in his condemnation of Scots whose facile nationalism blossomed only at Murrayfield or Burns Suppers:

'…they are wont to wash down haggis with whisky in honour of Robert Burns, and by the natural reaction of these national chemicals, preceeding within their paunches, generate a sententious aromatic fume that dislodges from their brains their little stock of platitudes.'

Hugh MacDiarmid, while acknowledging Burns's genius, also despised the uncritical adulation of Burns cult followers on whom he frequently vented his comic satire.

> *Mair nonsense has been uttered in his name*
> *Than in ony's barrin liberty and Christ.*

Hugh MacDiarmid *'A Drunk Man Looks at the Thistle'*

It is not the intention of this book to create yet another 'Immortal Memory' and risk adding to the 'nonsense'. The aim of this book is to make a selection of Burns's poems more accessible to readers who have little or no Scots. All the Scots poems have been transcribed into English, with full explanations of words and phrases that might seem obscure or present difficulty.

The poems are arranged chronologically so that they can be related to the major events in his life and the reader is encouraged to engage with the views expressed by the poet and to consider the poems in context.

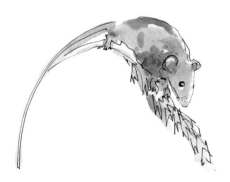

Handsome Nell (1774)

'I remember I composed it in a wild enthusiasm of passion…', said Burns of his first venture into poetry in 1774, when he was just 15. His 'muse' was Nelly Kilpatrick, the 14-year-old 'bonie, sweet, sonsie lass'[1] who was his partner in the harvest field. Burns wrote the words to be sung to a tune, '*I am a man unmarried*', allegedly Nell's favourite reel[2]. While it was not unusual for young men to sing songs to their sweethearts, it was highly unusual for a young man of that time to be able to write the words for a song, simply because most young men received little or no formal education. Burns, however, was not a simple peasant's son. From the age of 6, he had been tutored in reading, writing, grammar and arithmetic.

Like most people of his day, Burns spoke in Scots most of the time, with English reserved for theological discussion of the 'English' Bible or business matters. In most of his poems, Scots and English sit comfortably with each other, the rhymes often produced from using both languages. Notice verses 3 and 4 where the only Scots words are e'e, to rhyme with 'me', and a' to rhyme with 'flaw'. Verse 1 and the last two verses are wholly in English. This mixter-maxter of Scots and English is typical of most of his poetry.

At this time, the Burns family lived a life of incredible hardship and poverty at Mount Oliphant, a 75 acre farm outside Ayr. The soil was poor, there was no money to invest in the land and the threatening demands of the factor made life wretched for the whole family.

O, once I lov'd a bonnie lass,
Ay, and I love her still!
And, whilst that virtue warms my breast,
I'll love my handsome Nell.

O, once I loved a bonnie lass,
Yes, and I love her still
And as long as virtue warms my breast
I'll love my handsome Nell.

As bonnie lasses I hae seen,
And mony full as braw,
But for a modest gracefu' mien
The like I never saw.

I have seen some bonnie lasses
And many just as beautiful
But for a modest graceful demeanour,
The like I never saw.

A bonnie lass, I will confess,
Is pleasant to the e'e,
But without some better qualities
She's no a lass for me.

A pretty girl, I will confess,
Is pleasant to the eye
But without some better qualities,
She's not the girl for me.

But Nelly's looks are blythe and sweet,
And what is best of a'
Her reputation is complete,
And fair without a flaw.

But Nelly's looks are cheerful and sweet,
And what is best of all-
Her reputation is complete,
And fair without a flaw.

She dresses aye sae clean and neat,
Baith decent and genteel:
An' then there's something in her gait
Gars ony dress look weel.

She dresses always so clean and neat,
Both decent and genteel:
And then there's something in her gait
Makes any dress look well.

---

[1] Well-favoured, healthily attractive.
[2] Unfortunately, the tune has not survived.

A gaudy dress and gentle air
May slightly touch the heart;
But it's innocence and modesty
That polishes the dart.

'Tis this in Nelly pleases me,
'Tis this enchants my soul!
For absolutely in my breast
She reigns without control.

Mary Morison (1782)

From 1777 until William Burness's death in 1784, the Burns family lived at Lochlea in Tarbolton parish. To help out financially, Robert and his brother Gilbert rented a field to grow flax in and Robert went to Irvine to learn flax-dressing. The whole enterprise collapsed when the flax shop went up in flames in 1781 and everything was lost. At the same time, his father was seriously ill and suffering from the repercussions of an ongoing dispute about rents that was finally settled in his favour at the Court of Session in Edinburgh. Despite the miseries of ill-health, punishingly hard work and litigation, Robert managed to make a social life for himself. He founded the Tarbolton Bachelors' Club (1780) and joined the Masons (1781).

Mary Morison is arguably one of Burns's finest songs, even although it was written when he was only 23.

The first verse affirms that poverty and the exhausting slavery of work would be tolerable if he could win Mary Morison's love. The lines 'A weary slave frae sun to sun' suggest an experience of things beyond Scotland.

In verse 2, as the company of dancers moves through the hall, the lover is oblivious to everything but the love object. The 'trembling' string of the violins is almost a sympathetic echo of the lover's emotions, as he sits, not joining in, seeing , yet not seeing, other women because he was obsessed with only one.

When Hugh MacDiarmid was asked what he thought to be the finest line Burns ever wrote, his response was, 'Ye are na Mary Morison'. The understatement of the line serves to emphasise the overwhelming compulsive power of love.

Verse 3 sees the poet addressing the beloved in a traditional love-sick way: 'If you can't love me in return, at least pity me.' The last two lines, however, are a masterpiece of poetic economy.

O Mary, at thy window be!	O Mary at your window be!
It is the wish'd, the trysted hour.	It is the wished, the appointed hour.
Those smiles and glances let me see,	Those smiles and glances let me see,
That make the miser's treasure poor,	That make the miser's treasure poor,
How blithely wad I bide the stoure,	How cheerfully would I endure the struggle
A weary slave frae sun to sun,	A weary slave from sun to sun,
Could I the rich reward secure –	If I could secure the rich reward –
The lovely Mary Morison.	The lovely Mary Morison.
Yestreen, when to the trembling string	Yesterday evening, when to the trembling string
The dance gaed thro the lighted ha',	The dance travelled through the lighted hall,
To thee my fancy took its wing,	To thee my fancy took its wing,
I sat, but neither heard nor saw:	I sat, but neither heard nor saw:
Tho' this was fair, and that was braw,	Though this one was fair and another beautiful,
And yon the toast of a' the town,	And that one the toast of the whole town,
I sigh'd and said amang them a' –	I sighed and said among them all –
'Ye are na Mary Morison!'	'You're not Mary Morison!'

O Mary canst thou wreck his peace
Wha for thy sake wad gladly die[1]?
Or canst thou break that heart of his
Whase only faut is loving thee?
If love for love thou wilt na gie,
At least be pity to me shown:
A thought ungentle canna be
The thought o' Mary Morison.

O Mary, can you wreck his peace
Who, for your sake, would gladly die?
Or can you break that heart of his
Whose only fault is loving you?
If love for love you will not give,
At least show me some pity:
An ungentle thought cannot be
The thought of Mary Morison.

[1] Notice that 'die' in l.2 has to be pronounced 'dee' in Scots.

The Rigs o Barley (1782)

In 18th century Scotland the land was cultivated communally in long raised strips or rigs, separated by ditches. This was known as the run-rig system ('ridge and furrow' in England). Farmers rented these rigs from the landowner. In Burns's time, this system was coming to an end as the Agricultural Revolution got under way and fields were enclosed.

Lammas, August 1st, was traditionally a 'quarter day', when farm workers were forced to attend a hiring fair to be looked over by potential employers and hired for the next term. It would have been a day of intense stress and insecurity for the farm labourers – but what release and celebration there must have been when the business was done.

The rigs o barley are transformed from the place of slavish labour into a trysting place; they have become bonnie.

The atmospheric conditions are perfect: the wind still, the moon so full that the sky remains blue, dotted with stars. Most importantly, the lassie is willing: *'wi sma persuasion she agreed'* (a delightful touch of humorous understatement!) Small wonder the lover considers this night to have been worth more than all life's other pleasures put together! This is no ethereal, idealised love, but lusty, earthy, honest passion that has set the world in a spin.

Allegedly, the young woman who inspired it was Annie Ronald, a neighbour's daughter.

It was upon a Lammas night,
  When corn rigs are bonnie,
Beneath the moon's unclouded light,
  I held awa to Annie;
The time flew by, wi tentless heed;
  Till, 'tween the late and early,
Wi sma' persuasion she agreed
  To see me thro the barley.

Chorus:
  Corn rigs, an barley rigs,
  An corn rigs are bonnie:
I'll ne'er forget that happy night,
  Amang the rigs wi Annie.

The sky was blue, the wind was still,
  The moon was shining clearly.
I set her down, wi right good will,
  Amang the rigs o barley:
I ken't her heart was a' my ain;
  I lov'd her most sincerely;
I kiss'd her owre and owre again,
  Amang the rigs o barley.

It was on a Lammas night
  When corn rigs are bonnie
Beneath the moon's unclouded light
  I went to meet Annie.
The time flew by unnoticed
  Till between the late and early
With little persuasion she agreed
  To see me through the barley.

  Corn rigs and barley rigs
  And corn rigs are bonnie.
I'll never forget that happy night
  Among the rigs with Annie.

The sky was blue, the wind was still,
  The moon was shining clearly.
I set her down with right good will
  Among the rigs of barley.
I knew her heart was all my own
  I loved her most sincerely.
I kissed her over and over again
  Among the rigs of barley.

Chorus

I lock'd her in my fond embrace;
  Her heart was beating rarely:
My blessings on that happy place,
  Amang the rigs o barley!
But by the moon and stars so bright,
  That shone that hour so clearly!
She aye shall bless that happy night
  Amang the rigs o barley.

Chorus

I hae been blythe wi comrades dear;
  I hae been merry drinking;
I hae been joyfu gath'rin gear;
  I hae been happy thinking:
But a' the pleasures e'er I saw,
  Tho three times doubl'd fairly –
That happy night was worth them a',
  Amang the rigs o barley.

I locked her in my fond embrace,
  Her heart was beating rarely.
My blessings on that happy place,
  Among the rigs of barley!
But by the moon and stars so bright,
  That shone that hour so clearly!
She'll always bless that happy night
  Among the rigs of barley!

I have been cheerful with dear friends
  I have been merry drinking
I have been joyful gathering wordly goods
  I have been happy thinking.
But all the pleasures ever I saw
  Though three times doubled fairly
That happy night was worth them all
  Among the rigs of barley.

The Death and Dying Words of Poor Mailie (1782)

In this year, Burns became acquainted with Robert Fergusson's poetry and was inspired by the strength and vitality of Fergusson's imagination and the natural Scots with which he expressed it. Burns decided this was the way forward for him. He said, *"Rhyme I had given up; but meeting with Fergusson's Scotch poems, I strung anew my wildly-sounding rustic lyre with emulating vigour."*

This is Burns's earliest poem in sustained Scots. The mock elegy was not new in Scots poetry. Hamilton of Gilbertfield's *'Last Dying words of Bonny Heck, a famous greyhound in the shire of Fife'* appeared in Allan Ramsay's *Tea-table Miscellany* in 1724.

Beast fables are also traditional in European literature, the poems of Robert Henryson in the 15th century providing Scotland's finest examples of the genre. *'Poor Mailie'* is a descendant of both traditions.

Many of the themes, treated comically in this poem, are ones which Burns addresses more seriously and mournfully elsewhere. Comic reduction perhaps helps to make personal pain more objective and therefore more tolerable. This poem, despite its very playful tone, makes serious comment on moral and psychological issues.

The poem was actually written long before Mailie did die, but the incident is recorded by Gilbert Burns. Robert had bought the ewe with her two lambs from a neighbour and Hughoc did indeed report the incident with so much agitation and drama that Burns was inspired to record it in verse – even although Mailie was rescued and lived for some time afterwards!

The Death and Dying words of Poor Mailie

The Author's Only Pet Yowe:
(An Unco Mournfu' Tale)

As Mailie, an' her lambs thegither,
Was ae day nibblin on the tether,
Upon her cloot she coost a hitch,
An' owre she warsl'd in the ditch:
There, groanin, dying, she did lie,
When Hughoc he cam doytin by.

Wi' glowrin een, an' lifted han's
Poor Hughoc like a statue stan's;
He saw her days were near-hand ended,
But, wae's my heart! He could na mend it!
He gaped wide, but naething spak.
At length poor Mailie silence brak:-

The author's only pet ewe
(A very mournful tale)

As Mailie and her lambs together
Was one day nibbling on the hair rope
Her hoof became tangled in the rope
And she floundered in the ditch[1].
There groaning, dying, she did lie
When Hughoc[2] came wandering aimlessly[3] by.

With glowering eyes, and lifted hands
Poor Hughoc like a statue stands;
He saw her days were almost ended
But, alas, he could do nothing about it!
His mouth gaped wide but said nothing
At length poor Mailie broke the silence:-

---

[1] Warsle also implies a wrestling effort to try to right herself.

[2] Little Hugh. The 'oc' suffix added to an object or proper name means 'little' e.g. bullock, hillock.

[3] 'Wandering aimlessly' does not convey the 'daftness' implicit in the word 'doyt'. To say someone is doytit means their mind is a bit wandered as well as their feet.

'O thou, whase lamentable face
Appears to mourn my woefu' case!
My dying words attentive hear,
An' bear them to my Master dear.

'Tell him, if e'er again he keep
As muckle gear as buy a sheep –
O, bid him never tie them mair,
Wi' wicked strings o' hemp or hair!
But ca' them out to park or hill,
An' let them wander at their will:
So may his flock increase, an' grow
To scores o' lambs, an' packs o' woo'!
'Tell him, he was a Master kin',
An' ay was guid to me an' mine;
An' now my dying charge I gie him,
My helpless lambs, I trust them wi' him.

'O, bid him save their harmless lives,
Frae dogs, an' tods, an' butchers' knives!
But gie them guid cow-milk their fill,
Till they be fit to fend themsel;
An' tent them duly, e'en an' morn,
Wi' teats o' hay an' ripps o' corn.

'An' may they never learn the gaets,
Of ither vile, wanrestfu' pets –
To slink thro' slaps, an' reave an' steal,
At stacks o' pease, or stocks o' kail!
So may they, like their great forbears,
For monie a year come thro' the sheers:
So wives will gie them bits o' bread,
An' bairns greet for them when they're dead.

'My poor toop-lamb, my son an' heir,
O, bid him breed him up wi' care!
An' if he live to be a beast,
To pit some havins in his breast!
An' warn him – what I winna name –
To stay content wi' yowes at hame;
An' no to rin an' wear his cloots,
Like other menseless, graceless brutes.

'An' niest, my yowie, silly thing,
Gude keep thee frae a tether string!
O, may thou ne'er forgather up
Wi' onie blastit, moorland toop;

'O thou, whose lamentable face
Appears to mourn my woeful case!
Listen attentively to my dying words
And bear them to my dear master.

Tell him, if ever again he has
As much wealth as would buy a sheep
O tell him never to tie them up again
With wicked strands of hemp or hair
But drive them out to park or hill
And let them wander at their will
So may his flock increase and grow
To scores of lambs and packs of wool!
Tell him he was a kind master
And always was good to me and mine
And now I give him my dying charge,
My helpless lambs I entrust to him.

O bid him save their harmless lives
From dogs, and foxes and butchers' knives
But give them their fill of good cows' milk
Until they're fit to fend for themselves
And tend them duly, evening and morning,
With morsels of hay and handfuls of corn.

And may they never learn the ways
Of other vile, restless pets
To slink through gaps in walls and steal
At stacks of peas or stalks of cabbage!
So may they, like their great forebears
For many a year continue to be shorn
So women will give them bits of bread
And children weep for them when they die.

My poor tup lamb, my son and heir
O, bid him bring him up with care!
And if he lives to become a beast
To put some good sense in his breast
And warn him – what I will not name –
To stay content with ewes at home,
And not to run and wear out his hooves
Like other foolish, graceless brutes.

And next my little ewe, silly thing
God keep you away from a tether rope!
O, may you never become intimate
With any blasted moorland ram

But ay keep mind to moop an' mell,
Wi' sheep o' credit like thysel!

'An' now, my bairns, wi' my last breath,
I lea'e my blessin wi' you baith:
An' when you think upo' your mither,
Mind to be kind to ane anither.
'Now, honest Hughoc, dinna fail,
To tell my master a' my tale;
An' bid him burn this cursed tether,
An' for thy pains thou'se get my blether.'
This said, poor Mailie turn'd her head,
An' clos'd her een amang the dead!

But always take care to keep company and mingle
With well-bred sheep like yourself!

And now, my children, with my last breath
I leave my blessing with you both
And when you think of your mother
Take care you're kind to one another.
Now, honest Hughoc, do not fail
To tell my master all my tale
And bid him burn this cursed tether
And, for your pains you'll get my bladder[4].'
This said, poor Mailie turned her head
And closed her eyes among the dead!

[4] Although sheep bladders have, in the course of history, been used to make bag-pipes, condoms, floats and whiskey 'flasks', it is not known what value or usefulness Mailie's bladder might hold for the recipient! Whatever the case, the gift is inspirationally comic.

Green Grow the Rashes O (1784)

You can imagine this one being belted out in the Tarbolton Bachelors' Club, which Burns founded in 1780. One of the rules was: 'Every man proper for a member of this Society must have a frank, honest, open heart; above anything dirty or mean; and must be a professed lover of one or more of the female sex…'

This song, in its honest exuberance and enthusiasm for the opposite sex, is surely a hearty endorsement of the rule. Verse 5 is frequently quoted in a 'Toast tae the Lasses' at Burns' suppers. This toast is traditionally a gentle satire which can be totally overturned by the sentiments in the final verse.

Chorus
Green grow the rashes, O;
Green grow the rashes, O;
The sweetest hours that e'er I spend,
Are spent among the lasses, O.

Green grow the rushes, O
Green grow the rushes, O
The sweetest hours I ever spend
Are spent among the lasses, O.

1.
There's nought but care on ev'ry han',
In every hour that passes, O:
What signifies the life o' man,
An' 'twere na for the lasses, O.

There's nought but care on every hand
In every hour that passes, O
What is a man's life worth
If it were not for the lasses, O.

2.
The war'ly race may riches chase,
An' riches still may fly them, O;
An' tho' at last they catch them fast,
Their hearts can ne'er enjoy them, O.

The worldly race may chase riches
And riches still may elude them, O
And though at last they catch them fast,
Their hearts can never enjoy them, O.

3.
But gie me a cannie hour at e'en,
My arms about my dearie, O,
An' war'ly cares an' war'ly men
May a' gae tapsalteerie, O!

But give me a pleasant evening hour
My arms about my dear one, O
And wordly cares and wordly men
May all go topsy-turvy, O!

4.
For you sae douce, ye sneer at this;
Ye're nought but senseless asses, O;
The wisest man the warl' e'er saw,
He dearly lov'd the lasses, O.

For you, who are so sedate you sneer at this
You're nothing but senseless asses, O
The wisest man the world ever saw
He dearly loved the lasses, O.

5.
Auld Nature swears, the lovely dears
Her noblest work she classes, O:
Her prentice han' she try'd on man,
An' then she made the lasses, O.

Old Nature swears, the lovely dears
To be her noblest work she classes, O
Her apprentice hand she tried on man
And then she made the lasses, O.

Death and Dr. Hornbook (1785)

A hornbook was a primer for children, it consisting of a sheet of paper with the letters of the alphabet, mounted on a board and covered with a piece of very thin transparent horn.

For local people, it would not have been difficult to find out that Burns was directing this brillliant satire at the Tarbolton schoolmaster, John Wilson. To augment his paltry teacher's income, John had set up a small grocer's shop. Despite his lack of knowledge, he set himself up as an expert in medical matters, advertising that 'Advice would be given in common orders at the shop gratis'. There, cynically, he also sold medicines.

Burns met him at the masonic lodge where his pedantry had so bored the poet that he had invited him to, 'sit down, Dr. Hornbook'. In the poem, Burns inflates him to enormous proportions – so that he can then cut him right down to size.

Apart from its satiric content, this poem is simply very funny, almost a laugh a line. Notice in verses 3, 4 and 5 the hilarious self-mockery he adopts to convince the reader of his sobriety. It is also a marvellous example of 18th century colloquial speech, which is appropriate for the intimacy of the conversation.

The story

The storyteller is the worse for drink. As he lurches about, he meets 'something' – something long and reedy with a scythe over one shoulder and a big three-pronged poacher's fork over the other. The drunk greets him almost with a 'Hello Jimmy, how's it gaun?' and asks him if he'd been mowing (well, what else would you ask a man carrying a scythe?). When the creature introduces himself as 'Death', the terrified drunkard, in a great show of bravado, whips out his knife. Death tells him to put the puny thing away, they shake hands and settle down for a tête-a-tête.

Death chats about his job, but he has a bitter complaint. For all his 6,000 years of experience, someone is putting him out of business. He describes, with hilarious irony, how Hornbook's medicines have robbed him of customers and made the tools of his trade useless. Burns's biting ridicule of Hornbook escalates: how he diagnoses ailments at a distance and has erudite Latin names for the most ordinary items. The drunkard remarks that the graveyards will be empty, but the final comic reduction of Hornbook reveals that he kills off 20 for every one Death gets rid of. After giving a few humorous examples of this (note his ironic use of conventional euphemisms for death), Death vows he'll get even – but the kirk bell reminds him that it's time to go.

Some books are lies frae end to end,	Some books are lies from end to end
And some great lies were never penn'd:	And some great lies were never penned
Ev'n ministers, they ha'e been kenn'd,	Even ministers have been known
In holy rapture,	In holy rapture
A rousing whid, at times, to vend,	Sometimes to tell a big whopper
And nail't wi' Scripture.	And confirm it with Scripture.

But this that I am gaun to tell,
Which lately on a night befel,
Is just as true's the Deil's in Hell
   Or Dublin-city:
That e'er he nearer comes oursel
   'S a muckle pity.

The Clachan yill had made me canty,
I was na fou, but just had plenty;
I stacher'd whyles, but yet took tent ay
   To free the ditches;
An' hillocks, stanes, and bushes, kenn'd ay
   Frae ghaists an' witches.

The rising moon began to glow'r
The distant Cumnock hills out-owre:
To count her horns with a' my pow'r,
   I set mysel;
But whether she had three or four,
   I could na tell.

I was come round about the hill,
And todlin down on Willie's mill,
Setting my staff with a' my skill,
   To keep me sicker
Tho' leeward whyles, against my will,
   I took a bicker.

I there wi' something did forgather,
That put me in an eerie swither;
An awfu' scythe, out-owre ae shouther,
   Clear-dangling, hang;
A three-taed leister on the ither
   Lay, large an' lang.

Its stature seem'd lang Scotch ells twa,
The queerest shape that e'er I saw,
For fient a wame it had ava:
   And then, its shanks,
They were as thin, as sharp an' sma'
   As cheeks o' branks.

"Guid-een," quo' I; "Friend, hae ye been mawin,
When ither folk are busy sawin?"
It seem'd to mak a kind o' stan',
   But naething spak;
At length, says I, "Friend, whare ye gaun?
   Will ye go back?"

But this that I am going to tell
Which lately on a night befell
Is just as true as the Devil's in Hell
   Or Dublin city
That ever he comes closer to us
   Is a great pity.

The village ale had made me merry
I wasn't drunk, but just had plenty
I staggered occasionally, but was always careful
   To avoid the ditches
I could differentiate between small hills, stones –
   And ghosts and witches.

The rising moon began to glower
Out over the distant Cumnock hills
To count her horns with all my power
   I set myself
But whether she had three or four
   I couldn't tell.

I had come round about the hill
And walking unsteadily down on Willie's mill
Setting my staff with all my skill
   To keep me steady
Though sideways, occasionally, against my will
   I took a quick lurching movement.

There, I met something
That made me shake in my shoes.
An awful scythe over one shoulder
   Dangling clear, hang –
A three pronged fork[1] on the other
   Lay large and long.

It seemed about eight feet tall
The queerest shape I ever saw
For it had no stomach at all
   And then, its legs
They were as thin, as sharp and small
   As the narrow sides of a bridle.

'Good evening, said I,' 'Friend have you been mowing
When other folk are busy sowing?'
It seemed to make a kind of stand
   But said not a word
At length, said I, 'Friend where are you going?'
   Will you go back?'

[1] The leister is usually used to spear salmon.

It spak right howe, – "My name is Death,
But be na fley'd." – Quoth I, "Guid faith,
Ye're may be come to stap my breath;
    But tent me, billie;
I red ye weel, tak care o' skaith,
    See, there's a gully!"

"Guidman," quo' he, "put up your whittle,
I'm no design'd to try its mettle;
But if I did, I wad be kittle
    To be mislear'd,
I wad nae mind it, no that spittle
    Out-owre my beard."

"Weel, weel!" says I, "a bargain be't;
Come, gies your hand, an' sae we're gree't;
We'll ease our shanks an' tak a seat:
    Come, gie's your news!
This while ye hae been mony a gate
    At mony a house.

"Ay, ay!" quo' he, an' shook his head,
"It's e'en a lang, lang time indeed
Sin' I began to nick the thread,
    An' choke the breath:
Folk maun do something for their bread,
    An' sae maun Death.

"Sax thousand years are near hand fled
Sin' I was to the butchering bred,
An' mony a scheme in vain's been laid,
    To stap or scar me;
Till ane Hornbook's ta'en up the trade,
    An' faith, he'll waur me.

"Ye ken Jock Hornbook i' the Clachan,
Deil mak his kings-hood in a spleuchan!
He's grown sae weel acquaint wi' Buchan
    An' ither chaps,
The weans haud out their fingers laughin
    And pouk my hips.

"See, here's a scythe, and there's a dart,
They hae pierc'd mony a gallant heart;
But Doctor Hornbook, wi' his art
    And cursed skill,
Has made them baith no worth a fart,
    Damn'd haet they'll kill.

It spoke in a hollow, guttural voice – 'My name is Death
But don't be afraid.' Said I, 'Good Faith,
Maybe you've come to stop my breathing
    But listen to me, boyo!
I'm warning you, watch out or you'll get hurt
    See, there's a big knife.

'Mister,' said he, 'put away your knife,
I'm not designed to test its strength
But if I did I would be provoked
    Into being a bit mischievous
I would not mind it, not that useless thing[2]
    Over my beard.'

'Well, well', said I, 'a bargain be it,
Come, give me your hand, so we're agreed
We'll ease our legs and take a seat
    Come, give me your news!
Recently you've been out and about a lot
    At many a house.

'Yes, yes!' said he, and shook his head
It's been a long, long time indeed
Since I began to cut the thread
    And choke the breath
Folk must do something to earn their bread
    And so must Death.

'Six thousand years are almost fled
Since I was to the butchering bred
And many a scheme's been laid in vain
    To stop or scare me
Till one Hornbook's taken up the trade
    And faith, he'll get the better of me.

You know John Hornbook in the village
May the Devil make his stomach into a tobacco pouch
He's become so well acquainted with Buchan[3]
    And other chaps
The children hold out their fingers laughing
    And pluck at my hips.

See, here's a scythe, and there's a dart,
They have pierced many a gallant heart
But Doctor Hornbook, with his art
    And cursed skill,
Has made them both not worth a fart
    They would kill nothing.

---

[2] The knife.

[3] 'Buchan's Domestic Medicine' was a book that professed a cure for all domestic ailments.

"'Twas but yestreen, nae farther gane,
I threw a noble throw at ane;
Wi' less, I'm sure, I've hundreds slain;
    But-deil-ma-care,
It just play'd dirl on the bane,
    But did nae mair.

"Hornbook was by, wi' ready art,
And had sae fortify'd the part,
That when I looked to my dart,
    It was sae blunt,
Fient haet o't wad hae pierc'd the heart
    Of a kail-runt."

"I drew my scythe in sic a fury,
I near-hand cowpit wi' my hurry,
But yet the bauld Apothecary
    Withstood the shock;
I might as weel hae tried a quarry
    O' hard whin rock."

"Ev'n them he canna get attended,
Although their face he ne'er had kend it,
Just shite in a kail-blade, and send it,
    As soon's he smells't,
Baith their disease, and what will mend it,
    At once he tells't."

"And then a' doctor's saws and whittles,
Of a' dimensions, shapes, an' mettles,
A' kinds o' boxes, mugs, an' bottles,
    He's sure to hae;
Their Latin names as fast he rattles
    As A B C."

"Calces o' fossils, earths, and trees;
True *sal-marinum* o' the seas;
The *farina* of beans and pease,
    He has't in plenty;
Aqua-fortis, what you please,
    He can content ye.

"Forbye some new, uncommon weapons,
Urinus spiritus of capons;
Or mite-horn shavings, filings, scrapings,
    Distill'd *per se*;
Sal-alkali o' midge-tail clippings,
    And mony mae."

It was yesterday evening, no earlier than that
I threw a worthy throw at someone
With less, I'm sure, I've slain hundreds
    But no matter,
It just rattled against the bone
    But no more than that.

Hornbook was nearby, with ready art
And had so fortified the part
That when I looked to my dart,
    It was so blunt
Not a bit of it would have pierced the heart
    Of a withered cabbage stem.

I drew my scythe in such a fury
I almost fell over in my hurry
But yet the bold Apothecary
    Withstood the shock;
I might as well have tried a quarry
    Of hard whinstone.

Even those he cannot attend
Although he never knew their faces
Just shit in a cabbage leaf, and send it.
    As soon as he smells it
Both disease and what will cure it
    He can tell at once.

And then all doctor's saws and knives
Of all dimensions, shapes and strengths
All kinds of boxes, mugs and bottles
    He's sure to have;
Their Latin names he rattles off as fast
    As A B C.

Ashes of fossils, earths and trees
True salt of the seas
The flour of beans and peas
    He has plenty of it
Strong water, what you please
    He can sort you out.

'In addition he has, some new, uncommon weapons
Essence of urine of capons
Or shavings, filings, and scrapings from the horns of mites
    Distilled in their purity
Salt of midge-tail clippings
    And many more.'

"Waes me for Johnny Ged's-Hole now,"
Quoth I, "If that thae news be true!
His braw calf-ward whare gowans grew,
    Sae white and bonie,
Nae doubt they'll rive it wi' the plew;
    They'll ruin Johnie!"

The creature grain'd an eldritch laugh,
And says, "Ye need na yoke the pleugh,
Kirkyards will soon be till'd eneugh,
    Tak ye nae fear;
They'll a' be trench'd wi' mony a sheugh
    In twa-three year.

"Whare I kill'd ane a fair strae death,
By loss o' blood or want of breath,
This night I'm free to tak my aith,
    That Hornbook's skill
Has clad a score i' their last claith,
    By drap an' pill.

"An honest wabster to his trade,
Whase wife's twa nieves were scarce weel bred,
Gat tippence-worth to mend her head,
    When it was sair;
The wife slade cannie to her bed,
    But ne'er spak mair.

"A countra laird had ta'en the batts,
Or some curmurring in his guts,
His only son for Hornbook sets,
    An' pays him well:
The lad, for twa guid gimmer-pets,
    Was laird himsel.

"A bonnie lass – ye kend her name –
Some ill-brewn drink had hov'd her wame;
She trusts hersel, to hide the shame,
    In Hornbook's care;
Horn sent her aff to her lang hame,
    To hide it there.

"That's just a swatch o' Hornbook's way;
Thus goes he on from day to day,
Thus does he poison, kill, an' slay,
    An's weel paid for't;
Yet stops me o' my lawfu' prey,
    Wi' his damn'd dirt:

Alas for Johnny Ged's-Hole[4] now'
Said I, 'If that news is true!'
His lovely calf enclosure[5] where daisies grew
    So white and bonnie
No doubt they'll break it up with the plough;
    They'll ruin Johnnie!'

The creature groaned an unearthly laugh
And says, 'You need not yoke the plough,
Churchyards will soon be tilled enough
    Have no fear
They'll all be dug up with graves everywhere
    In two or three years.

Where I killed one (by) a natural death
By loss of blood or want of breath,
This night I'm free to take my oath
    That Hornbook's skill
Has dressed twenty in their shrouds
    By drop and pill.

"An honest weaver to his trade,
Whose wife's two fists were hardly well bred
Got twopence worth to mend her head,
    When it was sore;
The woman crept cautiously to bed
    But never spoke again.

A country laird had taken colic
Or some rumbling flatulence in his guts
His only son calls for Hornbook
    And pays him well;
The lad for the price of two good year-old ewes
    Became laird himself.

A bonnie lass, you knew her name
Some badly-brewed drink had swollen her womb
She entrusts herself, to hide the shame
    To Hornbook's care;
Horn sent her off to her long home[5]
    To hide it there.

That's just a sample of Hornbook's way
Thus he goes on from day to day,
Thus does he poison, kill and slay
    And is well paid for it
Yet robs me of my lawful prey
    With his damned dirt.

[4] The grave-digger.
[5] The graveyard was sometimes used as an enclosure for calves.
[6] Death.

"But, hark! I'll tell you of a plot,
Though dinna ye be speaking o't;
I'll nail the self-conceited sot,
    As dead's a herrin':
Niest time we meet, I'll wad a groat,
    He gets his fairin'!"

But just as he began to tell,
The auld kirk-hammer strak' the bell
Some wee short hour ayont the twal,
    Which rais'd us baith:
I took the way that pleas'd mysel',
    And sae did Daith

But hark! I'll tell you of a plot
Though don't you be speaking of it
I'll nail the self-conceited fool
    As dead as a herring;
Next time we meet, I'll wager a groat[7]
    He gets his come-uppance!

But just as he began to tell
The old church-hammer struck the bell
Some wee small hour after midnight
    Which roused us both;
I took the way that pleased me
    And so did Death.

[7] A small coin worth fourpence.

Epistle to Davie (1785)

1784 was a year of ill-health and depression. Burns's father died, worn out by a lengthy court case. Robert and his brother Gilbert took a lease on Mossgiel, a farm in Mauchline. The first year saw them defeated by bad seed, the second year by a late harvest. The bright spot in all of this was that he met Jean Armour who later became his wife.

Despite all the hardships, this was a prolific time for Burns's writing. The *Epistle to Davie* was one of many written in 1785. It is written in the *Cherry and the Slae* stanza form. *The Cherry and the Slae*, a famous poem by Alexander Montgomerie, was first published in 1597.

David Sillar, who had been temporary schoolmaster in Tarbolton before John Wilson of Dr. Hornbook fame got the job, was also a poet. He was a regular visitor to the Burns family and a firm friend of Robert. He records how impressed he was at Burns's facility to 'chat up' the lasses.

The poem highlights the harrowing contrasts between the lives of rich and poor. In this sense, it is a fore-runner to 'The Twa Dugs' and 'The Jolly Beggars', but spoiled by sentimentality and pious rhetoric.

Real anger and bitterness come across, reminding us that Burns knew well what he was talking about, having faced bankruptcy several times. However, while the terrible realities of poverty are painfully portrayed, Burns's idyllic vision of rural life could arguably be described as kailyard poetry, sentimental and accepting that ordinary folk can survive inequality, without questioning that inequality. This is a kind of escapism.

This sentimentality which sometimes creeps into Burns's poetry can be attributed to his admiration for Henry MacKenzie's novel, *The Man of Feeling* (1771). In this novel, the hero is constantly moved to tears of pity without any effort made to understand or consider any kind of social reform. Notice too how his language becomes almost entirely English as the sentimentality increases and the pious pomposity of verse 9, which seems to belong to another genre altogether. Should we doubt his sincerity?

1.

While winds frae aff Ben-Lomond blaw,	While winds from off Loch Lomond blow
And bar the doors wi' drivin' snaw,	And bar the doors with driving snow
And hing us owre the ingle,	And force us to drape ourselves round the fireplace
I set me down to pass the time,	I settle down to pass the time
And spin a verse or twa o' rhyme,	And spin a verse or two of poetry
In hamely, westlin jingle:	In homely, western rhyme;
While Frosty winds blaw in the drift,	While frosty winds blow in the drift
Ben to the chimla lug,	Through to the fireside
I grudge a wee the great-folk's gift,	I grudge the great folk's gift a bit
That live sae bien an' snug:	Who live so comfortably and snug
I tent less, and want less	I heed less and want less
Their roomy fire-side;	Their roomy fireside
But hanker, and canker,	But sit about, and fret
To see their cursed pride.	To see their cursed pride.

2.

It's hardly in a body's pow'r,	It's hardly in a person's power
To keep, at times, frae being sour,	To keep from being sour occasionally
To see how things are shar'd;	To see how things are shared.
How best o' chiels are whyles in want,	How the best of lads are sometimes in want
While coofs on countless thousands rant,	While fools with countless thousands make merry
And ken na how to ware't;	And don't know how to spend it
But, Davie, lad, ne'er fash your head	But, Davie, lad, don't bother your head
Tho' we hae little gear;	Though we have few possessions.
We're fit to win our daily bread,	We're fit to earn our daily bread,
As lang's we're hale and fier:	As long as we're healthy and strong
'Mair spier na, nor fear na',	Ask for no more, fear no more
Auld age ne'er mind a feg;	Don't give a fig for old age
The last o't, the warst o't,	The last of it, the worst of it
Is only but to beg.	Is only that we'll have to beg.

3.

To lie in kilns and barns at e'en,	To lie in kilns and barns at night
When banes are craz'd, and bluid is thin,	When bones are broken down and blood is thin,
Is, doubtless, great distress!	Is, doubtless, great distress!
Yet then content could make us blest;	Yet then content could make us blessed,
E'en then, sometimes, we'd snatch a taste	Even then, sometimes, we'd snatch a taste
Of truest happiness.	Of truest happiness.
The honest heart that's free frae a'	The honest heart that's free from all
Intended fraud or guile,	Intended fraud or guile,
However Fortune kick the ba',	However Fortune kicks the ball,
Has ay some cause to smile;	Has always some cause to smile.
And mind still, you'll find still,	And take heed, you'll still find
A comfort this nae sma';	A not inconsiderable comfort.
Nae mair then, we'll care then,	No more then we'll care then,
Nae further can we fa'.	No farther can we fall.

4.

What tho', like commoners of air,	What though, like arbitrators of air,
We wander out, we know not where,	We wander out, we know not where,
But either house or hal'?	Without either house or hall?
Yet Nature's charms, the hills and woods,	Yet Nature's charms, the hills and woods,
The sweeping vales, and foaming floods,	The sweeping vales and foaming floods
Are free alike to all.	Are free alike to all.
In days when daisies deck the ground,	In days when daisies deck the ground
And blackbirds whistle clear,	And blackbirds whistle clear,
With honest joy our hearts will bound,	With honest joy our hearts will bound
To see the coming year:	To see the coming years.
On braes when we please then,	On hill slopes, when we please then,
We'll sit an' sowth a tune;	We'll sit and whistle a tune,
Syne rhyme till't we'll time till't,	Then rhyme to it we'll time to it
An' sing't when we hae done.	And sing it when we've done.

5.

It's no in titles nor in rank:
It's no in wealth like Lon'on Bank,
To purchase peace and rest.
It's no in makin muckle, mair;
It's no in books, it's no in lear,
To make us truly blest:
If happiness hae not her seat
An' centre in the breast,
We may be wise, or rich, or great,
But never can be blest!
Nae treasures nor pleasures
Could make us happy lang;
The heart ay's the part ay
That makes us right or wrang.

It's not in titles nor in rank,
It's not in wealth like London Bank
To purchase peace and rest.
It's not in making a lot even more,
It's not in books, it's not in learning
To make us truly blessed:
If happiness does not have her seat
And centre in the breast,
We may be wise, or rich, or great,
But never can be blessed!
No treasures or pleasures
Could make us happy for long;
The heart is always the part
That make us right or wrong.

6.

Think ye, that sic as you and I,
Wha drudge and drive thro' wet and dry,
Wi' never ceasing toil;
Think ye, are we less blest than they,
Wha scarcely tent us in their way,
As hardly worth their while?
Alas! how oft, in haughty mood,
God's creatures they oppress!
Or else, neglecting a' that's guid,
They riot in excess!
Baith careless and fearless
Of either Heaven or Hell;
Esteeming and deeming
It a' an idle tale!

Do you think that such as you and I
Who drudge and drive through wet and dry
With never-ending toil,
Think, are we less blessed than they
Who scarcely notice us in their way
As hardly worth their while?
Alas, how often, in haughty mood,
God's creatures they oppress!
Or else, neglecting all that's good,
They riot in excess!
Both careless and fearless
Of either Heaven or Hell,
Esteeming and deeming
It all an idle tale!

7.

Then let us chearfu' acquiesce,
Nor make our scanty pleasures less
By pining at our state:
And, even should misfortunes come,
I here wha sit hae met wi' some,
An's thankfu' for them yet,
They gie the wit of age to youth:
They let us ken oursel;
They make us see the naked truth –
The real guid and ill:
Tho' losses and crosses
Be lessons right severe,
There's wit there, ye'll get there,
Ye'll find nae other where.

Then let us cheerfully acquiesce,
Nor make our scanty pleasures less
By pining at our state:
And, even should misfortunes come,
I, who sit here, have met with some,
And am thankful for them yet.
They give the wit of age to youth,
They let us know ourselves
They make us see the naked truth,
The real good and ill.
Though losses and crosses,
And very severe lessons
There's wit there you'll get there
That you'll find nowhere else.

8.

But tent me, Davie, ace o' hearts!	But heed me, Davie, Ace of Hearts,
(To say aught less wad wrang the cartes,	(To say anything less would wrong the cards,
And flatt'ry I detest)	and flattery I detest)
This life has joys for you and I;	This life has joys for you and I
And joys that riches ne'er could buy,	And joys that wealth could never buy,
And joys the very best.	And joys the very best.
There's a' the pleasures o' the heart,	There are all the pleasures of the heart,
The lover an' the frien':	The lover and the friend.
Ye hae your Meg, your dearest part,	You have your Meg, the dearest part,
And I my darling Jean!	And I my darling Jean!
It warms me, it charms me	It warms me, it charms me,
To mention but her name:	To mention but her name.
It heats me, it beets me,	It heats me, it heals me,
And sets me a' on flame!	And sets me all on flame!

9.

O all ye Pow'rs who rule above!	O all ye Powers who rule above,
O Thou whose very self art love!	O thou, whose very self is love!
Thou know'st my words sincere!	You know my words sincere!
The life-blood streaming thro' my heart,	The life-blood streaming through my heart
Or my more dear immortal part,	Or my more dear immortal part,
Is not more fondly dear!	Is not more fondly dear!
When heart-corroding care and grief	When heart-corroding care and grief
Deprive my soul of rest,	Deprive my soul of rest,
Her dear idea brings relief	Her dear idea brings relief
And solace to my breast.	And solace to my breast.
Thou Being All-seeing,	Thou being, all-seeing,
O, hear my fervent pray'r!	O hear my fervent prayer!
Still take her, and make her	Still take her and make her
Thy most peculiar care!	Your most particular care!

10.

All hail! ye tender feelings dear!	All hail! ye tender feelings dear!
The smile of love, the friendly tear,	The smile of love, the friendly tear,
The sympathetic glow!	The sympathetic glow!
Long since, this world's thorny ways	Long ago, this world's thorny ways
Had number'd out my weary days,	Would have numbered out my weary days
Had it not been for you!	Had it not been for you!
Fate still has blest me with a friend	Fate still has blest me with a friend
In every care and ill;	In every care and ill,
And oft a more endearing band,	And oft a more endearing band,
A tie more tender still.	A tie more tender still.
It lightens, it brightens	It lightens, it brightens
The tenebrific scene,	The tenebrific scene,
To meet with, and greet with	To meet with, and greet with
My Davie or my Jean!	My Davie or my Jean!

11.

O, how that Name inspires my style!	O, how that name inspires my style
The words come skelpin' rank an' file,	The words come rushing rank and file
Amaist before I ken!	Almost before I know!
The ready measure rins as fine,	The ready measure runs as fine
As Phoebus and the famous Nine	As if Phoebus and the famous nine[1]
Were glowrin owre my pen.	Were glowering over my pen.
My spaviet Pegasus will limp,	My disabled Pegasus[2] will limp
Till ance he's fairly het;	Until he's warmed up
And then he'll hilch, an' stilt, an' jimp,	And then he'll lurch, and walk stiffly and jump
And rin an unco fit;	And burst into an unprecedented run.
But least then, the beast then	But lest then the beast then
Should rue this hasty ride,	Should rue this hasty ride,
I'll light now, and dight now	I'll alight and wipe down now
His sweaty, wizen'd hide.	His sweaty wizened hide.

[1] In Greek mythology, Phoebus is the God of the Sun, or Apollo, and the famous nine are the nine Muses.
[2] The winged horse of Greek mythology.

Epistle to James Smith (1786)

James Smith was a Mauchline draper. Like Burns, he was a great pursuer of the opposite sex and received from Burns some of his more bawdy verses and letters which both of them must have chuckled over. Burns is therefore very relaxed and honest in this epistle. It is written to a friend, not for the general public.

From the very first line, this poem is firmly in Scottish idiom. Among Scots, affection is often shown by addressing people in a comically reductive way, in this case as a sly thief. The first three verses consist of hyperbolic praise of Smith, who charms everyone as if by magic, who has cost the poet twenty pairs of shoes to visit him (and each worn-out pair makes the poet value him more!). Indeed, Nature has made Smith the perfect creation.

This is Burns in the persona of the ploughman poet, claiming that he writes verses for fun (which, in this case, is largely true) and that this ability to make verses compensates for his lack of wealth. He tentatively tells Smith of his intention to get his poems in print. However, the consideration that the works of 'great' poets lie unread and in tattered volumes persuades him to give up any notions of fame and return to the obscure rustic life he knows!

From this conclusion, he begins to contemplate death and the necessity to live life to the full before he gets to the ripe old age of 45! This thought leads him to consider the easy lives of the rich and to conclude that his ability to rhyme makes up for everything.

The last four verses veer from the epistle genre as he attacks those who have no passion, with scathing irony. This raises the poem to a new level and perhaps heralds his 'Address to the unco guid'.

1.
Dear Smith, the slee'st, pawkie thief,
That e'er attempted stealth or rief!
Ye surely hae some warlock-breef
Owre human hearts;
For ne'er a bosom yet was prief
Against your arts.

Dear Smith, the slyest, wily thief
That ever attempted stealth or plunder
You surely have some wizardly spell
Over human hearts,
For never a bosom yet was proof
Against your arts.

2.
For me, I swear by sun an' moon,
And ev'ry star that blinks aboon,
Ye've cost me twenty pair o' shoon,
Just gaun to see you;
And ev'ry ither pair that's done,
Mair taen I'm wi' you.

For me, I swear by sun and moon,
And every star that blinks above,
You've cost me twenty pairs of shoes,
Just going to see you
And with every other pair that's done
I'm more taken with you.

3.
That auld, capricious carlin, Nature,
To mak amends for scrimpit stature,
She's turn'd you off, a human-creature
On her first plan;
And in her freaks, on ev'ry feature
She's wrote the Man.

4.
Just now I've taen the fit o' rhyme,
My barmie noddle's working prime,
My fancy yerkit up sublime,
Wi' hasty summon:
Hae ye a leisure-moment's time
To hear what's comin?

5.
Some rhyme a neebor's name to lash;
Some rhyme (vain thought!) for needfu' cash;
Some rhyme to court the countra clash,
An' raise a din;
For me, an aim I never fash;
I rhyme for fun.

6.
The star that rules my luckless lot,
Has fated me the russet coat,
An' damn'd my fortune to the groat;
But, in requit,
Has blest me with a random-shot
O' countra wit.

7.
This while my notion's taen a sklent,
To try my fate in guid, black prent;
But still the mair I'm that way bent,
Something cries, 'Hoolie!
I redd you, honest man, tak tent!
Ye'll shaw your folly:

8.
'There's ither poets, much your betters,
Far seen in Greek, deep men o' letters,
Hae thought they had ensur'd their debtors,
A' future ages;
Now moths deform, in shapeless tatters,
Their unknown pages.'

That old, capricious witch, Nature,
To make amends for your short stature
She's turned you out, a human creature,
On her first plan;
And in her freaks, on every feature
She's written the Man.

Just now I've taken the fit of rhyme,
My seething brain's working overtime
My fancy jerked up sublimely
With hasty summons:
Have you a leisure-moment's time
To hear what's coming?

Some rhyme a neighbour's name to slander
Some rhyme (vain thought) for needful cash,
Some rhyme to court the country gossip
And raise a rumpus.
For me, an aim I never bother with.
I rhyme for fun.

The star that rules my luckless lot,
Has fated me a coat of coarse cloth[1]
And damned my fortune to be a groat[2]
But in recompense
Has blessed me with a random shot
Of country wit.

Recently my notion is to take the chance
To try my fate in good, black print
But still the more I'm that way inclined,
Something cries, 'Careful!
I advise you, honest man, take heed
You'll give yourself a showing up:

There are other poets much better than you,
Accomplished in Greek, deep men of letters,
Have thought they had ensured as their debtors
All future ages:
Now moths deform, in shapeless tatters,
Their unknown pages.

[1] The garment of a poor man.
[2] An old coin worth about fourpence.

9.
Then farewell hopes o' laurel-boughs
To garland my poetic brows!
Henceforth I'll rove where busy ploughs
Are whistling thrang;
An' teach the lanely heights an' howes
My rustic sang.

Then farewell hopes of laurel boughs
To garland my poetic brows!
From now on, I'll rove where working ploughs
Are whistling busily
And teach the lonely heights and hollows
My rustic song.

10.
I'll wander on, wi' tentless heed
How never-halting moments speed,
Till Fate shall snap the brittle thread;
Then, all unknown,
I'll lay me with th' inglorious dead,
Forgot and gone!

I'll wander on, with careless heed
How never-halting moments speed,
Till Fate shall snap the brittle thread,
Then, all unknown,
I'll lie down with the inglorious dead,
Forgotten and gone!

11.
But why o' death begin a tale?
Just now we're living sound an' hale;
Then top and maintop crowd the sail,
Heave Care o'er-side!
And large, before Enjoyment's gale,
Let's tak the tide.

But why of death begin a tale?
Just now we're living sound and healthy;
Then top and maintop crowd the sail,
Heave Care over the side!
And large, before Enjoyment's gale,
Let's take the tide.

12.
This life, sae far's I understand,
Is a' enchanted fairy-land,
Where Pleasure is the magic-wand,
That, wielded right,
Maks hours like minutes, hand in hand,
Dance by fu' light.

This life, as far as I understand,
Is all enchanted fairy-land,
Where Pleasure is the magic wand
That, wielded right,
Makes hours like minutes, hand in hand,
Dance by full light.

13.
The magic-wand then let us wield;
For, ance that five-an'-forty's speel'd,
See, crazy, weary, joyless Eild,
Wi' wrinkl'd face,
Comes hostin, hirplin owre the field,
Wi' creepin pace.

The magic wand then let us wield
For once we've reached 45
See crazy, weary, joyless Age
With wrinkled face,
Comes coughing, limping over the field,
With creeping pace.

14.
When ance life's day draws near the gloamin,
Then fareweel vacant, careless roamin;
An' fareweel cheerfu' tankards foamin,
An' social noise:
An' fareweel dear, deluding Woman,
The joy of joys!

When once life's day draws near the twilight,
Then farewell vacant, careless roaming
And farewell cheerful tankards foaming
And social noise.
And farewell, dear, deluding Woman,
The joy of joys.

15.

O Life! how pleasant, in thy morning,	O Life! how pleasant, in the morning,
Young Fancy's rays the hills adorning!	Young Fancy's rays the hills adorning!
Cold-pausing Caution's lesson scorning,	Cold-pausing Caution's lesson scorning,
We frisk away,	We frisk away,
Like school-boys, at th' expected warning,	Like school-boys, at the expected warning,
To joy an' play.	To joy and play.

16.

We wander there, we wander here,	We wander there, we wander here,
We eye the rose upon the brier,	We eye the rose upon the brier,
Unmindful that the thorn is near,	Unmindful that the thorn is near,
Among the leaves;	Among the leaves;
And tho' the puny wound appear,	And though the puny wound appear,
Short while it grieves.	Short while it grieves.

17.

Some, lucky, find a flow'ry spot,	Some, lucky, find a flowery spot,
For which they never toil'd nor swat;	For which they never toiled nor sweated,
They drink the sweet and eat the fat,	They drink the sweet and eat the fat,
But care or pain;	Without care or pain
And haply eye the barren hut	And perhaps eye the barren hut
With high disdain.	With high disdain.

18.

With steady aim, some Fortune chase;	With steady aim, some Fortune chase,
Keen Hope does ev'ry sinew brace;	Keen hope braces every sinew;
Thro' fair, thro' foul, they urge the race,	Through fair and foul, they urge the race,
And seize the prey:	And seize the prey:
Then cannie, in some cozie place,	Then comfortable, in some cosy place,
They close the day.	They end the day

19.

And others like your humble servan',	And others, like your humble servant,
Poor wights! nae rules nor roads observin,	Poor valiant men! observing no rules nor roads,
To right or left eternal swervin,	Eternally swerving to right or left,
They zig-zag on;	They zig-zag on;
Till, curst with age, obscure an' starvin,	Till, cursed with age, obscure and starving,
They aften groan.	They often groan.

20.

Alas! what bitter toil an' straining –	Alas! What bitter toil and straining –
But truce with peevish, poor complaining!	But a truce to peevish poor complaining!
Is Fortune's fickle Luna waning?	Is Fortune's fickle moon waning?
E'en let her gang!	Then let her go!
Beneath what light she has remaining,	Beneath what light she has remaining,
Let's sing our sang.	Let's sing her song.

21.

My pen I here fling to the door,	My pen here I fling to the door,
And kneel, ye Pow'rs! and warm implore,	And kneel, ye powers, and warmly implore,
'Tho' I should wander Terra o'er,	Though I should wander the earth
In all her climes,	In all her climes,
Grant me but this, I ask no more,	Grant me but this, I ask no more,
Ay rowth o' rhymes.	Always abundance of rhymes.

22.

'Gie dreeping roasts to countra lairds,	Give dripping roasts to country lairds
Till icicles hing frae their beards;	Till icicles hang from their beards
Gie fine braw claes to fine life-guards	Give fine clothes to fine life-guards
And maids of honor;	And maids of honour
And yill an' whisky gie to cairds,	And ale and whisky give to tinkers
Until they sconner.	Until they feel nauseated

23.

'A title, Dempster merits it;	A title, Dempster deserves it[3]
A garter gie to Willie Pit;	The order of the garter, give it to William Pitt[4]
Gie wealth to some be-ledger'd cit,	Give wealth to some be-ledgered city dweller
In cent. per cent.;	In cent per cent;
But give me real, sterling wit,	But give me real sterling wit,
And I'm content	And I'm content.

24.

'While ye are pleas'd to keep me hale,	While you are pleased to keep me healthy,
I'll sit down o'er my scanty meal,	I'll sit down to my scanty meal
Be't water-brose or muslin-kail,	Whether it's pease meal mixed with water or thin cabbage soup
Wi' cheerfu' face,	With a cheerful face,
As lang's the Muses dinna fail	As long as the Muses don't fail
To say the grace.'	To say the grace.

25.

An anxious e'e I never throws	I never cast an anxious eye
Behint my lug, or by my nose;	Behind my ear or by my nose,
I jouk beneath Misfortune's blows	I duck beneath Misfotune's blows
As weel's I may;	As well as I am able,
Sworn foe to sorrow, care, and prose,	Sworn foe to sorrow, care and prose,
I rhyme away.	I rhyme away.

26.

O ye douce folk that live by rule,	O you sedate folk that live by the rules,
Grave, tideless-blooded, calm an' cool,	Grave, tideless-blooded, calm and cool,
Compar'd wi' you – O fool! Fool! Fool!	Compared with you – O Fool! Fool! Fool!
How much unlike!	How much unlike!
Your hearts are just a standing pool,	Your hearts are just a standing pool,
Your lives a dyke!	Your lives a wall!

---

[3] George Dempster, a progressive liberal M.P.

[4] William Pitt became Prime Minister in 1783 when he was only 24.

27.

Nae hair-brained, sentimental traces	No hare-brained, sentimental traces
In your unletter'd, nameless faces!	In your unlettered, nameless faces!
In arioso trills and graces	In airy trills and graces
Ye never stray;	You never stray,
But *gravissimo*, solemn, basses	But very gravely, solemn basses,
Ye hum away.	You hum away.

28.

Ye are sae grave, nae doubt ye're wise;	You are so grave, no doubt you're wise;
Nae ferly tho' ye do despise	No wonder though you do despise
The hairum-scairum, ram-stam boys,	The headstrong, impetuous boys
The rattling squad:	The rattling squad;
I see ye upward cast your eyes –	I see you roll your eyes –
Ye ken the road!	You know the road.

29.

Whilst I – but I shall haud me there,	While I – but I shall stop there,
Wi' you I'll scarce gang onie where –	With you I'd scarcely go anywhere
Then, Jamie, I shall say nae mair,	Then Jamie, I shall say no more
But quat my sang.	But quit my song
Content wi' you to mak a pair,	Content with you to make a pair,
Whare'er I gang.	Wherever I go.

Epitaph for a wag in Mauchline (1787)

Burns wrote a large number of pithy epitaphs, and the subject was not necessarily deceased. It has been suggested that the wag of this epitaph was James Smith.

Lament him Mauchline husbands a',	Lament him, all you Mauchline husbands,
He aften did assist ye;	He often helped you out;
For had ye staid hale weeks awa',	For if you had stayed away for weeks at a time
Your wives they ne'er had miss'd ye.	Your wives would never have missed you.

Ye Mauchline bairns as on ye pass	You Mauchline children as you pass by
To school in bands thegither,	To school in groups together,
O, tread ye lightly on his grass –	O, tread lightly where he is buried –
Perhaps he was your father!	Perhaps he was your father!

Epistle to John Lapraik (1785)

John Lapraik was a farmer in Muirkirk. In 1773, the failure of the Ayr Bank forced him to sell his farm and he was jailed for debt. While in prison, he started to write poetry and published his collection in 1788. Although Burns admires his work – excessively – the admiration was not universal. This verse by another 'bard', James Maxwell, has a rather different view of Lapraik's publication:

> *'For some devoted theirs unto the flame;*
> *Bumfodder also others made of them.*
> *Some turn'd to dung, and others they were burn'd,*
> *And so to dirt and ashes all were turn'd.'*

Burns, however, praises Lapraik to the skies, rating him alongside Allan Ramsay and Robert Fergusson (verse 14). You can be forgiven if you think Burns is a bit OTT, especially in verses 4 to 8 where his hyperbole is not only excessive but expressed in mundane language.

His ranting, in verses 8-14 show Burns disingenuously denying the excellent education he received from John Murdoch. Burns was not the simple ploughman poet he is pretending to be, but even the reek of false modesty cannot diminish the sheer vigour and poetic merit of verses 11 and 12, where the plosive consonants contribute to the impassioned rhetoric.

Verses 20 and 21 show the poet's honest emotion in his utter condemnation of those who value money above all else. These verses are a prelude to the great *A Man's a Man for a' that*.

1

While briers an' woodbines budding green,	While briars and woodbines are in budding green
An' paitricks scraichin loud at e'en,	And partridges screeching loudly in the evening
An' morning poussie whiddin seen,	And hare seen moving back and forwards in the morning
Inspire my muse,	Inspire my Muse
This freedom, in an unknown frien'	This freedom in an unknown friend
I pray excuse.	I pray excuse.

2

On Fasten-e'en we had a rockin[1],	On Shrove Tuesday, we had a gathering of neighbours
To ca' the crack and weave our stockin;	To enjoy a gossip and weave our stockings
And there was muckle fun and jokin,	And there was much fun and joking,
Ye need na doubt;	You need not doubt
At length we had a hearty yokin	At length we had a hearty good time
At sang about.	and sang in turn.

3

There was ae sang, amang the rest,	There was one song among the rest
Aboon them a' it pleas'd me best,	Above them all it pleased me best
That some kind husband had addrest	That some kind husband had addressed
To some sweet wife;	To some sweet wife.
It thirl'd the heart-strings thro' the breast,	It pierced the heart strings through the breast
A' to the life.	All to the life.

[1] Rockin: This could be a work party or a social occasion or both. The word comes from 'rock' – the distaff that held the unspun wool or flax.

4

I've scarce heard ought describ'd sae weel,
What gen'rous, manly bosoms feel;
Thought I "Can this be Pope, or Steele,
Or Beattie's wark?"
They tauld me 'twas an odd kind chiel
About Muirkirk.

I've hardly ever heard anything described so well
What generous, manly bosoms feel
Thought I 'Can this be Pope or Steele,
Or Beattie's work?'
They told me it was an odd kind fellow
About Muirkirk.

5

It pat me fidgin-fain to hear't,
An' sae about him there I speir't;
Then a' that kent him round declar'd
He had ingine;
That nane excell'd it, few cam near't,
It was sae fine:

It made me restlessly eager to hear it
And so I enquired about him there;
Then all who knew him roundly declared
He had genius;
That none excelled it, few came near it
It was so fine.

6

That, set him to a pint of ale,
An' either douce or merry tale,
Or rhymes an' sangs he'd made himsel,
Or witty catches –
'Tween Inverness an' Teviotdale,
He had few matches.

That, set him before a pint of ale,
And either sober or merry tale,
Or rhymes or songs he'd made himself,
Or witty quips –
Between Inverness and Teviotdale,
There were few to equal him.

7

Then up I gat, an' swoor an aith,
Tho' I should pawn my pleugh an' graith,
Or die a cadger pownie's death,
At some dyke-back,
A pint an' gill I'd gie them baith,
To hear your crack.

Then up I got, and swore an oath
Though I should (have to) pawn my plough and equipment
Or die a hawker's pony's death
Behind some wall,
A pint and gill, I'd give them both
To hear your conversation.

8

But, first an' foremost, I should tell,
Amaist as soon as I could spell,
I to the crambo-jingle fell;
Tho' rude an' rough –
Yet crooning to a body's sel'
Does weel eneugh.

But first and foremost, I should tell,
Almost as soon as I could spell
I fell to rhyming,
Though rude and rough
Yet crooning to oneself
Does well enough.

9

I am nae poet, in a sense;
But just a rhymer like by chance,
An' hae to learning nae pretence;
Yet, what the matter?
Whene'er my muse does on me glance,
I jingle at her.

I am no poet, in a sense
But just a kind-of rhymer by chance,
And have to learning no pretence.
Yet, what does it matter?
Whenever my Muse glances at me
I make rhymes for her.

10

Your critic-folk may cock their nose,
And say, "How can you e'er propose,
You wha ken hardly verse frae prose,
To mak a sang?"
But, by your leaves, my learned foes,
Ye're maybe wrang.

Your critics may be a bit snooty
And say 'How can you ever propose,
You who hardly know verse from prose
To make a song?'
But, by your leave, my learned foes
Maybe you're wrong.

11

What's a' your jargon o' your schools –
Your Latin names for horns an' stools?
If honest Nature made you fools,
What sairs your grammars?
Ye'd better taen up spades and shools,
Or knappin-hammers.

What's all your jargon of your schools –
Your Latin names for horns and stools?
If honest Nature made you fools
What use are your grammars?
You'd have been better taking up spades and shovels
Or stone-breaking hammers.

12

A set o' dull, conceited hashes
Confuse their brains in college classes!
They gang in stirks, and come out asses,
Plain truth to speak;
An' syne they think to climb Parnassus
By dint o' Greek!

A set of dull conceited fools
Confuse their brains in college classes!
They go in as bullocks, and come out asses
To tell you the truth;
And then they think to climb Parnassus
By dint of Greek!

13

Gie me ae spark o' nature's fire,
That's a' the learning I desire;
Then tho' I drudge thro' dub an' mire
At pleugh or cart,
My muse, tho' hamely in attire,
May touch the heart.

Give me one spark of nature's fire
That's all the learning I desire;
Then though I toil through puddle and bog
At the plough or cart
My Muse, although homely in attire
May touch the heart.

14

O for a spunk o' Allan's glee,
Or Fergusson's the bauld an' slee,
Or bright Lapraik's, my friend to be,
If I can hit it!
That would be lear eneugh for me,
If I could get it.

O for a spark of Allan's glee[2]
Or Fergusson's the bold and sly
Or bright Lapraik's, my friend to be,
If I could pull it off!
That would be learning enough for me,
If I could get it.

15

Now, sir, if ye hae friends enow,
Tho' real friends, I b'lieve, are few;
Yet, if your catalogue be fu',
I'se no insist:
But, gif ye want ae friend that's true,
I'm on your list.

Now, sir, if you've sufficient friends enough
Though real friends, I believe, are few
Yet, if your catalogue is full
I won't insist
But if you want one friend that's true
I'm on your list.

[2] The poet Allan Ramsay.

16

I winna blaw about mysel,
As ill I like my fauts to tell;
But friends, an' folk that wish me well,
They sometimes roose me;
Tho' I maun own, as mony still
As far abuse me.

I will not boast about myself
As I don't like to reveal my faults
But friends, and folk who wish me well
They sometimes praise me;
Though I must admit, just as many
Abuse me to the same extent.

17

There's ae wee faut they whiles lay to me,
I like the lasses – Gude forgie me!
For mony a plack they wheedle frae me
At dance or fair;
Maybe some ither thing they gie me,
They weel can spare.

There's one small fault they sometimes accuse me of
I like the lasses, God forgive me!
For many a farthing they wheedle from me
At a dance or a fair;
Maybe some other thing they give me
They well can spare.

18

But Mauchline Race, or Mauchline Fair,
I should be proud to meet you there;
We'se gie ae night's discharge to care,
If we forgather;
An' hae a swap o' rhymin-ware
Wi' ane anither.

But at Mauchline Races or Mauchline Fair,
I should be proud to meet you there
We'd give care a night off
If we meet,
And exchange poems
With one another

19

The four-gill chap, we'se gar him clatter,
An' kirsen him wi' reekin water;
Syne we'll sit down an' tak our whitter,
To cheer our heart;
An' faith, we'se be acquainted better
Before we part.

The four-gill cup, we'll make it clatter
And christen him with steaming water
Then we'll sit down and take our liquor
To cheer our heart;
And faith, we'll be acquainted better
Before we part.

20

Awa ye selfish, war'ly race,
Wha think that havins, sense, an' grace,
Ev'n love an' friendship should give place
To catch-the-plack!
I dinna like to see your face,
Nor hear your crack

Away you selfish wordly race
Who think that manners, sense and grace
Even love and friendship should give place
To making money!
I do not like to see your face,
Nor hear your conversation.

21

But ye whom social pleasure charms,
Whose hearts the tide of kindness warms,
Who hold your being on the terms,
"Each aid the others,"
Come to my bowl, come to my arms,
My friends, my brothers!

But you whom social pleasure charms,
Whose hearts, the tide of kindness warms,
Who hold your being on the terms,
"Each aid the others."
Come to my bowl, come to my arms,
My friends, my brothers!

22

But, to conclude my lang epistle,
As my auld pen's worn to the gristle,
Twa lines frae you wad gar me fissle,
Who am, most fervent,
While I can either sing or whistle,
Your friend and servant.

But, to conclude my long epistle
As my old pen's worn to the gristle
Two lines from you would fire me up
(I) Who am, most fervently,
While I can either sing or whistle
Your friend and servant.

Halloween (1785)

Halloween, October 31st, is a time when witches and warlocks can enter human territory, all sorts of magical spells can be tried out and people can thoroughly scare themselves.

Much of Burns's folklore, as well as his songs, came from his mother and her relative, Betty Davidson, of whom Burns said, *'She had the largest collection in the county of tales and songs concerning devils, ghosts, fairies, brownies, witches, warlocks, spunkies, kelpies, elf-candles, dead-lights, wraiths, apparitions, cantraips, giants, inchanted towers, dragons and other trumpery.'* Quite a list!

The poem 'Halloween' is full of warmth, humour and incident – an absorbing description of folklore and society in Burns's time. In this poem, Burns does not make the metaphysical leap that he often makes to consider a moral or religious principle, or simply the lot of man. This is observation, invention and description, much of it comic and all of it rich in humanity. The customs described are as follows:

Kail stalks
The crowd of young people went blindfolded into the field to pull a kail stalk, the size and straightness of which would foretell the kind of wife/husband they will get. The earth sticking to it was a measure of the wealth or tocher; the taste – sweet or sour – a measure of the significant other's temperament.

Corn stalks
The girls had to pull three different stalks. If the third had no grain at the top, i.e. no 'top-pickle', the girl would not be a virgin when she married.

Nuts
Two nuts were burned, each nut secretly named. How the nuts burned would foretell how the relationship would turn out.

Blue Yarn
A person went alone to the kiln and threw a length of blue yarn into the pot. The yarn from the pot was rewound on another spool. As the rewinding neared an end, it would be caught up – by 'something'. The question, 'Who holds?' was asked and the answer that came from the pot would be the wife or husband of the diviner.

Apples and Mirror
This meant eating an apple (and some said combing your hair at the same time) as you looked in the mirror, where you would see your future wife/husband.

Hemp seed
This had to be done alone. You had to sow some hemp seed and say the words 'Come after me and shaw (show) thee' and your true love would appear behind you pulling up the plant – or alternatively, just say the spell and the person should appear behind your left shoulder.

Dipping your sleeve

For this you had to go to where three lairds' lands met and dip your left shirt sleeve in a south-running stream. When you went to bed, you had to leave the sleeve by the fire to dry and the future spouse would appear to 'turn' the sleeve to dry the other side.

Three basins

One dish had clean water, one dirty water and one was empty. Blindfolded, a person had to dip the left hand in a basin. Whichever basin the hand dipped in foretold the fate: clean = bachelor or spinster, dirty = widow/widower, empty = no marriage at all. This was repeated three times with the bowls being moved around.

Supper

Sowans are made from the bran or husks of oats, boiled and left to ferment. Sowans with butter instead of milk was always the Halloween supper.

As the Scots is fairly dense and the poem almost entirely descriptive, it is presented here simply with its direct transcription.

Upon that night, when fairies light	Upon that night when fairies light
On Cassilis Downans dance,	On the hillocks of Cassilis[1] dance
Or owre the lays, in splendid blaze,	Or over the leas, in splendid blaze
On sprightly coursers prance;	On sprightly courses prance;
Or for Colean the route is ta'en,	Or for Culzean[2] the route is taken
Beneath the moon's pale beams;	Beneath the moon's pale beams;
There, up the cove, to stray and rove,	There, up the Cove[3], to stray and rove
Among the rocks and streams	Among the rocks and streams
To sport that night.	To sport that night.
Among the bonny winding banks,	Among the bonnie winding banks
Where Doon rins, wimplin' clear;	Where Doon runs, meandering, clear
Where Bruce ance ruled the martial ranks,	Where Bruce once ruled the martial ranks
And shook his Carrick spear;	And shook his Carrick spear[4]
Some merry, friendly, country-folks,	Some merry, friendly country folks
Together did convene,	Together did convene
To burn their nits, and pou their stocks,	To burn their nuts, and pull their stalks
And haud their Halloween	And hold their Halloween
Fu' blithe that night.	So cheerfully that night.
The lasses feat, and cleanly neat,	The lasses trim and cleanly neat
Mair braw than when they're fine;	Prettier than when they're fine
Their faces blithe, fu' sweetly kythe,	Their happy faces sweetly show
Hearts leal, and warm, and kin';	Hearts loyal, warm and kind
The lads sae trig, wi' wooer-babs	The lads so smart with love-knots
Weel knotted on their garten,	well knotted on their garters
Some unco blate, and some wi' gabs	some really shy, and some with patter
Gar lasses' hearts gang startin'	make girls' hearts begin to
Whiles fast at night.	beat fast at times that night.

[1] Cassilis Downans was considered a favourite haunt of the fairies. The name is still used in Ayrshire.
[2] Culzean Castle near Maybole in Ayrshire.
[3] The cove of Culzean, allegedly another favourite haunt of fairies.
[4] In 1295, Robert the Bruce (King of Scotland 1306-1329) became Earl of Carrick.

Then, first and foremost, through the kail,	Then first and foremost through the kail
Their stocks maun a' be sought ance;	Their stalks must all be sought.
They steek their een, and graip and wale,	They squeeze their eyes shut, grope and grasp
For muckle anes and straught anes.	for big ones and straight ones.
Poor hav'rel Will fell aff the drift,	Poor silly Will got separated from the crowd
And wander'd through the bow-kail,	And wandered through the cabbage
And pou't, for want o' better shift,	And pulled, for the lack of anything better
A runt was like a sow-tail	A withered stump, bent just like
Sae bow't that night.	a sow's tail that night.
Then, staught or crooked, yird or nane,	Then, straight or crooked, earthy or not
They roar and cry a' throu'ther;	They roar and shout in an uproar.
The very wee things, todlin', rin,	Even the wee things, toddling, run
Wi' stocks out owre their shouther;	With stalks hanging over their shoulders
And gif the custoc's sweet or sour.	And if the kail stem's sweet or sour
Wi' joctelegs they taste them;	With clasp-knives they taste them
Syne cozily, aboon the door,	Then cosily, above the door
Wi cannie care, they've placed them	With cautious care they've placed them
To lie that night.	To lie that night.
The lasses staw frae 'mang them a'	The girls steal away from them all
To pou their stalks of corn:	To pull their stalks of corn
But Rab slips out, and jinks about,	But Rab slips out, and dodges about
Behint the muckle thorn:	Behind the big hawthorn
He grippet Nelly hard and fast;	He gripped Nellie hard and fast
Loud skirl'd a' the lasses;	Loud screamed all the lasses
But her tap-pickle maist was lost,	But most of her top-pickle[5] was lost,
When kitlin' in the fause-house	When cuddling in the false-house[6]
Wi' him that night.	With him that night.
The auld guidwife's well-hoordit nits,	The old woman's well hoarded nuts
Are round and round divided,	Are round and round divided
And monie lads' and lasses' fates	And many lads' and lasses' fates
Are there that night decided:	Are there that night decided
Some kindle coothie, side by side,	Some kindle sociably, side by side
And burn thegither trimly;	And burn together trimly
Some start awa, wi' saucy pride,	Some jump away with saucy pride
And jump out-owre the chimlie	And jump to the other side of the fireplace
Fu' high that night.	Really high that night.
Jean slips in twa wi' tentie ee;	Jean slips in two, with watchful eye
Wha 'twas she wadna tell;	Who it was she would not tell
But this is Jock, and this is me,	But this is Jock, and this is me
She says in to hersel:	She says into herself.
He bleez'd owre her, and she owre him,	He blazed over her, and she over him
As they wad never mair part;	As if they'd never part
Till, fuff! he started up the lum,	Till fuff! he jumped up the chimney

---

5 See 'Corn Stalks' p.40.
6 'A conical structure of wooden props built inside a corn stack to facilitate drying' (*Dictionary of Scots Language*).

And Jean had e'en a sair heart To see't that night.	And Jean had a sore heart To see it that night.
Poor Willie, wi' his bow-kail runt, Was brunt wi' primsie Mallie; And Mallie, nae doubt, took the drunt, To be compared to Willie; Mall's nit lap out wi' pridefu' fling, And her ain fit it brunt it; While Willie lap, and swore by jing, 'Twas just the way he wanted To be that night.	Poor Willie with his cabbage stump Was burnt with straight-laced Mallie And Mallie, no doubt, took the huff To be paired off with Willie Mall's nut leapt out, with prideful fling And burnt her on the foot While Willie leapt and swore by jing It was just the way he wanted To be that night.
Nell had the fause-house in her min', She pits hersel and Rob in; In loving bleeze they sweetly join, Till white in ase they're sobbin'; Nell's heart was dancin' at the view, She whisper'd Rob to leuk for't: Rob, stowlins, prie'd her bonny mou', Fu' cozie in the neuk for't, Unseen that night.	Nell had the false-house in her mind She puts herself and Rob in In loving blaze they sweetly join Till white in ash they're sobbing. Nell's heart was dancing at the view She whispered to Rob to look at it Rob stealthily sampled her bonnie mouth Very cosy in the corner for it Unseen that night.
But Merran sat behint their backs, Her thoughts on Andrew Bell; She lea'es them gashin' at their cracks, And slips out by hersel: She through the yard the nearest taks, And to the kiln goes then, And darklins graipit for the bauks, And in the blue-clue throws then, Right fear't that night.	But Merran sat behind their backs Her thoughts on Andrew Bell; She leaves them chattering loudly And slips out by herself. She takes the first track through the yard And to the kiln she goes then And in the dark groped for the wooden beams And throws the blue yarn in then Really scared that night.
And aye she win't, and aye she swat – I wat she made nae jaukin'; Till something held within the pat, Guid Lord! but she was quakin'! But whether 'twas the deil himsel, Or whether 'twas a bauk-en', Or whether it was Andrew Bell, She didna wait on talkin' To spier that night.	On and on she wound, and sweated I tell you she did not slacken Till something held, inside the pot Good Lord! but she was quaking! But whether it was the Devil himself Or whether it was a beam end Or whether it was Andrew Bell She did not wait to talk And ask questions that night.
Wee Jennie to her grannie says, "Will ye go wi' me, grannie? I'll eat the apple at the glass I gat frae Uncle Johnnie:"	Wee Jennie to her granny says "Will you go with me, granny? I'll eat the apple at the mirror I got from Uncle Johnnie"

She fuff't her pipe wi' sic a lunt,
In wrath she was sae vap'rin',
She notice't na, an aizle brunt
Her braw new worset apron
Out through that night.

"Ye little skelpie-limmer's face!
I daur you try sic sportin',
As seek the foul thief ony place,
For him to spae your fortune.
Nae doubt but ye may get a sight!
Great cause ye hae to fear it;
For mony a ane has gotten a fright,
And lived and died deleeret
On sic a night.

"Ae hairst afore the Sherramoor,
I mind't as weel's yestreen –
I was a gilpey then, I'm sure
I wasna past fifteen:
The simmer had been cauld and wat,
And stuff was unco green;
And aye a rantin' kirn we gat,
And just on Halloween
It fell that night.

"Our stibble-rig was Rab M'Graen,
A clever sturdy fallow:
His son gat Eppie Sim wi' wean,
That lived in Achmacalla:
He gat hemp-seed, I mind it weel,
And he made unco light o't;
But mony a day was by himsel,
He was sae sairly frighted
That very night."

Then up gat fechtin' Jamie Fleck,
And he swore by his conscience,
That he could saw hemp-seed a peck;
For it was a' but nonsense.
The auld guidman raught down the pock,
And out a hanfu' gied him;
Syne bade him slip frae 'mang the folk,
Some time when nae ane see'd him,
And try't that night.

She puffed her pipe with so much smoke
In wrath she was so steaming.
She did not notice a spark burned
Her lovely new worsted apron
Right through that night.

"You naughty little girl!
I defy you to try such sport
And seek the Foul Thief anywhere
For him to tell your fortune.
No doubt you might get a sight!
Great cause you have to fear it
For many a one has had a fright
And lived and died demented
On such a night".

"One harvest, before the Battle of Sheriffmuir,
I remember as if it was yesterday
I was a girl then, I'm sure
I wasn't past fifteen.
The summer had been cold and wet
And grain was really green
Yet still we had a boisterous harvest-home
And just on Halloween
It fell that night.

Our chief harvester was Rab McGean,
A clever, sturdy fellow.
His son got Eppie Sim pregnant
She lived in Achmachalla.
He got hemp-seed, I remember it well
And he really made light of it
But many a day was beside himself,
He was so badly frightened
That very night.

Then up got fighting Jamie Fleck,
And he swore by his conscience
That he'd sow hempseed – a peck[7]
For it was all just nonsense
The old good man reached down the bag
And out a handful gave him
Then invited him to slip out from the gathering
When no one could see him
And try it that night.

[7] A large quantity (equal to 16 pints dry volume).

He marches through amang the stacks,
Though he was something sturtin;
The graip he for a harrow taks.
And haurls it at his curpin;
And every now and then he says,
"Hemp-seed, I saw thee,
And her that is to be my lass,
Come after me, and draw thee
As fast this night."

He whistled up *Lord Lennox' march*
To keep his courage cheery;
Although his hair began to arch,
He was say fley'd and eerie:
Till presently he hears a squeak,
And then a grane and gruntle;
He by his shouther gae a keek,
And tumbled wi' a wintle
Out-owre that night.

He roar'd a horrid murder-shout,
In dreadfu' desperation!
And young and auld came runnin' out
To hear the sad narration;
He swore 'twas hilchin Jean M'Craw,
Or crouchie Merran Humphie –
Till, stop! she trotted through them a';
And wha was it but grumphie
Asteer that night!

Meg fain wad to the barn hae gaen,
To win three wechts o' naething;
But for to meet the deil her lane,
She pat but little faith in:
She gies the herd a pickle nits,
And two red-cheekit apples,
To watch, while for the barn she sets,
In hopes to see Tam Kipples
That very nicht.

She turns the key wi cannie thraw,
And owre the threshold ventures;
But first on Sawnie gies a ca',
Syne bauldly in she enters:
A ratton rattled up the wa',
And she cried, Lord, preserve her!
And ran through midden-hole and a',

He marches through among the (hay) stacks
Though he was staggering a bit
He takes the pitchfork for a harrow
And drags it at his rump
And every now and then, he says
"Hemp-seed I sow thee,
And her that is to be my lass,
Come after me and draw you
As fast this night."

He whistled up Lord Lennox's March[8]
To keep his courage cheery
Although his hair began to arch
He was so scared and uneasy
Till presently he hears a squeak
And then a groan and grunt
Over his shoulder he dared a peek
And tumbled in a somersault
Right over that night.

He roared a horrid murder-shout
In dreadful desperation!
And young and old came running out
To hear the sad narration
He swore it was crippled Jean McCraw
Or hump-backed Merran Humphie
Till stop! she trotted through them all
Who was it but the pig
Astir that night?

Meg would gladly have gone to the barn
To win three weights of nothing
As for meeting the devil on her own
She put little faith in it.
She gave the shepherd a few nuts
And two red-cheeked apples
To watch, while for the barn she sets out
Hoping to see Tam Kipples
That very night.

She carefully turns the key
And over the threshold ventures
But first on Sandy gives a call,
Then boldly in she enters.
A rat scarpered up the wall
And she cried Lord preserve her!
And ran through the dung heap and all

[8] Traditional tune.

And pray'd wi' zeal and fervour,	And prayed with zeal and fervour
Fu' fast that night;	Steadfastly that night.
They hoy't out Will wi' sair advice;	They urged Will out, with harsh advice
They hecht him some fine braw ane;	They promised him some fine beauty.
It chanced the stack he faddom'd thrice	It happened that the stack he fathomed[9] thrice
Was timmer-propt for thrawin';	Was timber-propped for turning;
He taks a swirlie, auld moss-oak,	He mistakes a gnarled old moss-oak
For some black grousome carlin;	For some black gruesome old witch
And loot a winze, and drew a stroke,	Let out a curse and aimed a blow
Till skin in blypes cam haurlin'	Till skin came flying in ribbons
Aff's nieves that night.	Off his fists that night.
A wanton widow Leezie was,	A wanton widow Lizzie was
As canty as a kittlin;	As lively as a kitten
But, och! that night amang the shaws,	But oh! that night among the shaws
She got a fearfu' settlin'!	She got a fearful settling!
She through the whins, and by the cairn,	She through the gorse, and past the cairn
And owre the hill gaed scrievin,	And over the hill went striding
Whare three lairds' lands met at a burn	Where three lairds' lands met at a stream
To dip her left sark-sleeve in,	To dip her left shirt-sleeve in
Was bent that night.	Was determined that night.
Whyles owre a linn the burnie plays,	Sometimes the stream tumbles over a waterfall
As through the glen it wimpl't;	As it winds through the glen
Whyles round a rocky scaur it strays;	Sometimes it strays round a rocky outcrop
Whyles in a wiel it dimpl't;	Sometimes whirls in an eddy
Whyles glitter'd to the nightly rays,	Sometimes glittered to the nightly rays
Wi' bickering, dancing dazzle;	With sparkling, dancing dazzle
Whyles cookit underneath the braes,	Sometimes hidden under the slopes
Below the spreading hazel	Below the spreading hazel
Unseen that night.	Unseen that night.
Among the brackens, on the brae,	Among the brackens on the valley side
Between her and the moon,	Between her and the moon
The deil, or else an outler quey,	The Devil, or else an outdoor cow
Gat up and gae a croon:	Got up and gave a croon.
Poor Leezie's heart maist lap the hool!	Poor Lizzie's heart nearly leapt over the hill
Near lav'rock-height she jumpit;	Nearly lark high she jumped
but mist a fit, and in the pool	But missed her footing, and in the pool
Out-owre the lugs she plumpit,	Right over her ears she fell
Wi' a plunge that night.	With a plunge that night.
In order, on the clean hearth-stane,	In order, on the clean hearth stone
The luggies three are ranged,	Three wooden dishes are ranged
And every time great care is ta'en',	And every time great care is taken
To see them duly changed:	To see them duly changed (around):

[9] Another Halloween custom – to encircle the stack with outstretched arms to call up the vision of the future spouse.

Auld Uncle John, wha wedlock's joys
Sin' Mar's year did desire,
Because he gat the toom dish thrice,
He heaved them on the fire,
In wrath that night.

Wi' merry sangs, and friendly cracks,
I wat they didna weary;
And unco tales, and funny jokes,
Their sports were cheap and cheery;
Till butter'd sowans, wi' fragrant lunt,
Set a' their gabs a-steerin';
Syne, wi' a social glass o' strunt,
They parted aff careerin'
Fu' blythe that night.

Old Uncle John who wedlock's joys
Since Mar's year[10] did desire
Because he got the empty dish three times
He heaved them on the fire
In wrath that night.

With merry songs, and friendly talk
I warrant they did not weary
And weird tales, and funny jokes
Their sports were cheap and cheery
Till buttered sowans, with fragrant steam
Set all their tongues wagging
Then with a social glass of whisky
They parted off careering
Very happy that night.

[10] 1715, the year John Erskine, Earl of Mar, began the Jacobite Rebellion.

Holy Willie's Prayer (1785)

Many critics would say that Burns is at his best in religious satire. To appreciate these poems fully, some knowledge of the religious beliefs of his time is essential. The following is a brief summary of the main Calvinist doctrines which Burns attacks:

> The Elect
> Original Sin
> Hell
> Predestination
> Justification by faith

The Elect are the people chosen by God: they have grace, they go to heaven after death. This might seem like a licence to misbehave as one's fate was already gloriously fixed. However, alongside this is the conviction that the Elect would behave like the Elect, filled with the Holy Spirit here on earth and therefore incapable of sin. It was the need to behave like a sinless person that led to all kinds of hypocrisy.

This is linked with **predestination** – that God has every detail of our lives planned for each of us and we cannot escape our fate.

Original sin is the evil that exists in all of us as part of our nature. We are born with it and it is a legacy from Adam.

Hell is where those who are not 'the elect' go after they die. The Calvinist version of Hell was based on the New Testament vision of a place of eternal fire and total damnation.

"The Son of Man will send out his angels, and they will weed out of his kingdom everything that causes sin and all who do evil. They will throw them into the fiery furnace, where there will be weeping and gnashing of teeth."
(Matthew 13:40-42, quoting Jesus)

Justification by faith: a person is justified when he/she is seen to be righteous (i.e. free from sin) in the sight of God. A lifetime of good works will not make a person justified: only faith will. Unfortunately, faith is also a matter of predestination: you either have it or you don't!

Although by Burns's time, the religious moderates were gaining ground, there were still many people who held to an uncompromising Calvinism. Burns was probably a pious young man , but he became less and less religious as he grew older.

Background to Holy Willie's Prayer

Holy Willie's original was William Fisher, who lived in Mauchline. He was a church elder of the old school (Auld Licht), where the ministers and elders kept an assiduous (and perhaps prurient) eye on the morals of the congregation and called them to account for their sins, mainly drinking and fornication. People could be arraigned, for example, for 'anti-nuptial fornication' if they had a child less than nine months after they were married. Burns was arraigned several times.

The eponymous William Fisher was renowned for his lack of tolerance and also for his own secret vices; in other words, he was almost a caricature of Calvinist hypocrisy.

Gavin Hamilton, who was a lawyer and a good friend of Burns, was a moderate Presbyterian elder (a 'New Licht'). He had been called to account before Mauchline Kirk Session for having been absent from church on several occasions and for having journeyed to Carrick on a Sunday, even although the minister had admonished him. In addition, it was alleged that he had neglected the worship of God within his family, written an abusive letter to the session and, most heinously, sent a servant out to the garden on a Sunday to bring in some potatoes (note that they too are cursed in the poem!).

After the Mauchline session had condemned him, an appeal was sent to the Presbytery of Ayr where Hamilton was vindicated, thanks in great measure to the pleading of Robert Aiken, another lawyer friend of both Burns and Hamilton. In 1785, the Synod, the governing body above the presbytery, granted him 'free from all ground of church censure'.

Style and Structure of Holy Willie's Prayer

The poem is a wonderfully comic dramatic monologue, which reveals this form of relentless Calvinism in all its drama and horror. The tone of the Calvinist purist is at once sycophantic, self-righteous, elitist and fanatical – and ultimately self-revealing in its ludicrous hypocrisy. Note too the subtlety of linguistic variation, from Biblical English to pulpit rhetoric to vituperative vernacular!

Elements of Christian Prayer

Certain elements are always contained in Christian prayer. Among these would be adoration, confession, thanksgiving and supplication. Willie's prayer contains all of these – in some form.

Verses 1-5 begin with adoration and then it becomes apparent that Willie is praising God for making Willie so special, divinely chosen by God. In short, the adoration becomes self-adulation.

These five verses contain almost all of the ideas mentioned above.

In verse 3, Willie is referring to original sin, which should have damned him to Hell as soon as he was born. This makes his grace all the more 'amazing'! Notice the physical details of this Hell, drawn from the quotation from Matthew (above).

Verses 6-10 contain Willie's confession. It may seem strange that a person so full of grace could ever sin. However, if everyone is predestined to behave in God-ordained ways, Willie can have grace – and sin as well: God, who has put temptation in his way to test him, is really responsible for his lust.

Verse 6 sees him professing his zeal in observing and reporting on the sins of others, namely drinking, swearing and dancing, which he manages to steer clear of, only to admit haltingly (and embarrassedly?) to several sexual encounters. With startling irony, he blames his sexual lapse on drink (verse 9), which he had earlier claimed he avoided.

Verse 10 clearly shows that, in Willie's eyes, the lust that daily torments him is sent by God to keep Willie from becoming too proud because he is so 'holy'. Poor Willie! This God-sent daily thirst for drink and sexual gratification is the cross he has to bear with resignation!

Verses 10-17

Having dealt with the formalities, Willie now loses the prayer-plot and embarks on a crescendo of vituperation against Gavin Hamilton. He starts off mildly enough by asking for a blessing on all the elect in 'this place', but his real feelings emerge very quickly; jealousy and humiliation, as a consequence of Ayr presbytery's overturning of Gavin Hamilton's arraignment. Willie has been laughed at and been made to look a fool. Verse 15 shows the extent of his anger and embarrassment in his description of physical incontinence that he was reduced to. Notice too how he loses the formal language of the pulpit as his real emotions burst out – in the vernacular.

The final verse is the calm after the storm, when Willie returns to prayer-mode, promising God all the glory – provided Willie gets more than his share of grace and worldly goods.

1

O Thou, wha in the heavens dost dwell,	O Thou, who in the heavens dost dwell
Wha, as it pleases best thysel',	Who, as it pleases best Thyself
Sends ane to Heaven and ten to Hell,	Sends one to Heaven and ten to Hell
A' for Thy glory,	All for Thy glory
And no for onie guid or ill	And not for any good or ill
They've done afore Thee:	They've done before Thee.

2

I bless and praise Thy matchless might,	I bless and praise Thy matchless might
Whan thousands Thou hast left in night,	When thousands Thou have left in night
That I am here, afore Thy sight,	That I am here, before Thy sight
For gifts and grace,	For gifts and grace
A burnin' and a shining' light	A burning and a shining light
To a' this place.	To all this place.

3

What was I, or my generation,	What was I, or my generation
That I should get sic exaltation?	That I should get such exaltation?
I wha deserve sic just damnation	I who deserve such just damnation
For broken laws,	For broken laws
Five thousand years 'fore my creation,	Five thousand years before my creation
Thro' Adam's cause.	Through Adam's cause.

4

When frae my mither's womb I fell,	When from my mother's womb I fell
Thou might hae plung'd me deep in Hell,	Thou might have plunged me deep in Hell
To gnash my gums, and weep and wail,	To gnash my gums and weep and wail
In burnin lake,	In burning lake
Where damned devils roar and yell,	Where damned devils roar and yell
Chain'd to a stake.	Chained to a stake.

5

Yet I am here a chosen sample,	Yet I am here a chosen sample
To show thy grace is great and ample:	To show thy grace is great and ample:
I'm here a pillar in Thy temple,	I'm here a pillar in Thy temple
Strong as a rock,	Strong as a rock
A guide, a buckler, and example,	A guide, a shield, and an example
To a' Thy flock!	To all Thy flock!

6

O Lord, Thou kens what zeal I bear,	O Lord, Thou knowest what zeal I bear
When drinkers drink, an' swearers swear,	When drinkers drink and swearers swear
And singing here, and dancing there,	And singing here, and dancing there
Wi' great and sma';	With great and small
For I am keepit by Thy fear	For I am kept by Thy fear
Free frae them a'.	Free from them all.

7

But yet, O Lord! confess I must,	But yet, O Lord! confess I must
At times I'm fash'd wi' fleshly lust:	At times I'm troubled with fleshly lust
And sometimes, too, wi' warldly trust,	And sometimes too, with wordly trust
Vile self gets in;	Vile self gets in
But Thou remembers we are dust,	But You remember we are dust
Defil'd wi' sin.	Defiled with sin.

8

O Lord! yestreen, Thou kens, wi' Meg –	O lord, yesterday evening, you know, with Meg
Thy pardon I sincerely beg –	Thy pardon I sincerely beg
O may it ne'er be a livin' plague	O may it never be a living plague
To my dishonour!	To my dishonour
An' I'll ne'er lift a lawless leg	And I'll never lift a lawless leg
Again upon her.	Again upon her.

9

Besides, I farther maun avow,	Besides, I farther must admit
Wi' Leezie's lass, three times I trow –	With Leezie's daughter, three times I believe –
But Lord, that Friday I was fou,	But Lord, that Friday I was drunk
When I cam near her;	When I came near her.
Or else, Thou kens, Thy servant true	Otherwise, you know, your servant true
Wad never steer her.	Would never sleep with her.

10

Maybe Thou lets this fleshly thorn	Maybe You let this fleshly thorn
Beset Thy servant e'en and morn,	Beset Your servant evening and morn
Lest he owre proud and high should turn,	Lest he should turn over proud and high
That he's sae gifted:	Because he's so gifted.
If sae, Thy han' maun e'en be borne,	If so, Your hand must even be borne
Until Thou lift it.	Until You lift it.

11

Lord, bless Thy chosen in this place,
For here Thou has a chosen race!
But God confound their stubborn face,
And blast their name,
Wha bring Thy elders to disgrace
An' public shame.

Lord bless Thy chosen in this place
For here Thou has a chosen race
But God confound their stubborn face
And blast their name
Who bring Thy elders to disgrace
And public shame.

12

Lord, mind Gaw'n Hamilton's deserts;
He drinks, an' swears, an' plays at cartes,
Yet has sae mony takin arts,
Wi' great an' sma',
Frae God's ain priests the people's hearts
He steals awa'.

Lord take care that Gavin Hamilton gets his come-uppance
He drinks and swears and plays at cards
Yet has so many taking arts (charisma)
With great and small,
From God's own priests the people's hearts
He steals away.

13

And when we chasten'd him therefore,
Thou kens how he bred sic a splore,
And set the world in a roar
O' laughing at us;
Curse Thou his basket and his store,
Kail an' potatoes!

And when we chastised him for this
You know how he made such a commotion
And set the world in a roar
Of laughing at us.
Curse Thou his basket and his store
Kail and potatoes.

14

Lord, hear my earnest cry and pray'r,
Against that Presbyt'ry o' Ayr;
Thy strong right hand, Lord mak it bare
Upo' their heads;
Lord weigh it down, and dinna spare,
For their misdeeds!

Lord, hear my earnest cry and prayer
Against that Presbytery of Ayr;
Thy strong right hand, Lord, make it bear
Upon their heads
Lord weigh it down, and do not spare
For their misdeeds.

15

O Lord my God! that glib-tongu'd Aiken,
My very heart and saul are quakin',
To think how we stood sweatin, shakin,
An' pish'd wi' dread,
While he, wi' hingin lip an' snakin,
Held up his head.

O Lord, my God! that glib-tongued Aiken
My very heart and soul are quaking
To think how we stood sweating, shaking
And wet ourselves with dread
While he, with hanging lip and sneering
Held up his head.

16

Lord, in Thy day o' vengeance try him!
Lord, visit them wha did employ him!
And pass not in Thy mercy by them,
Nor hear their pray'r,
But for Thy people's sake destroy them,
An' dinna spare.

Lord, in Thy day of vengeance try him!
Lord, visit them who did employ him!
And pass not in Thy mercy by them
Nor hear their prayer
But for Thy people's sake destroy them
And do not spare.

17
But, Lord, remember me and mine
Wi' mercies temporal and divine,
That I for grace an' gear may shine,
Excell'd by nane,
And a' the glory shall be Thine –
Amen, Amen!

But, Lord, remember me and mine
With mercies temporal and divine
That I for grace and wordly possessions may shine
Excelled by none
And all the glory shall be Thine
Amen, Amen!

Man was made to mourn (1785)

An elegantly-penned poem like this makes nonsense of Burns's persona as a 'heaven-taught ploughman'. It was not heaven that taught him this polished formal English, but John Murdoch, his tutor, as well as William Burness, his father.

As the poem is not in Burns's first language, it lacks the spontaneity and vigour of his vernacular Scots.

The poem is rightly described as a 'dirge' and its tum-te-tum-tum rhythm makes for a monotonous read that emphasises its dirge status. Despite that, it contains one of the poet's most quoted lines:

"Mans' inhumanity to man
Makes countless thousands mourn."

The sentiments it contains have resulted in left-wing politicians claiming Burns for their own – although there are other poems where he seems to lean to the other side.

1.
When chill November's surly blast
Made fields and forest bare,
One ev'ning, as I wand'red forth
Along the banks of Ayr,
I spied a man, whose aged step
Seem'd weary, worn with care,
His face was furrow'd o'er with years,
And hoary was his hair.

2.
'Young stranger, whither wand'rest thou?'
Began the rev'rend Sage;
'Does thirst of wealth thy step constrain,
Or youthful pleasure's rage?
Or haply, prest with cares and woes,
Too soon thou hast began
To wander forth, with me to mourn
The miseries of Man.

3.
The sun that overhangs yon moors,
Out-spreading far and wide,
Where hundreds labour to support
A haughty lordling's pride:
I've seen yon weary winter-sun
Twice forty times return;
And ev'ry time has added proofs,
That man was made to mourn.

4.

'O Man! while in thy early years,
How prodigal of time!
Mis-spending all thy precious hours,
Thy glorious, youthful prime!
Alternate follies take the sway,
Licentious passions burn:
Which tenfold force gives Nature's law,
That Man was made to mourn.

5.

Look not alone on youthful prime,
Or manhood's active might;
Man then is useful to his kind,
Supported is his right:
But see him on the edge of life,
With cares and sorrows worn;
Then Age and Want – O ill match'd pair! –
Shew Man was made to mourn.

6.

'A few seem favourites of Fate,
In Pleasure's lap carest;
Yet think not all the rich and great
Are likewise truly blest:
But oh! what crowds in ev'ry land,
All wretched and forlorn,
Thro' weary life this lesson learn,
That Man was made to mourn.

7.

'Many and sharp the num'rous ills
Inwoven with our frame!
More pointed still we make ourselves
Regret, remorse, and shame!
And Man, whose heav'n-erected face
The smiles of love adorn, –
Man's inhumanity to man
Makes countless thousands mourn!

8.

'See yonder poor, o'erlabour'd wight,
So abject, mean, and vile,
Who begs a brother of the earth
To give him leave to toil;
And see his lordly fellow-worm
The poor petition spurn,
Unmindful, tho' a weeping wife
And helpless offspring mourn.

9.

'If I'm design'd yon lordling's slave –
By Nature's law design'd –
Why was an independent wish
E'er planted in my mind?
If not, why am I subject to
His cruelty, or scorn?
Or why has Man the will and pow'r
To make his fellow mourn?

10.

'Yet let not this too much, my son,
Disturb thy youthful breast:
This partial view of human-kind
Is surely not the last!
The poor, oppressed, honest man,
Had never, sure, been born,
Had there not been some recompense
To comfort those that mourn!

11.

'O Death! the poor man's dearest friend,
The kindest and the best!
Welcome the hour my aged limbs
Are laid with thee at rest!
The great, the wealthy fear thy blow,
From pomp and pleasure torn;
But, oh! a blest relief to those
That weary-laden mourn!'

Scotch Drink (1785)

The main inspiration for this poem was the oppression of distilleries by the excisemen (tax-collectors), which resulted in many of them being closed because the taxes were so high.

With the closure of distilleries, demand for barley dropped and, as the price of barley fell, the landowners raised objections, with the result that an Act was passed to curtail the power of the excisemen. Burns was delighted!

Another inspiration for this poem was *'Caller Water'* by Robert Fergusson (1750-1774), Burns's acknowledged 'elder brother in the muse'. Fergusson too opens his poem with a Biblical reference, to Adam, who drank from a silvery stream that ran through the garden of Eden. His descendants were consequently much sturdier than those of Noah – who drank wine! He deplores poets who sing the praises of wine and Bacchus, claiming that his muse will stay at home and sing in praise of cool water. Like Burn's alcoholic equivalent, Fergusson's cool water is a panacea for the joints, colic, heartburn etc. Most importantly, it is the source of beauty, the reason Edinburgh's lasses are so bonnie – and long may it continue to be so, says Fergusson!

Burns takes the theme much farther into the realm of hyperbole – with some justification perhaps, as he's lauding whisky, not just water. This whisky will oil the wheels of life, ease the stress of the overworked, lighten despair, give zest to homely fare, inspire religious zeal and mend quarrels.

Verses 15-17 are a little diatribe on foreign alcohol which, apart from making people ill, gives money to the enemy.

Burns begins this poem with a little introit, a Biblical justification for drink no less, translated into Scots from the Book of Proverbs! Strong drink would appear to acceptable for those facing death or despair, but also permissible for those suffering from poverty and misery to enable them to forget their wretchedness for a while. How encouraging it must have been for Burns to find this text!

This is the King James Bible version:

Proverbs Ch 31, verses 6, 7
6. Give strong drink unto him that is ready to perish; and wine unto those that be of heavy hearts.
7. Let him drink, and forget his poverty, and remember his misery no more.

Gie him strong drink until he wink,	*Give him strong drink until he winks,*
That's sinking in despair;	*That's sinking in despair;*
An' liquor guid to fire his bluid,	*And liquor good, to fire his blood*
That's prest wi' grief an' care:	*That's pressed with grief and care –*
There let him bouse, and deep carouse,	*Then let him drink and drink to excess*
Wi' bumpers flowing o'er,	*With drinking cups overflowing*
Till he forgets his loves or debts,	*Till he forgets his loves or debts,*
An' minds his griefs no more.	*And remembers his griefs no more.*
Solomon's Proverbs, xxxi. 6, 7.	

1.

Let other poets raise a fracas	Let other poets raise a fracas
'Bout vines, an' wines, an' drucken Bacchus,	About vines, and wines and drunken Bacchus[1]
An' crabbit names an' stories wrack us,	And bad-tempered names and stories upset us
An' grate our lug:	And grate upon our ear.
I sing the juice Scotch beare can mak us,	I sing of the juice Scotch barley can make us,
In glass or jug.	In glass or jug.

2.

O thou, my Muse! guid auld Scotch drink!	O thou my Muse, good old Scotch drink!
Whether thro' wimplin worms thou jink,	Whether through winding worms[2] you dodge
Or, richly brown, ream owre the brink,	Or richly brown, froth over the edge
In glorious faem,	In glorious foam,
Inspire me, till I lisp an' wink,	Inspire me till I lisp and wink,
To sing thy name!	To sing thy name!

3.

Let husky wheat the haughs adorn,	Let husky wheat adorn the valley floors,
An' aits set up their awnie horn,	And oats set up their bearded horn,
An' pease an' beans, at e'en or morn,	And peas and beans at even and morn,
Perfume the plain:	Perfume the plain:
Leeze me on thee, John Barleycorn,	I'll vote for you, John Barleycorn,
Thou king o' grain!	Thou king of grain!

4.

On thee aft Scotland chows her cood,	On you often, Scotland chews her cud
In souple scones, the wale o' food!	In supple scones, the prime choice of food
Or tumbling in the boiling flood	Or tumbling in the boiling flood
Wi' kail an' beef;	With cabbage and beef
But when thou pours thy strong heart's blood,	But where you pour your strong heart's blood,
There thou shines chief.	There you shine as chief.

5.

Food fills the wame, an' keeps us livin;	Food fills the stomach and keeps us living,
Tho' life's a gift no worth receivin,	Though life's a gift not worth receiving,
When heavy-dragg'd wi' pine an' grievin;	When dragged down with pain and grieving.
But oil'd by thee,	But oiled by thee,
The wheels o' life gae down-hill, scrievin,	The wheels of life glide downhill smoothly
Wi' rattlin glee.	With rattling glee.

6.

Thou clears the head o' doited Lear,	You clear the head of foolish learning
Thou cheers the heart o' drooping Care;	You cheer the heart that droops with care,
Thou strings the nerves o' Labour sair,	You string the nerves of the hard-working labourer
At's weary toil;	At his weary toil
Thou ev'n brightens dark Despair	You even brighten dark despair
Wi' gloomy smile.	With gloomy smile.

[1] Roman God of Wine.
[2] Coiled copper tube, part of the condensing process.

7.

Aft, clad in massy siller weed,	Often, clad in solid silver (jugs)
Wi' gentles thou erects thy head;	You raise your head among gentlefolk
Yet, humbly kind in time o' need,	Yet, humbly clad, in times of need,
The poor man's wine:	The poor man's wine:
His wee drap parritch, or his bread,	His small portion of porridge or his bread
Thou kitchens fine.	You give relish to it.

8.

Thou art the life o' public haunts:	You are the life of public haunts.
But thee, what were our fairs and rants?	Without you, what are our fairs and merrymaking?
Even godly meetings o' the saunts,	Even godly meetings of the saints,
By thee inspired,	By you inspired,
When, gaping, they besiege the tents,	When, gaping, they besiege the tents[3],
Are doubly fired.	Are doubly fired.

9.

That merry night we get the corn in,	That merry night we get the corn in,
O sweetly, then, thou reams the horn in!	O sweetly then you froth in the horn (cup)
Or reekin on a New-Year mornin	Or steaming on a New-Year morn
In cog or bicker,	In wooden bowl or beaker
An' just a wee drap sp'ritual burn in,	And burn in just a small amount of spirit
An' gusty sucker!	And tasty sugar.

10.

When Vulcan gies his bellows breath,	When Vulcan[4] blows into his bellows
An' ploughmen gather wi' their graith,	And ploughmen gather with their implements,
O rare! to see thee fizz an freath	O wondrous! to see you fizz and froth
I' the lugget caup!	In the (wooden) cup (with 'ears')
Then Burnewin comes on like death	Then the blacksmith comes on like death
At ev'ry chap.	At every stroke.

11.

Nae mercy, then, for airn or steel:	No mercy then for iron or steel:
The brawnie, bainie, ploughman chiel,	The muscular, bony ploughman lad
Brings hard owrehip, wi' sturdy wheel,	Brings over his shoulder, in a sturdy whirl
The strong forehammer,	The strong forehammer,
Till block an' studdie ring an' reel,	Till block and anvil ring and reel,
Wi' dinsome clamour.	With noisy clamour.

12.

When skirlin weanies see the light,	When screaming new-borns see the light
Thou make the gossips clatter bright,	You make the gossips' chatter bright
How fumbling cuifs their dearies slight;	How fumbling fools their darlings slight
Wae worth the name!	Woe worth the name!
Nae howdie gets a social night,	No midwife gets a social night
Or plack frae them.	Or small coin from them.

[3] See 'The Holy Fair'.
[4] Roman God of Fire.

59

13.

When neebors anger at a plea,
An' just as wud as wud can be,
How easy can the barley-brie
Cement the quarrel!
It's aye the cheapest lawyer's fee,
To taste the barrel.

When neighbours are angry at a plea,
And just as mad as mad can be
How easily can the barley brew i.e. whisky
Cement the quarrel!
It's always the cheapest lawyer's fee,
To taste the barrel.

14.

Alake! that e'er my Muse has reason,
To wyte her countrymen wi' treason!
But monie daily weet their weason
Wi' liquors nice,
An' hardly, in a winter season,
E'er spier her price.

Alas! that ever my Muse has reason
To accuse her countrymen of treason!
But many daily wet their whistle
With dainty liquors
And hardly, in a winter season,
Ever ask her price.

15.

Wae worth that brandy, burnin trash!
Fell source o' monie a pain an' brash!
'Twins monie a poor, doylt, drucken hash,
O' half his days;
An' sends, beside, auld Scotland's cash
To her warst faes.

Woe to that brandy, burning trash!
Painful source of many a pain and illness!
Deprives many a poor, daft drunken fool
Of half his days:
And sends, besides, old Scotland's cash
To her worst enemies.

16.

Ye Scots, wha wish auld Scotland well!
Ye chief, to you my tale I tell,
Poor, plackless devils like mysel!
It sets you ill,
Wi' bitter, dearthfu' wines to mell,
Or foreign gill.

You Scots, who wish old Scotland well
Chiefly to you my tale I tell,
Poor, penniless devils like myself!
It ill becomes you
With bitter, highly-priced wines to mingle
Or foreign measures.

17.

May gravels round his blather wrench,
An' gouts torment him, inch by inch,
Wha twists his gruntle wi a glunch
O' sour disdain,
Out owre a glass o' whisky-punch
Wi' honest men!

May kidney stones twist round his bladder
And gouts torment him, inch by inch,
Who wrinkles his snout with a scowl
Of sour disdain
Over a glass of whisky punch
With honest men.

18.

O Whisky! soul o' plays an' pranks!
Accept a Bardie's gratefu' thanks!
When wanting thee, what tuneless cranks
Are my poor verses!
Thou comes – they rattle i' their ranks
At ither's arses!

O whisky! soul of plays and pranks!
Accept a poet's grateful thanks
When lacking you, what rough noises
My poor verses are!
You appear – they rattle in their ranks
At one another's arses!

19.

Thee, Ferintosh! O sadly lost!
Scotland's lament frae coast to coast!
Now colic grips, an' barkin' hoast
May kill us a';
For loyal Forbes' chartered boast
Is taen awa!

Thee, Ferintosh[5] – o sadly lost!
Scotland's lament from coast to coast!
Now colic grips and barking cough
May kill us all:
For loyal Forbes'[6] chartered boast
Is taken away!

20.

Thae curst horse-leeches o' th' Excise,
Wha mak the whisky stells their prize!
Haud up thy han', Deil! ance, twice, thrice!
There, seize the blinkers!
An' bake them up in brunstane pies
For poor damn'd drinkers.

Those cursed horse leeches of the Excise
Who make the whisky stills their prize
Hold up your hand, Devil, once, twice, thrice!
There, seize the excisemen!
And bake them up in brimstone pies
For poor damned drinkers.

21.

Fortune! if thou'll but gie me still
Hale breeks, a scone, an' whisky gill,
An' rowth o' rhyme to rave at will,
Tak a' the rest,
An' deal't about as thy blind skill
Directs thee best.

Fortune! if you'll but give me still
Whole breeches, a scone, a dram of whisky,
And abundance of rhyme to rave at will,
Take all the rest
And distribute it as your blind skill
Directs you best.

[5] Ferintosh: a malt whisky distilled at Ferintosh, near Dingwall.

[6] The distillery belonged to Forbes of Culloden and the whisky was exempted from duty from 1695 to 1785 as reparation for damages by the Jacobites in 1689. When the taxes were reintroduced, because of complaints from other distilleries, Ferintosh closed in 1785.

The Cottar's Saturday Night (1785)

Many people think this poem shows Burns at his best; many equally believe it shows Burns at his worst. On first hearing it, his brother Gilbert was 'electrified' and claimed the 5th, 6th and 18th stanzas 'thrilled with peculiar ecstacy through my soul'. Does it do it for you?

Fergusson's *The Farmer's Ingle (The Farmer's Fireside)*

Once again, Burns's model came from Robert Fergusson, whose poem *The Farmer's Ingle* was published in 1773. Like this poem, *The Cottar's Saturday Night* is almost in Spenserian stanza form. Both describe the life of the cottar and his family, but where Fergusson 'tells it like it is', Burns veers off into moralising, sentimentality and pious cant.

This is particularly evident in the passages which describe the young women and their amorous adventures. Here is Fergusson's matter-of-fact description:

How Jock woo'd Jenny here to be his bride,	How Jock wooed Jenny here to be his bride,
And there how Marion, for a bastard son,	And there how Marion, for having a bastard son
Upo' the cutty-stool was forc'd to ride,	Had to sit on the confession stool and put up with
The waefu scald o' our Mess John to bide.	The woeful scolding of our Minister.

(*Mess* – was a common and often humorous way to refer to the minister)

Compare this with Burns's rhetoric below. In view of Burns's own sexual peccadilloes, dare we say his attitude is a little hypocritical?

> *Is there, in human form, that bears a heart,*
> *A wretch! a villain! lost to love and truth!*
> *That can, with studied, sly, ensnaring art,*
> *Betray sweet Jenny's unsuspecting youth?*
> *Curse on his perjur'd arts! dissembling, smooth!*
> *Are honour, virtue, conscience, all exil'd?*

Fergusson's poem is written in vernacular Scots, as he says it will be in the first stanza: '*Begin, my Muse, and chant in hamely strain.*' Almost half of '*The Cottar's Saturday Night*' is written in English – and not just ordinary English as would befit humble cottagers, but the poetic diction common to English poets of that time. This polished diction rather undercuts Burns's claim to be singing '*in simple Scottish lays*'. (Stanza 1, line 5)

The poem begins with a stanza from Gray's '*Elegy written in a country churchyard*'

> *Let not Ambition mock their useful toil,*
> *Their homely joys, and destiny obscure;*
> *Nor Grandeur hear, with a disdainful smile,*
> *The short and simple annals of the poor.*
>
> Gray.

The poem is dedicated to Robert Aiken, the lawyer friend of the poet. This is the same Aiken who successfully defended Gavin Hamilton. He also found about a quarter of the number of subscribers to the Kilmarnock edition.

Both Burns and Fergusson loved to depict the freezing weather outside and contrast it with the warmth, both physical and human, inside.

1.

My lov'd, my honour'd, much respected friend!	My loved, my honoured, much respected friend!
No mercenary bard his homage pays;	No mercenary bard his homage pays;
With honest pride, I scorn each selfish end,	With honest pride, I scorn each selfish end,
My dearest meed, a friend's esteem and praise:	My dearest reward, a friend's esteem and praise:
To you I sing, in simple Scottish lays,	To you I sing, in simple Scottish lays,
The lowly train in life's sequester'd scene;	The lowly train in life's sequester'd scene;
The native feelings strong, the guileless ways;	The native feelings strong, the guileless ways;
What Aiken in a cottage would have been;	What Aiken in a cottage would have been;
Ah! tho' his worth unknown, far happier there I ween!	Ah! tho' his worth unknown, far happier there I surmise!

2.

November chill blaws loud wi' angry sugh;	November chill blows loud with deep sighs,
The short'ning winter-day is near a close;	The shortening winter day is near its close,
The miry beasts retreating frae the pleugh;	The miry beasts retreating from the plough,
The black'ning trains o' craws to their repose:	The blackening trains of crows to their repose.
The toil-worn Cotter frae his labour goes –	The toil-worn cottager from his labour goes
This night his weekly moil is at an end,	This night his weekly toil is at an end,
Collects his spades, his mattocks, and his hoes,	Collects his spades, his pick-axes and hoes,
Hoping the morn in ease and rest to spend,	Hoping to spend the morning in ease and rest
And weary, o'er the moor, his course does hameward bend.	And weary, over the moor, his course bends homeward.

The picture of domesticity is idyllic, even as their morality is honed by the patriach's advice.

3.

At length his lonely cot appears in view,	At length his lonely cottage appears in view
Beneath the shelter of an aged tree;	Beneath the shelter of an aged tree.
Th' expectant wee-things, toddlin, stacher through	The expectant infants, toddling, stagger through
To meet their dad, wi' flichterin' noise and glee.	To meet their dad with fluttering noise and glee,
His wee bit ingle, blinkin bonilie,	His humble fireside blinking bonnily
His clean hearth-stane, his thrifty wifie's smile,	His clean hearth-stone, his thrifty little wife's smile,
His lisping infants, prattling on his knee,	His lisping infants, prattling on his knee,
Does a' his weary carking cares beguile,	Does all his weary anxious cares beguile,
And makes him quite forget his labour and his toil.	And makes him quite forget his labour and his toil.

4.

Belyve, the elder bairns come drapping in,	Soon, the elder children come dropping in
At service out, amang the farmers roun';	From out at service among the neighbouring farmers.
Some ca' the pleugh, some herd, some tentie rin	Some drive the plough, some herd, some heeedful run
A cannie errand to a neebor town:	A careful errand to a neighbouring town.
Their eldest hope, their Jenny, woman grown,	Their eldest hope, their Jenny, woman grown,
In youthfu' bloom, love sparkling in her e'e,	In youthful bloom, love sparkling in her eye
Comes hame; perhaps, to shew a braw new gown,	Comes home, perhaps, to show off a lovely new gown
Or deposite her sair-won penny-fee,	Or deposit her hard-earned penny fee
To help her parents dear, if they in hardship be.	To help her dear parents, if they are in hardship.

5.

With joy unfeign'd, brothers and sisters meet,	With unfeigned joy, brothers and sisters meet,
And each for other's weelfare kindly spiers:	And each asks kindly after the other's welfare:
The social hours, swift-wing'd, unnotic'd fleet;	The social hours, swift-winged, un-noticed fleet
Each tells the uncos that he sees or hears.	Each tells the news that he sees or hears
The parents partial eye their hopeful years;	The partial parents eye their hopeful years;
Anticipation forward points the view;	They look forward with anticipation;
The mother, wi' her needle and her sheers	The mother with her needle and scissors
Gars auld claes look amaist as weel's the new;	Makes old clothes look almost as good as new
The father mixes a' wi' admonition due.	The father mixes everything with due admonition.

6.

Their master's and their mistress's command	Their master's and their mistress's command
The younkers a' are warned to obey;	The youngsters all are warned to obey
And mind their labours wi' an eydent hand,	And pay diligent attention to their labours
And ne'er, tho' out o' sight, to jauk or play:	And never, though out of sight, to slack or play
'And O! be sure to fear the Lord alway,	And O! be sure to fear the Lord always,
And mind your duty, duly, morn and night;	And mind your duty, duly, morn, and night.
Lest in temptation's path ye gang astray,	Lest in temptation's path you go astray,
Implore His counsel and assisting might:	Implore His counsel and assisting might:
They never sought in vain that sought the Lord aright.'	They never sought in vain that sought the Lord aright.

A touch of gentle drama and the quality of Jenny's shyness enliven this passage.

7.

But hark! a rap comes gently to the door;	But hark! a rap comes gently to the door.
Jenny, wha kens the meaning o' the same,	Jenny, who knows what it means,
Tells how a neebor lad came o'er the moor,	Tells how a neighbour lad came over the moor
To do some errands, and convoy her hame.	To do some errands and walk her home.
The wily mother sees the conscious flame	The wily mother sees the conscious flame
Sparkle in Jenny's e'e, and flush her cheek;	Sparkle in Jenny's eye, and flush her cheek.
With heart-struck anxious care, enquires his name,	With heart-struck anxious care, enquires his name
While Jenny hafflins is afraid to speak;	While Jenny is half-afraid to speak.
Weel-pleas'd the mother hears, it's nae wild worthless rake.	Well pleased the mother hears it's no wild, worthless rake.

8.

With kindly welcome, Jenny brings him ben;	With kindly welcome, Jenny brings him through,
A strappin' youth, he takes the mother's eye;	A strapping youth, he takes the mother's eye.
Blythe Jenny sees the visit's no ill taen;	Happy Jenny sees the visit's not disapproved of
The father cracks of horses, pleughs, and kye.	The father talks of horses, ploughs and cows,
The youngster's artless heart o'erflows wi' joy,	The youngster's artless heart overflows with joy,
But blate and laithfu', scarce can weel behave;	But shy and bashful, scarcely can behave well.
The mother, wi' a woman's wiles, can spy	The other, with a woman's wiles, can spy
What makes the youth sae bashfu' and sae grave;	What makes the youth so bashful and so grave,
Weel-pleas'd to think her bairn's respected like the lave.	Well pleased to think her child's respected like the rest.

At this point, would you agree Burns goes into overdrive? It must be remembered that, in the same year that stanza 10 was written, Elizabeth Paton, a simple servant girl, gave birth to his first illegitimate daughter.

9.

O happy love! where love like this is found:	O happy love! where love like this is found:
O heart-felt raptures! bliss beyond compare!	O heart-felt raptures! bliss beyond compare!
I've paced much this weary, mortal round,	I've paced much this weary, mortal round,

And sage experience bids me this declare:-
'If Heaven a draught of heavenly pleasure spare,
One cordial in this melancholy vale,
'Tis when a youthful, loving, modest pair,
In other's arms, breathe out the tender tale
Beneath the milk-white thorn that scents the ev'ning gale.'

And sage experience bids me this declare, –
'If Heaven a draught of heavenly pleasure spare
One cordial in this melancholy vale,
It's when a youthful, loving, modest pair
In other's arms, breathe out the tender tale,
Beneath the milk-white thorn that scents the evening gale.'

10.

Is there, in human form, that bears a heart,
A wretch! a villain! lost to love and truth!
That can, with studied, sly, ensnaring art,
Betray sweet Jenny's unsuspecting youth?
Curse on his perjur'd arts! dissembling, smooth!
Are honour, virtue, conscience, all exil'd?
Is there no pity, no relenting ruth,
Points to the parents fondling o'er their child?
Then paints the ruin'd maid, and their distraction wild?

Is there, in human form, that bears a heart,
A wretch! a villain! lost to love and truth!
That can, with studied, sly, ensnaring art,
Betray sweet Jenny's unsuspecting youth?
Curse on his perjured arts! dissembling, smooth!
Are honour, virtue, conscience, all exiled?
Is there no pity, no relenting remorse
Points to the parents fondling over their child?
Then paints the ruined maid, and their distraction wild?

Stanza 11 gets the poem back on track, with the cow chewing the cud behind the wall (Animals and people shared the same house.) and the presentation of the matured cheese. Warm humanity and mutual respect define the young man's first meeting with the family.

11.

But now the supper crowns their simple board,
The healsome parritch, chief o' Scotia's food;
The soupe their only hawkie does afford
That, 'yont the hallan snugly chows her cood;
The dame brings forth, in complimental mood,
To grace the lad, her weel-hain'd kebbuck, fell;
And aft he's prest, and aft he ca's it guid;
The frugal wifie, garrulous, will tell,
How 'twas a towmond auld, sin' lint was i' the bell.

But now the supper crowns their simple table,
The wholesome porridge, chief of Scotland's food,
The supper their only milk cow can afford,
That, beyond the partition snugly chews her cud,
The dame brings forth in complimentary mood,
To welcome the lad, her well preserved strong cheese
And often he's pressed, and often proclaims it good.
The frugal wife, garrulous, will tell
How it was a year old, since lint was in the bell[1].

Stanzas 12 and 13, with their blend of religion and patriotism, are a realistic description of a family gathering at this time.

12.

The chearfu' supper done, wi' serious face,
They, round the ingle, form a circle wide;
The sire turns o'er, wi' patriarchal grace,
The big ha'-Bible, ance his father's pride.
His bonnet rev'rently is laid aside,
His lyart haffets wearing thin and bare;
Those strains that once did sweet in Zion glide,
He wales a portion with judicious care,
And 'Let us worship God!' he says, with solemn air.

The cheerful supper done, with serious face
They form a wide circle round the fireside.
The father turns over, with patriarchal grace,
The big family Bible, once his father's pride.
His bonnet reverently is laid aside,
His grey side-locks wearing thin and bare.
Those strains that once did sweet in Zion glide,
He chooses a passage with judicious care,
And, 'Let us worship God!' he says with solemn air.

13.

They chant their artless notes in simple guise,
They tune their hearts, by far the noblest aim;
Perhaps Dundee's wild-warbling measures rise,
Or plaintive Martyrs, worthy of the name;
Or noble Elgin beets the heaven-ward flame,
The sweetest far of Scotia's holy lays:
Compar'd with these, Italian trills are tame;

They chant their artless notes in simple guise,
They tune their hearts, by far the noblest aim
Perhaps Dundee's[2] wild-warbling measures rise,
Or plaintive Martyrs, worthy of the name;
Or noble Elgin kindles the heaven-ward flame,
The sweetest far of Scotland's holy tunes
Compared with these, Italian trills are tame;

[1] Since the lint (flax) was flowering.

[2] Dundee, Martyrs and Elgin are hymn tunes.

The tickl'd ears no heart-felt raptures raise;
Nae unison hae they, with our Creator's praise.

The tickled ears no heart-felt raptures raise;
No unison have they with our Creator's praise.

Some readers might be tempted to skip to the familiar lines of stanza 19 and avoid the laboured accounts of Biblical heroes.

14.

The priest-like father reads the sacred page,
How Abram was the friend of God on high;
Or, Moses bade eternal warfare wage
With Amalek's ungracious progeny;
Or, how the royal Bard did groaning lie
Beneath the stroke of Heaven's avenging ire;
Or Job's pathetic plaint, and wailing cry;
Or rapt Isaiah's wild, seraphic fire;
Or other holy Seers that tune the sacred lyre.

The priest-like father reads the sacred page,
How Abram was the friend of God on high;
Or, Moses bade eternal warfare wage
With Amalek's ungracious progeny;
Or, how the royal Bard did groaning lie
Beneath the stroke of Heaven's avenging ire;
Or Job's pathetic plaint, and wailing cry;
Or rapt Isaiah's wild, seraphic fire;
Or other holy Seers that tune the sacred lyre.

15.

Perhaps the Christian volume is the theme:
How guiltless blood for guilty man was shed;
How He, who bore in Heaven the second name,
Had not on earth whereon to lay His head;
How His first followers and servants sped;
The precepts sage they wrote to many a land:
How he, who lone in Patmos banished,
Saw in the sun a mighty angel stand,
And heard great Bab'lon's doom pronounc'd by Heaven's command.

Perhaps the Christian volume is the theme:
How guiltless blood for guilty man was shed;
How He, who bore in Heaven the second name,
Had not on earth whereon to lay His head;
How His first followers and servants sped;
The precepts sage they wrote to many a land:
How he, who lone in Patmos banished,
Saw in the sun a mighty angel stand,
And heard great Babylon's doom pronounced
by Heaven's command.

16.

Then kneeling down to Heaven's Eternal King,
The saint, the father, and the husband prays:
Hope 'springs exulting on triumphant wing.'
That thus they all shall meet in future days,
There, ever bask in uncreated rays,
No more to sigh or shed the bitter tear,
Together hymning their Creator's praise,
In such society, yet still more dear;
While circling Time moves round in an eternal sphere.

Then kneeling down to Heaven's Eternal King,
The saint, the father, and the husband prays:
Hope 'springs exulting on triumphant wing.'
That thus they all shall meet in future days,
There, ever bask in uncreated rays,
No more to sigh or shed the bitter tear,
Together hymning their Creator's praise,
In such society, yet still more dear;
While circling Time moves round in an
eternal sphere.

17.

Compar'd with this, how poor Religion's pride,
In all the pomp of method, and of art;
When men display to congregations wide
Devotion's ev'ry grace, except the heart!
The Power, incens'd, the pageant will desert,
The pompous strain, the sacerdotal stole:
But haply, in some cottage far apart,
May hear, well-pleas'd, the language of the soul,
And in His Book of Life the inmates poor enroll.

Compared with this, how poor Religion's pride,
In all the pomp of method, and of art;
When men display to congregations wide
Devotion's every grace, except the heart!
The Power, incensed, the pageant will desert,
The pompous strain, the sacerdotal stole:
But haply, in some cottage far apart,
May hear, well-pleased, the language of the soul,
And in His Book of Life the inmates poor enroll.

18.

Then homeward all take off their sev'ral way;
The youngling cottagers retire to rest:
The parent-pair their secret homage pay,

Then homeward all take off their several way;
The younger cottagers retire to rest:
The parent-pair their secret homage pay,

And proffer up to Heaven the warm request,
That He who stills the raven's clam'rous nest,
And decks the lily fair in flow'ry pride,
Would, in the way His wisdom sees the best,
For them and for their little ones provide;
But, chiefly, in their hearts with Grace Divine preside.

And proffer up to Heaven the warm request,
That He who stills the raven's clamorous nest,
And decks the lily fair in flowery pride,
Would, in the way His wisdom sees the best,
For them and for their little ones provide;
But, chiefly, in their hearts with Grace Divine preside.

This is Burns, the social leveller; political, patriotic and, above all, passionate! Despite the rhetoric, real sentiment comes through that convinces you of his sincerity.

19.

From scenes like these, old Scotia's grandeur springs
That makes her lov'd at home, rever'd abroad:
Princes and lords are but the breath of kings,
'An honest man's the noblest work of God';
And certes, in fair Virtue's heavenly road,
The cottage leaves the palace far behind;
What is a lordling's pomp? a cumbrous load,
Disguising oft the wretch of human kind,
Studied in arts of Hell, in wickedness refin'd!

From scenes like these, old Scotia's grandeur springs
That makes her loved at home, revered abroad:
Princes and lords are but the breath of kings,
'An honest man's the noblest work of God';
And certes, in fair Virtue's heavenly road,
The cottage leaves the palace far behind;
What is a lordling's pomp? a cumbrous load,
Disguising oft the wretch of human kind,
Studied in arts of Hell, in wickedness refined!

20.

O Scotia! my dear, my native soil!
For whom my warmest wish to Heaven is sent!
Long may thy hardy sons of rustic toil
Be blest with health, and peace, and sweet content!
And O! may Heaven their simple lives prevent
From Luxury's contagion, weak and vile!
Then, howe'er crowns and coronets be rent,
A virtuous populace may rise the while,
And stand a wall of fire around their much-lov'd Isle.

O Scotia! my dear, my native soil!
For whom my warmest wish to Heaven is sent!
Long may thy hardy sons of rustic toil
Be blest with health, and peace, and sweet content!
And O! may Heaven their simple lives prevent
From Luxury's contagion, weak and vile!
Then, however crowns and coronets be rent,
A virtuous populace may rise the while,
And stand a wall of fire around their much-loved Isle.

21.

O Thou! who pour'd the patriotic tide,
That stream'd thro' Wallace's undaunted heart,
Who dar'd to, nobly, stem tyrannic pride,
Or nobly die, the second glorious part:
(The patriot's God, peculiarly Thou art,
His friend, inspirer, guardian, and reward!)
O never, never Scotia's realm desert;
But still the patriot, and the patriot-bard
In bright succession raise, her ornament and guard!

O Thou! who poured the patriotic tide,
That streamed through Wallace's undaunted heart,
Who dared to, nobly, stem tyrannic pride,
Or nobly die, the second glorious part:
(The patriot's God, peculiarly Thou art,
His friend, inspirer, guardian, and reward!)
O never, never Scotia's realm desert;
But still the patriot, and the patriot-bard
In bright succession raise, her ornament and guard!

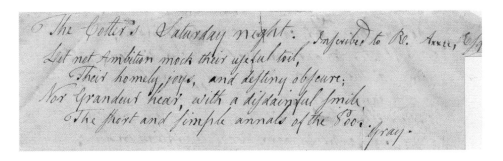

The Jolly Beggars *or*
Love and Liberty – a Cantata (1785)

The cantata consists of a collection of songs from a collection of society's misfits and outcasts, a 'merry core o' randy gangrel bodies' (loud and boisterous vagrants). This is an alternative society which, as Burns demonstrates, has its own values – and these are just as valid as those of the agricultural community or the Edinburgh Literati.

The songs are linked by recitativoes and the songs are mainly in English while the recitativoes are in fluid vernacular Scots. One can perhaps speculate that Burns wrote in English to capture a wider audience. It is also suggested that he writes in two languages to demonstrate that he is not parochial – though those who speak only English may be accused of that too! The English he uses is often the ornamental English of polite society which he exposes for its artificiality by setting it alongside good honest Scots. The latter he uplights by dropping into it Classical allusions, which demonstrate the knowledge and education of the speaker.

Burlesque cantatas like '*The Beggar's Opera*' were not new, but Burns's empathy with the participants is; indeed he himself is a member of the cast. The cantata arose from a visit paid to Poosie Nansie's infamous dive in Mauchline where Burns was deeply affected by the camaraderie, loyalty and, indeed, happiness of the social misfits and vagrants who were making a night of it. They did not care that they were misfits. Indeed, as misfits, they had a freedom which Burns envied. He does not patronise, nor does he sentimentalise. The beggars are what they are – honest about themselves (if not in their professional dealings), free of hypocrisy, loyal, and with an immense zest for life, despite the horrors of their past experiences.

While *The Jolly Beggars* was much admired by other writers e.g. Sir Walter Scott, Thomas Carlyle, Matthew Arnold, Burns himself claimed later in life that he had forgotten all about it. This may have been a convenient lapse of memory because, by that time, he was employed as an exciseman and had been warned that political indiscretion could endanger his employment. The pro-Jacobite song the old woman sings would certainly not have gone down well with his Hanoverian employers, nor would the final chorus.

Recitativo to The Soldier's Song

Notice how rhythmic the song is and how the rhythm, like a drum-beat, is accentuated by internal rhymes. As happens often, Burns paints a picture of the outdoors, north winds stirring up dead leaves, battering hailstones and frost. By contrast, the interior of the tavern is cosy and intimate, with blankets, whisky and sex.

It becomes clear that the soldier has fought many times for his country and would do so again, even although his only rewards are homelessness and a missing arm and leg.

When lyart leaves bestrow the yird,	When grey leaves lie scattered over the earth
Or, wavering like the bauckie bird,	Or, wavering like the bat
Bedim cauld Boreas' blast;	Dim the cold North Wind's blast
When hailstanes drive wi' bitter skyte,	When hailstones drive with bitter striking blows

And infant frosts begin to bite,	And infant frosts begin to bite
In hoary cranreuch drest;	In hoar dressed,
Ae night at e'en a merry core	One night at even a merry party
O' randie, gangrel bodies,	Of boisterous vagrants
In Poosie-Nansie's held the splore.	Had a drinking spree in Poosie Nansie's
To drink their orra duddies;	To drink their worthless rags.
Wi' quaffing and laughing,	With quaffing and laughing
They ranted an' they sang,	They made merry and they sang.
Wi' jumping an' thumping,	With jumping and thumping,
The vera girdle rang.	The very griddle rang
First, niest the fire, in auld red rags,	First, next to the fire , in old red rags,
Ane sat, weel brac'd wi' mealy bags,	One sat, well braced with meal bags
And knapsack a' in order;	And knapsack all in order.
His doxy lay within his arm;	His sweetheart lay within his arm
Wi' usquebae an' blankets warm	Warm with whisky and blankets
She blinket on her sodger:	She blinked at her soldier.
An' ay he gies the tousie drab	And continually he gives the dishevelled floozy
The tither skelpin kiss,	Yet another smacker of a kiss
While she held up her greedy gab	While she held up her greedy mouth
Just like an aumous dish:	Just like an alms dish.
Ilk smack still did crack still	Each smack still did crack still
Like onie cadger's whup;	Like any hawker's whip
Then, swaggering an' staggering,	Then, swaggering and staggering,
He roar'd this ditty up:–	He roared this ditty up.

AIR
Tune: *Soldier's Joy*

I am a son of Mars, who have been in many wars.
And show my cuts and scars wherever I come:
This here was for a wench, and that other in a trench
When welcoming the French at the sound of the drum.
Lal de daudle, etc.

My 'prenticeship I past, where my leader breath'd his last,
When the bloody die was cast on the heights of Abram[1]:
And I served out my trade when the gallant game was play'd,
And the Moro[2] low was laid at the sound of the drum.

I lastly was with Curtis[3] among the floating batt'ries,
And there I left for witness an arm and a limb;
Yet let my country need me, with Eliott[4] to head me
I'd clatter on my stumps at the sound of the drum.

And now, tho' I must beg with a wooden arm and leg,
And many a tatter'd rag hanging over my bum,

[1] Capture of Quebec, September 1759.
[2] Morro – a castle defending Havana Harbour in Cuba: stormed by the British in 1762.
[3] Admiral Sir Roger Curtis.
[4] General Sir George Elliot.

I'm as happy with my wallet, my bottle, and my callet[5],
As when I us'd in scarlet to follow a drum.

What though with hoary locks I must stand the winter shocks,
Beneath the woods and rocks oftentimes for a home?
When the t'other bag I sell, and the t'other bottle tell,
I could meet a troop of Hell at the sound of a drum.

Recitavo

He ended, and the kebars sheuk	He ended and the cabers shook
Aboon the chorus roar;	Above the chorus roar,
While frighted rattons backward leuk	While frightened rats backward look
An' seek the benmost bore	And seek the farthest away hole
A fairy fiddler frae the neuk,	An excited fiddler from the corner
He skirled out "Encore!"	He cried shrilly, "Encore!"
But up arose the martial chuck,	But up arose the camp follower
And laid the loud uproar.	And calmed the loud uproar.

Although the soldier earns the encore, it is his doxy who performs next. Her song trips along befitting the personality of the woman rather than her physical appearance or her years. She has been around, and she's not coy about her lusty sexual appetite and adventures. There's a hint of her infirmity in the last verse where she reveals that she needs two hands to hold the glass steady.

AIR
Tune: *Sodger Laddie*   Soldier Lad

I once was a maid, tho' I cannot tell when,
And still my delight is in proper young men.
Some one of a troop of dragoons was my daddie,
No wonder I'm fond of a sodger laddie!
Sing, lal de dal, etc.

The first of my loves was a swaggering blade,
To rattle the thundering drum was his trade;
His leg was so tight, and his cheek was so ruddy,
Transported I was with my sodger laddie.

But the godly old chaplain left him in the lurch,
The sword I forsook for the sake of the church;
He ventured the soul, and I risked the body,
Twas then I prov'd false to my sodger laddie.

Full soon I grew sick of my sanctified sot,
The regiment at large for a husband I got;
From the gilded spontoon[6] to the fife[7] I was ready,
I asked no more but a sodger laddie

[5] Wench.
[6] A half-pike.
[7] A small high-pitched flute.

But the Peace it reduc'd me to beg in despair,
Till I met my old boy at a Cunningham[8] Fair:
His rags regimental they flutter'd so gaudy,
My heart it rejoiced at a sodger laddie.

And now I have lived – I know not how long!
And still I can join in a cup and a song;
But whilst with both hands I can hold the glass steady,
Here's to thee, my hero, my sodger laddie!

Merry Andrew is the next performer. He is a social misfit because, as he claims, he is 'a fool by profession' – and, like all professional fools, he speaks words of anarchy. The last two verses attack the state and the church.

Recitativo

Poor Merry Andrew in the neuk
Sat guzzling wi' a tinkler hizzie;
They mind't na wha the chorus teuk,
Between themselves they were sae busy.
At length wi' drink and courting dizzy,
He stoiter'd up and made a face;
Then turned and laid a smack on Grizzie,
Syne tuned his pipes wi' grave grimace:–

Poor Merry Andrew in the corner
Sat guzzling with a tinker hussy
They did not care who took up the chorus
They were so preoccupied with each other.
At length, dizzy with drink and courting
He struggled up and made a face
Then turned and gave Grizzie a smacking kiss
Then tuned his pipes with grave grimace.

AIR
Tune: *Auld Sir Symon*

Sir Wisdom's a fool when he's fou:
Sir Knave is a fool in a session:
He's there but a 'prentice I trow,
But I am a fool by profession.

Sir Wisdom's a fool when he's drunk,
Sir Knave is a fool in court.
He's only an apprentice there I trust
But I am a fool by profession.

My grannie she bought me a beuk,
And I held awa' to the school:
I fear I my talent misteuk,
But what will ye hae of a fool?

My granny she bought me a book
And I went away to school.
I fear I mistook my talent
But what will you have of a fool?

For drink I would venture my neck;
A hizzie's the half o' my craft:
But what could ye other expect,
Of ane that's avowedly daft?

For drink I would venture my neck
A hussy's the half of my craft
But what else could you expect
Of one who's avowedly daft?

I ance was tied up like a stirk
For civilly swearing and quaffin';
I ance was abused in the kirk,
For touzling a lass in my daffin'.

I once was tied up like a bullock
For civilly swearing and quaffing
I once was rebuked in the church
For fondling a lass in my fun (i.e. sexual fun).

[8] District in North Ayrshire.

Poor Andrew that tumbles for sport
Let naebody name wi' a jeer:
There's even, I'm tauld, i' the court
A tumbler ca'd the Premier.

Observed ye yon reverend lad
Mak's faces to tickle the mob?
He rails at our mountebank squad –
It's rivalship just i' the job!

And now my conclusion I'll tell,
For faith I'm confoundedly dry:
The chiel that's a fool for himsel',
Gude Lord! he's far dafter than I.

Poor Andrew that tumbles for sport
Let nobody name with a jeer
There's even, I'm told, in the court.
A tumbler called the Premier.

Did you notice that reverend lad
Makes faces to entertain the mob?
He denounces our charlatan squad.
It's just rivalry in the job!

And now my conclusion I'll tell,
For faith, I'm confoundedly dry
The lad that's a fool for himself
Good Lord! he's far dafter than I.

He is followed by the old pickpocket woman, who sings of the loss of her lover, her handsome John Highlandman:

Then neist outspak' a raucle carlin,
Wha kent fu' weel to cleek the sterling;
For mony a pursie she had hooked,
And had in mony a well been ducked:
Her love had been a Highland laddie,
But weary fa' the waefu' woodie!
Wi' sighs and sobs she thus began
To wail her braw John Highlandman

Then next spoke up a rough old woman
Who knew full well how to grab the money
For many a purse she had snatched
And had been ducked in many a well.
Her love had been a Highland lad
But weary falls the woeful gallows rope!
With sighs and sobs she thus began
To bewail her handsome John Highlandman.

John Highlandman, the lover, was a Jacobite who had been hanged after the 1745 rebellion and Bonnie Prince Charlie's final defeat at Culloden. After this defeat, Highlanders (whether or not they supported the prince) were forbidden to wear tartan, carry arms or speak Gaelic. If caught doing any of these, they were imprisoned or banished. Highlanders are bitter about this death blow to Gaelic culture. Tartans had to be dipped in black dye and the language suffered a near fatal setback from which it never recovered. The author John Prebble talks of tartan as 'the shroud' and many Highlanders cannot bear to wear it even to this day.

Burns, who was not a Highlander and therefore not a member of a Highland clan, never wore the kilt. His traditional garb was 'hodden gray', the rough undyed homespun cloth worn by the poor Lowlander.

John Highlandman, the old woman's lover, is a lawbreaker – but the laws he defies are the Hanoverian ones which have attempted to destroy his culture.

The tune is *The White Cockade*. The white cockade was worn on the hat to demonstrate support for the Jacobite cause.

A Highland lad my love was born,
The Lalland laws he held in scorn
But he still was faithfu' to his clan,
My gallant, braw John Highlandman.

A Highland lad my love was born
The Lowland laws he held in scorn
But he still was faithful to his clan
My gallant, handsome John Highlandman.

CHORUS

Sing, hey my braw John Highlandman!
Sing, ho my braw John Highlandman!
There's no a lad in a' the lan'
Was match for my John Highlandman!

Sing, hey my handsome John Highlandman!
Sing, ho my handsome John Highlandman!
There's not a lad in all the land
Was match for my John Highlandman.

With his philabeg an' tartan plaid,	With his short kilt and tartan plaid
And guid claymore down by his side,	And good claymore[9] down by his side
The ladies' hearts he did trepan,	The ladies' hearts he did capture
My gallant, braw John Highlandman.	My gallant, handsome John Highlandman.
We ranged a' from Tweed to Spey,	We travelled from Tweed to Spey
And lived like lords and ladies gay,	And lived like lords and ladies gay
For a Lawland face he feared none,	For he feared no Lowland face
My gallant, braw John Highlandman.	My gallant, handsome John Highlandman.
They banished him beyond the sea,	They banished him beyond the sea
But ere the bud was on the tree,	But before the buds were on the tree
Adown my cheeks the pearls ran,	The pearly tears ran down my cheeks
Embracing my John Highlandman.	Embracing my John Highlandman.
But, och! they catch'd him at the last,	But, oh! they caught him at the last,
And bound him in a dungeon fast:	And bound him in a dungeon fast:
My curse upon them every one,	My curse upon them every one,
They've hanged my braw John Highlandman!	They've hanged my braw John Highlandman!
And now a widow, I must mourn	And now a widow, I must mourn
The pleasures that will ne'er return:	The pleasures that will never return
No comfort but a hearty can,	No comfort but a hearty can,
When I think on John Highlandman.	When I think on John Highlandman.

The vertically challenged violinist or 'pigmy fiddler' then does his thing, preceded by his introduction: Burns uses Italian musical terms to depict the fiddler's self-importance – then cuts him right down to size (or even less than his size!) by describing him reductively as 'the wee Apollo'.

Recitativo

A pigmy scraper, wi' his fiddle,	A pygmy scraper, with his fiddle
Wha us'd at trysts and fairs to driddle,	Who used to play the fiddle at meetings and fairs
Her strappin limb and gausy middle	Her strapping limb and ample middle
(He reached nae higher)	(He reached no higher)
Had holed his heartie like a riddle,	Had holed his heart like a riddle
And blawn't on fire	And blown it on fire.
Wi' hand on haunch, and upward e'e	With hand on haunch and upward eye
He crooned his gamut, one, two, three	He hummed his musical scale, one, two, three,
Then in an *arioso* key,	Then in a melodic key
The wee Apollo	The dinky Apollo
Set off wi' *allegretto* glee	Set off at a moderately fast and cheerful pace
His *giga* solo	His fast-paced solo.

AIR
Tune: *Whistle owre the lave o't*   *Whistle over the rest of it*

[9] A large two-edged sword.

Let me ryke up to dight that tear,
And go wi' me and be my dear;
And then your every care and fear
May whistle owre the lave o't.

Let me reach up to wipe that tear
And go with me and be my dear
And then your every care and fear
May whistle over the rest of it.

CHORUS

I am a fiddler to my trade,
And a' the tunes that e'er I played
The sweetest still to wife or maid,
Was whistle owre the lave o't.

I am a fiddler to my trade
And all the tunes that ever I played
The sweetest still to wife or maid
Was whistle over the rest of it.

At kirns and weddings we'se be there,
And oh! sae nicely's we will fare!
We'll bouse about till Daddie Care
Sings whistle owre the lave o't

At harvest homes and weddings we'll be there
And oh! so nicely we will fare,
We'll drink until Daddie Care
Sings whistle over the rest of it.

Sae merrily the banes we'll pyke,
And sun oursel's about the dyke;
And at our leisure, when ye like,
We'll whistle owre the lave o't!

So merrily the bones we'll pick
And sun ourselves about the wall
And at our leisure, when you like,
We'll whistle over the rest of it.

But bless me wi' your heav'n o' charms,
And while I kittle hair on thairms,
Hunger, cauld, and a' sic harms,
May whistle owre the lave o't.

But bless me with your heaven of charms
And while I tickle hair on guts (i.e. fiddle strings),
Hunger, cold and all such ills
May whistle over the rest of it.

Unfortunately, the pigmy fiddler had chosen the wrong woman to woo with his song. The caird (Tinker or brass worker), who fancies her himself, reacts badly with violence and ridicule. Wee Apollo now becomes Tweedle-dee, a light-weight nursery rhyme character, who begs for mercy then manages a gesture of defiance by sniggering up his sleeve at the caird's rough wooing.

Recitativo

Her charms had struck a sturdy caird,
As weel as poor gut-scraper;
He tak's the fiddler by the beard,
And draws a roosty rapier;

Her charms had struck a sturdy tinker
As well as the poor fiddler
He takes the fiddler by the beard
And draws a rusty rapier.

He swore by a' was swearing worth,
To speet him like a pliver,
Unless he wad from that time forth
Relinquish her for ever.

He swore by everything it was worth swearing by
To spit him like a plover
Unless he would from that time forth
Relinquish her for ever.

Wi' ghastly e'e, poor Tweedle-dee
Upon his hunkers bended,
And prayed for grace wi' ruefu' face,
And sae the quarrel ended.

With ghastly eye, poor Tweedle-dee
Bent down in a crouch
And prayed for grace with rueful face
And so the quarrel ended.

But tho' his little heart did grieve	But though his little heart did grieve
When round the tinkler prest her,	When roundly the tinker pressed her
He feigned to snirtle in his sleeve,	He pretended to snigger in his sleeve
When thus the caird addressed her:–	When thus the tinker addressed her.

To 'Clout the Cauldron' means to patch up the cauldron or pot, in other words the caird's work. The first verse of his address to the lady sounds more like a CV than a love song!

Notice again how Burns uses a mixture of Scots and English words and pronunciationto make the rhymes work.

AIR
TUNE: *Clout the Cauldron*

My bonny lass, I work in brass,	My bonnie lass, I work in brass
A tinkler is my station:	A tinker is my station.
I've travelled round all Christian ground	I've travelled round all Christian ground
In this my occupation;	In this my occupation.
I've taen the gold, an' been enrolled	I've taken the gold, I've been enrolled
In many a noble squadron;	In many a noble squadron
But vain they searched, when off I marched	But vain they searched, when off I marched
To go and clout the cauldron.	To go and patch up pots.
Despise that shrimp, that withered imp,	Despise that shrimp, that withered imp
Wi' a' his noise and cap'rin';	With all his noise and capering
And tak' a share wi' those that bear	And take a share with those that bear
The budget and the apron!	The budget and the apron,
And by that stoup, my faith an' houp,	And by that tankard, my faith and hope
And by that dear Kilbagie!	And by that dear Kilbagie[10]!
If e'er ye want, or meet wi' scant,	If ever you are in need or are hard up
May I ne'er weet my craigie!	May I never wet my throat.

Despite the decidedly unromantic wooing, the lady is his. Burns manages to introduce Cupid, Homer and Bacchus into the recitativo, a demonstration perhaps that his use of his native Scots does not preclude a much wider knowledge and that the two can sit comfortably together.

Notice the polite almost cliché-d language Burns uses at the start of the recitativo – only to shatter it with, 'and partly she was drunk'.

Recitativo

The caird prevailed – th' unblushing fair	The tinker prevailed – the unblushing fair
In his embraces sunk;	In his embraces sunk.
Partly wi' love o'ercome sae sair,	Partly with love sorely overcome
And partly she was drunk.	And partly she was drunk.
Sir Violino, with an air	Sir Violino, with an air
That showed a man of spunk,	That showed a man of spirit
Wished unison between the pair,	Wished unison between the pair
And made the bottle clunk	And made the bottle clunk
To their health that night!	To their health that night.

[10] Whisky.

But hurchin Cupid shot a shaft,	But urchin Cupid shot an arrow
That played a dame a shavie;	That played a trick on a lady.
The fiddler raked her fore and aft,	The fiddler raked her fore and aft[11]
Behint the chicken cavie.	Behind the kitchen hen-coop.
Her lord, a wight o' Homer's craft,	Her lord, a creature of Homer's craft,
Though limpin wi' the spavie	Though limping with rheumatics
He hirpled up, and lap like daft,	He limped up and leaped about like a madman
And shor'd them Dainty Davie	And offered them 'Dainty Davie'
O' boot that night.	For free that night.
He was a care-defying blade	He was a care-defying blade
As ever Bacchus listed!	As ever Bacchus listed.
Though Fortune sair upon him laid,	Though Fortune gave him a hard time
His heart she ever miss'd it.	She always missed his heart.
He had nae wish but – to be glad,	He had no wish but – to be glad
Nor want but – when he thirsted;	Nor want but – when he thirsted
He hated nought but – to be sad,	He hated nothing but – to be sad
And thus the Muse suggested	And thus the Muse suggested
His sang that night.	His song that night.

The poet's song, which comes next, has even more Classical allusions. This is subtle irony since he uses the Greek poetic allusions to claim he has not the learned poetic craft that others may have. He is also putting himself at the same level of his companions, all of whom 'gentle folks' would have 'no regard' for. When Burns wrote this, he had not yet received the recognition of the Edinburgh literati.

AIR
TUNE: *For a' that*

I am a bard of no regard,	I am a bard of no regard
Wi' gentle folks, and a' that,	With gentle folks and all that
But Homer-like, the glowrin' byke,	But Homer-like, the staring crowd
Frae town to town I draw that.	From town to town I attract.

CHORUS

For a' that, and a' that,	*For all that, and all that*
And twice as muckle's a' that,	*And twice as much as all that*
I've lost but ane, I've twa behin',	*I've lost but one, I've two behind*
I've wife eneugh for a' that.	*I've wife enough for all that.*
I never drank the Muses' stank,	I never drank from the Muses' watercourse,
Castalia's burn, and a' that;	Castalia's[12] stream, and all that
But there it streams, and richly reams –	But there it streams and richly froths
My Helicon I ca' that.	My Helicon[13] I call that.
For a' that, etc.	*For all that etc.*
Great love I bear to a' the fair,	Great love I bear to all the fair
Their humble slave, and a' that;	Their humble slave and all that,
But lordly will, I hold it still	But lordly will, I hold it still

[11] Sexual euphemism.

[12] Castalia was a nymph whom Apollo transformed into a fountain. Those who drank its waters were inspired to write poetry.

[13] Mountain in Greece where the Muses had sanctuaries.

A mortal sin to thraw that.
For a' that, etc.

In raptures sweet, this hour we meet,
Wi' mutual love, and a' that;
But for how lang the flie may stang,
Let inclination law that!
For a' that, etc.

Their tricks and craft have put me daft,
They've ta'en me in, and a' that;
But clear your decks, and here's – The Sex!
I like the jads for a' that.

For a' that, and a' that,
An' twice as muckle's a' that,
My dearest bluid, to do them gude,
They're welcome till't for a' that!

A mortal sin to oppose that
For all that, etc.

In raptures sweet, this hour we meet
With mutual love and all that,
But for how long the fly may sting
Let inclination decide that!
For all that, etc.

Their tricks and craft have made me daft
They've taken me in and all that
But clear your decks, and here's – The Sex!
I like the women for all that.

For all that and all that
And twice as much as all that,
My dearest blood to do them good
They're welcome to it for all that.

The poet must have sung well for his song to earn tumultuous applause! The very walls shake and the drinkers scream for more, even as they empty their pockets and pawn the shirts off their backs to buy more drink.

Recitavo

So sang the bard – and Nansie's wa's
Shook with a thunder of applause,
Re-echoed from each mouth!
They toomed their pocks, and pawned their duds,
They scarcely left to co'er their fuds,
To quench their lowin' drouth.
Then owre again, the jovial thrang
The poet did request
To loose his pack and wale a sang,
A ballad o' the best:
He rising, rejoicing,
Between his twa Deborahs,
Looks round him, and found them
Impatient for the chorus:–

So sang the bard – and Nansie's walls
Shook with a thunder of applause
Re-echoed from each mouth.
They emptied their pockets and pawned their clothes
They scarcely left anything to cover their bums
To quench their burning thirst.
Then over again, the jovial crowd
The poet did request
To loose his pack and pick a song
A ballad of the best.
He rising, rejoicing
Between his two Deborahs
Looks round him, and found them
Impatient for the chorus.

The poet's song is in English, but it plants the poet firmly in the ranks of the common man. Rank and obedience to the church and convention do not make for a better life. This rousing finale turns conventional society and morality on their heads.

AIR
Tune: *Jolly Mortals, fill your Glasses*

See the smoking bowl before us,
Mark our jovial ragged ring!
Round and round take up the chorus,
And in raptures let us sing:

CHORUS

A fig for those by law protected!
Liberty's a glorious feast!
Courts for cowards were erected,
Churches built to please the priest!

What is title? what is treasure?
What is reputation's care?
If we lead a life of pleasure,
'Tis no matter how or where!
A fig, etc.

With the ready trick and fable,
Round we wander all the day;
And at night, in barn or stable,
Hug our doxies on the hay.
A fig, etc.

Does the train-attended carriage
Through the country lighter rove?
Does the sober bed of marriage
Witness brighter scenes of love?
A fig, etc.

Life is all a variorum[14]
We regard not how it goes;
Let them cant about decorum,
Who have characters to lose!
A fig, etc.

Here's to budgets, bags, and wallets!
Here's to all the wandering train!
Here's our ragged brats and callets![15]
One and all cry out, Amen!
A fig etc.

In March 1784, Burns wrote, *'I have often courted the acquaintance of that part of mankind commonly known by the ordinary phrase of Blackguards, sometimes farther than was consistent with the safety of my character; those who by thoughtless Prodigality, or headstrong Passions have been driven to ruin... I have yet found among them, in not a few instances, some of the noblest virtues – Magnanimity, Generosity, disinterested friendship, and even modesty, in the highest perfection.'*

---

[14] Constant change.
[15] Loose women.

Epistle to John Rankine (1785)

It is extraordinary that the man who wrote such a tender welcome to his love-begotten daughter (page 140), is the same man who wrote this epistle, to describe the circumstances under which she was conceived! In this letter to a friend, he is both boastful of his sexual conquest and raging at the 'unco guid' for reprimanding him for the offence.

John Rankine was a farmer at Adamhill near Tarbolton and a co-founder of Tarbolton Bachelors' Club.

Verses 1 and 2 refer to incidents in Rankine's life. His dreams refer to a humorous story he had concocted, which had been circulating about the countryside. The 'saint' referred to ironically in verse 2 is a church elder whom Rankine had managed to get roaring drunk. Verses 3 and 4 show techniques similar to those Burns adopts in '*Holy Willie's Prayer*' to uplight hypocrisy.

Verse 7 sees the emergence of the main topic of the epistle. Burns's use of the bawdy vernacular and the crudity of the poaching allegory to describe his sexual conquest makes the reader think he is attempting to show Rankine that he can be just as 'rough, rude and ready-witted' as he is – one of the boys.

His sustained poaching metaphor is very cleverly done – even if in the 21st century it would not be considered politically correct and there would be a definite uneasiness in sniggering at it.

1.

O rough, rude, ready-witted Rankine,	O rough, rude, ready-witted Rankine
The wale o' cocks for fun an' drinkin!	The pick of lads for fun and drinking!
There's monie godly folks are thinkin'	There are many godly folks thinking
Your dreams and tricks	Your dreams and tricks
Will send you, Korah-like, a-sinkin	Will send you, Korah[1]-like, sinking
Straught to Auld Nick's.	Straight to the Devil's [Hell].

2.

Ye hae sae monie cracks an' cants,	You have so many tales and stories
And in your wicked drucken rants,	And in your wicked, drunken rants
Ye mak a devil o' the saunts,	You make a devil of the saints
An' fill them fou';	And get them drunk
And then their failings, flaws, an' wants,	And then their failings, flaws and wants
Are a' seen thro'.	Are all seen through.

3.

Hypocrisy, in mercy spare it!	Hypocrisy, in mercy spare it!
That holy robe, O, dinna tear it!	That holy robe, o, do not tear it!
Spare't for their sakes, wha aften wear it –	Spare it for their sakes, who often wear it –
The lads in black;	The lads in black.
But your curst wit, when it comes near it,	But your cursed wit, when it comes near it,
Rives't aff their back.	Rips it off their backs.

[1] Korah was one of the assembly of Israel who rebelled against Moses. God intervened and the rebels were swallowed up by the earth.

4.

Think, wicked sinner, wha ye're skaithing:	Think, wicked sinner, who you're harming
It's just the Blue-gown badge an' claithing	It's just the Blue-gown badge[2] and clothing
O' saunts; tak that, ye lea'e them naething	Of saints: take that, you leave them nothing
To ken them by	To know them by
Frae onie unregenerate heathen,	From any unregenerate heathen
Like you or I.	Like you or I.

5.

I've sent you here some rhyming ware,	I've sent you here some rhyming ware
A' that I bargain'd for, an' mair;	All that I bargained for and more
Sae, when ye hae an hour to spare,	So, when you have an hour to spare,
I will expect,	I will expect
Yon sang ye'll sen't, wi' cannie care,	You will send that song, with prudent care
And no neglect.	And don't neglect to do it.

6.

Tho' faith, sma' heart hae I to sing:	Though faith, small heart have I to sing,
My Muse dow scarcely spread her wing!	My Muse can scarcely spread her wing!
I've play'd mysel a bonie spring,	I've played myself a lovely dance tune
An' danc'd my fill!	And danced my fill!
I'd better gaen an' sair't the King	I'd be better to have gone and served the king
At Bunker's Hill.	At Bunker's Hill.

7.

'Twas ae night lately, in my fun,	One night lately, in my fun
I gaed a rovin wi' the gun,	I went roving with the gun
An' brought a paitrick to the grun' –	And brought a partridge to the ground
A bonie hen;	A lovely hen;
And, as the twilight was begun,	And, as the twilight had begun,
Thought nane wad ken.	Thought no one would know.

8.

The poor, wee thing was little hurt;	The poor little thing was hardly hurt.
I straikit it a wee for sport,	I stroked it a little
Ne'er thinkin they wad fash me for't;	Never thinking they would harass me for it
But, Deil-ma-care!	But, Devil may care!
Somebody tells the Poacher-Court	Somebody tells the Poacher-Court[3]
The hale affair.	The whole affair.

9.

Some auld, us'd hands had taen a note,	Some old, used hands had taken a note
That sic a hen had got a shot;	That such a hen had got a shot;
I was suspected for the plot;	I was suspected for the plot;
I scorn'd to lie;	I scorned to lie;
So gat the whissle o' my groat,	So I lost my money[4]
An' pay't the fee.	And paid the fee.

[2] Badge worn by a Bedesman (a man who was paid to pray for other people's souls).
[3] The kirk session.
[4] Literally, 'got the whistle of my coin'.

10.

But, by my gun, o' guns the wale,
An' by my pouther an' my hail,
An' by my hen, an' by her tail,
I vow an' swear!
The game shall pay, owre moor an' dale,
For this, niest year!

But, by my gun, the pick of guns
And by my powder and my shot
And by my hen, and by her tail
I vow and swear
The game shall pay, over moor and dale
For this next year!

11.

As soon's the clockin-time is by,
An' the wee pouts begun to cry,
Lord, I'se hae sportin by an' by
For my gowd guinea,
Tho' I should herd the buckskin kye
For't, in Virginia!

As soon as the hatching[5] is over
And the small chicks begin to cry
Lord, I shall have sport by and by
For my golden guinea,
Though I should herd the buckskin cattle
For it, in Virginia!

12.

Trowth, they had muckle for to blame!
'Twas neither broken wing nor limb,
But twa-three chaps about the wame,
Scarce thro' the feathers;
An' baith a yellow George to claim
An' thole their blethers!

Truth, they had a lot to blame me for
It was neither broken wing nor limb,
But two or three knocks about the belly
Scarcely through the feathers;
And both a guinea to claim
And endure their chatter.

13.

It pits me ay as mad's a hare;
So I can rhyme nor write nae mair;
But pennyworths again is fair,
When time's expedient:
Meanwhile I am, respected Sir,
Your most obedient.

It makes me always as mad as a hare
So that I can neither rhyme nor write any more;
But tit-for-tat
When time's expedient
Meanwhile I am, respected Sir,
Your most obedient.

[5] Child-birth.

To a Mouse (1785)

This is perhaps Burns's most quoted and best-known poem. What makes it so successful? These suggestions might help to provide part of the answer:

- His holistic perception of the mouse – from its size, to its sleek coat, its panic, its position in relation to him and the plough.

- Burns's knack in moving from the concrete to the abstract. The shift to English in verse 2 marks a move from the particular to the general. Man is no longer part of nature, because man is in charge – and yet, both man and mouse are subject to the basic laws of nature, life and death.

- The real empathy Burns has for the mouse and the real ruin faced by it. The mouse's plight could be that of the poor peasant. 'But mousie, thou art no thy lane' etc. brings this empathy to a real fullness. The plight of the mouse is not just the plight of the peasant farmer but of any member of the human race.

- The very personal sentiment of the last verse. The poet realises that his pain is much worse because he can remember the bitterness of the past and also fear the future.

During this period people were being cleared from the land all over Scotland to make way for a form of agriculture, which brought the landlords more income than rents did. The Highland Clearances are well documented, but the Lowland ones were just as vicious. Perhaps this is the poet's underlying fear, for many people suffered the same fate as Burns's timorous beastie.

There is real scorching pain in the final stanzas, born of insecurity and fear. This is the particular made universal.

Wee, sleekit, cowrin, tim'rous beastie,	Small, sleek, cowering, timorous beast
O, what a panic's in thy breastie!	O, what a panic's in your breast!
Thou need na start awa sae hasty,	There's no need to run away so hastily
Wi bickering brattle!	With a rushing patter of feet
I wad be laith to rin an' chase thee,	I would be loathe to run and chase you
Wi' murdering pattle.	With murdering pattle.[1]
I'm truly sorry man's dominion	I'm truly sorry man's dominion
Has broken Nature's social union,	Has broken Nature's social union,
An' justifies that ill opinion,	And justifies that ill opinion,
Which makes thee startle	Which makes thee startle
At me, thy poor, earth born companion,	At me, thy poor, earth born companion,
An' fellow mortal!	And fellow mortal!
I doubt na, whyles, but thou may thieve;	I doubt not that sometimes you steal
What then? poor beastie, thou maun live!	What then? poor wee beast, you must live!
A daimen icker in a thrave	An occasional ear of corn in a big measure
'S a sma' request;	Is a small request;

---

[1] A tool like a small spade for cleaning the ploughshare.

I'll get a blessin wi' the lave,
An' never miss't.

Thy wee-bit housie, too, in ruin!
It's silly wa's the win's are strewin!
An' naething, now, to big a new ane,
O' foggage green!
An' bleak December's win's ensuin,
Baith snell an' keen!

Thou saw the fields laid bare an' waste,
An' weary winter comin fast,
An' cozie here, beneath the blast,
Thou thought to dwell,
Till crash! the cruel coulter past
Out thro' thy cell.

That wee bit heap o' leaves an' stibble,
Has cost thee monie a weary nibble!
Now thou's turned out, for a' thy trouble,
But house or hald,
To thole the winter's sleety dribble,
An' cranreuch cauld!

But Mousie, thou art no thy lane,
In proving foresight may be vain:
The best laid schemes o' mice an' men
Gang aft agley,
An' lea'e us nought but grief an' pain,
For promis'd joy!

Still thou are blest, compared wi' me!
The present only toucheth thee:
But och! I backward cast my e'e,
On prospects drear!
An' forward, tho' I canna see,
I guess an' fear!

I'll get a blessing with the rest
And never miss it.

Your tiny little house, too in ruin!
The winds are scattering its weak walls
And nothing, now, to build a new one
Of green grass!
And bleak December's winds ensuing
Both biting and keen.

Thou saw the fields laid bare and waste,
And weary winter coming fast,
And cosy here, beneath the blast,
Thou thought to dwell,
Till crash! the cruel coulter past
Out through thy cell.

That little heap of leaves and stubble
Has cost you many a weary nibble!
Now you're turned out for all your trouble
Without house or home
To endure the winter's sleety dribble
And frosty cold.

But, little mouse, you are not alone
In proving foresight may be vain:
The best laid schemes of mice and men
Often go awry
And leave us nothing but grief and pain
For promised joy!

Still you are blessed, compared with me!
The present only concerns you
But oh! I cast my eye back
On dreary prospects
And forward, though I cannot see,
I guess and fear.

83

Address to the unco guid, or the rigidly righteous (1786)

Burns knew all about human failings and yielding to temptation. In April of this year, his attestation of marriage to Jean Armour (acknowledgement of her as his common law wife) was repudiated by her family. James Armour, master mason in Mauchline, had no wish to have Robert Burns as his son-in-law and the pregnant Jean was sent to live with relatives in Paisley. Devastated, Burns's intention was then to emigrate to Jamaica. At the same time, he renewed his relationship with Mary Campbell (Highland Mary), whom he also intended to marry. Tragically, Mary died of typhus, perhaps in premature childbirth, when she went home to tell her parents of her intentions. Meanwhile, Jean Armour had given birth to twins after both she and Burns had been called to account in the church and been publicly admonished. Small wonder that this poem is making a plea for the understanding of human frailty!

Here, he is addressing the Holy Willies of the world whose 'rigid righteousness' makes them less than human. He says they are like mills that clatter constantly, as they document the failings of others. In verse 5, he accuses them of the worst hypocrisy, claiming that what they really fear about having a good time is the calculation of what it would cost – rather than the fear of Hell! Verse 6 sees him appearing to titillate the virtuous ladies in their 'godly laces', but then tells them that nobody would be likely to fancy them anyway.

The poet's skilled crafsmanship gives each stanza different imagery and figures of speech:

1. mill-working
2. legal terminology
3. balancing accounts
4. the sea
5. social gatherings
6. sexual encounters
7. & 8. God's role

The final verse shows Burns's thoughts on predestination: God made us as we are and we can't change it. Notice the mixed imagery of this stanza – music, clockwork and book-keeping – which Burns manages to blend together into a single idea. We can partially understand what makes human beings err, but we do not know to what extent they have tried to resist temptation. Only God can fully understand.

The theme of the poem comes from Ecclesiastes chapter 7, verse 16: *Be not righteous over much: neither make thyself over wise; why shouldest thou destroy thyself?*

Burns's concrete corn and chaff metaphor lightens the abstract moralising of the introduction.

My son, these maxims make a rule,
An' lump them ay thegither:
The Rigid Righteous is a fool,
The Rigid Wise anither;

My son, these maxims make a rule
And always lump them together
The rigidly righteous person is a fool
The rigidly wise another;

The cleanest corn that e'er was dight
May hae some pyles o' caff in;
So ne'er a fellow-creature slight
For random fits o' daffin.
Solomon. (Ecclesiastes vii. 16)

The cleanest corn that ever was sifted
May have a fair amount of chaff in it
So never slight a fellow creature
For occasional spells of fun.

1.

O ye, wha are sae guid yoursel,
Sae pious and sae holy,
Ye've nought to do but mark and tell
Your neebours' fauts and folly!
Whase life is like a weel-gaun mill,
Supplied wi' store o' water;
The heapet happer's ebbing still,
An' still the clap plays clatter!

O you, who are so good yourself
So pious and so holy
You've nothing to do but mark and tell
Your neighbour's faults and folly,
Whose life is like a well-running mill
Supplied with a store of water
The heaped hopper is ebbing still
And still the clapper clatters!

2.

Hear me, ye venerable core,
As counsel for poor mortals
That frequent pass douce Wisdom's door
For glaikit Folly's portals:
I for their thoughtless, careless sakes
Would here propone defences –
Their donsie tricks, their black mistakes,
Their failings and mischances.

Hear me, ye venerable company
As counsel for poor mortals
That frequently pass by sober Wisdom's door
For daft Folly's portals.
I for their thoughtless, careless sakes
Would here propone defences –
Their stupid tricks, their black mistakes,
Their failings and mischances.

3.

Ye see your state wi' theirs compared,
And shudder at the niffer;
But cast a moment's fair regard,
What makes the mighty differ?
Discount what scant occasion gave;
That purity ye pride in;
And (what's aft mair than a' the lave)
Your better art o' hidin.

You see your state with theirs compared
And shudder at the exchange,
But cast a moment's fair regard,
What makes the mighty differ?
Discount what scant occasion gave
That purity ye pride in
And (what's often more than all the rest)
Your better art of hiding.

4.

Think, when your castigated pulse
Gies now and then a wallop,
What ragings must his veins convulse,
That still eternal gallop!
Wi' wind and tide fair i' your tail,
Right on ye scud your sea-way;
But in the teeth o' baith to sail,
It makes an unco lee-way.

Think, when your castigated pulse
Gives now and then a wallop
What ragings must his veins convulse
That still eternal gallop!
With the wind and a fair tide at your back
You sail by at speed
But in the teeth of both to sail
It makes an enormous lee-way.

5.

See Social-life and Glee sit down,
All joyous and unthinking,
Till, quite transmugrify'd, they're grown
Debauchery and Drinking:
O, would they stay to calculate
Th' eternal consequences,
Or – your more dreaded hell to state –
Damnation of expenses!

See Social-life and Glee sit down
All joyous and unthinking
Till, quite transformed, they've become
Debauchery and Drinking:
O, would they stay to calculate
The eternal consequences
Or – your more dreaded hell to state –
Damnation of expenses!

6.

Ye high, exalted, virtuous dames,
Tied up in godly laces,
Before ye gie poor Frailty names,
Suppose a change o' cases:
A dear-lov'd lad, convenience snug,
A treach'rous inclination–
But, let me whisper i' your lug,
Ye're aiblins nae temptation.

You high exalted virtuous dames
Tied up in godly laces
Before you call poor Frailty names
Imagine a change of cases:
A dearly loved lad, a snug opportunity
A treacherous inclination–
But, let me whisper in your ear
You're perhaps no temptation.

7.

Then gently scan your brother man,
Still gentler sister woman;
Tho' they may gang a kennin wrang,
To step aside is human:
One point must still be greatly dark,
The moving why they do it;
And just as lamely can ye mark,
How far perhaps they rue it.

Then gently scan your brother man
Still gentler sister woman
Though they may knowingly go wrong
To err is human:
One point must still be greatly dark
The moving why they do it
And just as lamely can you mark
How far perhaps they rue it.

8.

Who made the heart, 'tis He alone
Decidedly can try us:
He knows each chord, its various tone,
Each spring, its various bias:
Then at the balance let's be mute,
We never can adjust it;
What's done we partly may compute,
But know not what's resisted.

Who made the heart, 'tis He alone
Decidedly can try us:
He knows each chord, its various tone
Each spring, its various bias.
Then at the balance let's be mute
We never can adjust it.
What's done we partly may compute
But know not what's resisted.

The Twa Dugs (1786)

As in so many of Burns's poems, the focus here is on the rich-poor divide in society. In this case, it becomes clear how class divisions affect individual lives, how neither group has a clue about how the other half lives and that the poor, whose labour provides most of the luxuries for the rich, are, paradoxically, happier with their lot.

Burns's skill is consummate in this dialogue between two dogs who, in the beast-fable tradition, can hold inspired and informed discussion. They demonstrate a whole range of emotions, which enrich the discussion – empathy, surprise and indignation, sarcasm, naivety – and Burns reminds us neatly every so often that it's a dog who's speaking!

Caesar, named after a Roman Emperor, is the rich man's pet, a Newfoundland breed *'whalpit some place far abroad, Whare sailors gang to fish for cod.'* Despite his prestigious name and pedigree, however, Caesar is no snob, happy to piss on the stones with any 'tawted tyke' (mangy mongrel). He begins his discourse mainly in English, but shows he has natural vernacular speech when he gets disturbed and indignant.

Luath, whose name means 'swift' in Gaelic, is the ploughman's collie.

While Luath has a naive optimistic view of the gentry, Caesar is abysmally ignorant about the peasants. Each has to enlighten the other and correct the misconceptions. By the end of the dialogue, there is a perceptive, often humorous and certainly satirical commentary on society and its class values. Regardless of the poem's purpose, Burns conjures up a wonderful sense of 'dog-ness'. Look at lines 37–46 to see how alliteration and onomatopoeia enhance the dog's snuffling and burrowing.

Caesar starts by confessing his ignorance of how peasants survive and commenting on the huge amounts of food his masters – and their flunkies – eat. Luath explains that, although life is hard, the people are 'wonderfu contented' and that this kind of life breeds sturdy, handsome offspring. Caesar then comments on the harsh treatment the tenants often receive from the lairds. Luath's answer is that they live so close to poverty that it doesn't scare them and the peasants delight in their domestic life and children. Sometimes some drink will help them to relax and they'll venture into deep discussions of politics and religion. He describes the sociability of winter evenings round the fire with a few beers and smokes and snuff. He admits however that some tenants are evicted by middlemen – the fault of absentee landlords who, Luath believes, are working for Britain's good. *'For Britain's guid! Guid faith, I doubt it'*, Caesar interjects – they just do what the leader tells them then set off on European tours of dissipation. Burns undercuts the European experience with humorous irony. Luath is appalled. He then suggests that rich folk, with no fear of hunger or cold, must have a life of pleasure. Caesar claims that, free of such worries, the fools invent worries. When the peasant finishes his day's work, he can relax – but the gentry don't work and so their nights are restless and disturbed. Even their recreation is marred by the need to show off – scandal is rife and they might gamble some poor man's stackyard on the turn of a playing card.

Some will suggest that Burns is rather biased in this poem – a piece of social propaganda? However, before the dogs go their separate ways, Caesar concedes there are exceptions. Nevertheless, it has been a key theme of western literature for generations that simple folk have a greater understanding of what is moral/ethical than the rich do.

'Twas in that place o' Scotland's isle,
That bears the name o' auld King Coil,
Upon a bonnie day in June,
When wearin' thro' the afternoon,
Twa dogs, that were na thrang at hame,
Forgather'd ance upon a time.
The first I'll name, they ca'd him Caesar,
Was keepit for 'his Honor's' pleasure:
His hair, his size, his mouth, his lugs,
Shew'd he was nane o' Scotland's dogs;
But whalpit some place far abroad,
Whare sailors gang to fish for cod.

His locked, letter'd, braw brass collar
Shew'd him the gentleman an' scholar;
But tho' he was o' high degree,
The fient a pride, nae pride had he;
But wad hae spent an hour caressin,
Ev'n wi' a tinkler-gipsy's messin:
At kirk or market, mill or smiddie,
Nae tawted tyke, tho' e'er sae duddie,
But he wad stan't, as glad to see him,
An' stroan't on stanes an' hillocks wi' him.

The tither was a ploughman's collie,
A rhyming, ranting, raving billie,
Wha for his friend an' comrade had him,
And in his freaks had Luath ca'd him,
After some dog in Highland sang,
Was made lang syne – Lord knows how lang.

He was a gash an' faithfu' tyke,
As ever lap a sheugh or dyke.
His honest, sonsie, baws'nt face
Ay gat him friends in ilka place;
His breast was white, his tousie back
Weel clad wi' coat o' glossy black;
His gawsie tail, wi' upward curl,
Hung owre his hurdies wi' a swirl.

Nae doubt but they were fain o' ither,
And unco pack an' thick thegither,
Wi' social nose whyles snuff'd an' snowkit;
Whyles mice an' moudieworts they howkit;
Whyles scour'd awa' in lang excursion,
An' worry'd ither in diversion;
Till tir'd at last wi' monie a farce,

'Twas in that place of Scotland's Isle[1]
That bears the name of Old King Cole
Upon a pleasant day in June
When wearing through the afternoon
Two dogs, that were not busy at home
Foregathered once upon a time.
The first I'll name, they called him Caesar
Was kept for 'his Honour's' pleasure.
His hair, his size, his mouth, his ears
Showed he was not one of Scotland's dogs
But whelped some place far abroad
Where sailors go to fish for cod.

His locked, lettered, handsome brass collar
Showed him (to be) the gentleman and scholar
But though he was of high degree
Devil a bit of pride, no pride had he
But would have spent an hour cavorting
Even with a tinker gipsy's mongrel.
At church or market, mill or blacksmith's
No tattered mongrel, though ever so scruffy
But he would have stood, as glad to see him
And piss on stones and hillocks with him.

The other was a ploughman's collie
A rhyming, riotous, wild rascal
Who had him for his friend and comrade
And in his boldness called him Luath
After some dog in Highland song
That was written long ago – Lord knows how long.

He was a smart and faithful dog
As ever leapt a ditch or stone wall.
His honest, pleasant, white-streaked face
Always found him friends everywhere.
His breast was white, his shaggy back
Well clad with coat of glossy black;
His cheerful tail, with upward curl
Hung over his buttocks with a swirl.

No doubt but they were happy with each other
And very intimate and thick together
With social nose sometimes sniffed and poked
Sometimes mice and moles they dug up
Sometimes scampered away in a long excursion
And worried each other for a bit of sport
Till tired at last with many a farce

[1] Kyle, a district of Ayrshire.

They sat them down upon their arse,
An' there began a lang digression
About the 'lords o' the creation'.

CAESAR

I've aften wonder'd, honest Luath,
What sort o' life poor dogs like you have;
An' when the gentry's life I saw,
What way poor bodies liv'd ava.
Our laird gets in his racked rents,
His coals, his kain, an' a' his stents:
He rises when he likes himsel;
His flunkies answer at the bell;
He ca's his coach; he ca's his horse;
He draws a bonie silken purse,
As lang's my tail, whare, thro' the steeks,
The yellow letter'd Geordie keeks.

Frae morn to e'en it's nought but toiling,
At baking, roasting, frying, boiling;
An' tho' the gentry first are stechin,
Yet ev'n the ha' folk fill their pechan
Wi' sauce, ragouts, an' sic like trashtrie,
That's little short o' downright wastrie.
Our whipper-in, wee, blastit wonner,
Poor, worthless elf, it eats a dinner,
Better than onie tenant-man
His Honor has in a' the lan';
An' what poor cot-folk pit their painch in,
I own it's past my comprehension.

LUATH

Trowth, Caesar, whyles they're fash't enough:
A cotter howkin in a sheugh,
Wi' dirty stanes biggin a dyke,
Baring a quarry, an' sic like;
Himsel, a wife, he thus sustains,
A smytrie o' wee duddie weans,
An' nought but his han' darg to keep
Them right an' tight in thack an' rape.
An' when they meet wi' sair disasters,
Like loss o' health or want o' masters,
Ye maist wad think, a wee touch langer,
An' they maun starve o' cauld and hunger:
But how it comes, I never kend yet,
They're maistly wonderfu' contented;
An' buirdly chiels, an' clever hizzies,
Are bred in sic a way as this is.

They sat themselves down upon their arse
And there began a long digression
About the 'lords of the creation'.

CAESAR

I've often wondered, honest Luath,
What sort of life poor dogs like you have
And when the gentry's life I saw
[In] What way poor folk lived at all.
Our laird gets in his excessive rents
His coals, his payments in kind and all his dues:
He rises when he likes himself
His flunkies answer at the bell
He calls his coach, he calls his horse
He produces a lovely silken purse
As long as my tail, where, through the stitches,
The yellow lettered Guinea peeps out.

From morn to evening it's nothing but toiling,
At baking, roasting, frying, boiling
And thought the gentry are crammed full first
Yet even the servants fill their bellies
With sauce, ragouts and such-like rubbish
That's little short of downright wasteful.
Our huntsman, wee, blasted wonder
Poor worthless elf, it eats a dinner
Better than any tenant farmer
His Honour has in all the land.
And what poor cottagers put in their stomach
I admit it's past my comprehension.

LUATH

Indeed, Caesar, sometimes they're bothered enough:
A cottager digging in a ditch
With dirty stones building a wall
Clearing a quarry, and such like
Himself, a wife, he thus sustains
A litter of small ragged children
And nothing but his own manual labour to keep
Them right and secure in thatch and rope.
And when they meet with sore disasters
Like loss of health or want of masters
You would probably think, a little longer
And they would starve of cold and hunger.
But how it happens, I never yet found out
They're mostly wonderfully contented
And sturdy lads and clever lasses
Are bred just in this way.

CAESAR

But then to see how ye're negleckit,
How huff'd an' cuff'd, an' disrespecket!
Lord man, our gentry care as little
For delvers, ditchers, an' sic cattle;
They gang as saucy by poor folk,
As I wad by a stinking brock.
I've notic'd, on our laird's court-day,
(An' monie a time my heart's been wae),
Poor tenant bodies, scant o' cash,
How they maun thole a factor's snash:
He'll stamp an' threaten, curse an' swear
He'll apprehend them, poind their gear;
While they maun staun', wi' aspect humble,
An' hear it a', an' fear an' tremble!
I see how folk live that hae riches;
But surely poor-folk maun be wretches!

LUATH

They're nae sae wretched 's ane wad think:
Tho' constantly on poortith's brink,
They're sae accustom'd wi' the sight,
The view o't gies them little fright.
Then chance an' fortune are sae guided,
They're ay in less or mair provided;
An' tho' fatigu'd wi' close employment,
A blink o' rest's a sweet enjoyment.
The dearest comfort o' their lives,
Their grushie weans an' faithfu' wives;
The prattling things are just their pride,
That sweetens a' their fire-side.

An' whyles twalpennie worth o' nappy
Can mak the bodies unco happy:
They lay aside their private cares,
To mind the Kirk and State affairs;
They'll talk o' patronage an' priests,
Wi' kindling fury i' their breasts,
Or tell what new taxation's comin,
An' ferlie at the folk in Lon'on.

As bleak-fac'd Hallowmass returns,
They get the jovial, ranting kirns,
When rural life, of every station,
Unite in common recreation;
Love blinks, Wit slaps, an' social Mirth
Forgets there's Care upo' the earth.

CAESAR

But then to see how you're neglected
How upset and browbeaten and disrespected!
Lord man, our gentry care as little
For diggers, ditchers and such cattle
They go so saucily past poor folk
As I would past a stinking badger.
I've noticed in our laird's court-day
(And many a time my heart's been sad)
Poor tenant folk, short of cash
How they must endure a factor's snash:
He'll stamp and threaten, curse and swear
He'll apprehend them, confiscate their goods
While they must stand, with aspect humble
And hear it all, and fear and tremble!
I see how people live who have riches
But surely poor folk must be wretches.

LUATH

They're not as wretched as one would think
Though constantly on poverty's brink
They're so accustomed to the sight
The view of it gives them little fright.
Then chance and fortune are so guided
They're always more or less provided for
And though tired out with unremitting employment
A blink of rest's a sweet enjoyment.
The dearest comfort of their lives,
Their thriving children and faithful wives
The prattling things are just their pride
That sweetens all their fireside.

And sometimes twelve pence worth of drink
Can make them extraordinarily happy
They lay aside their private cares
To consider church and state affairs;
They'll talk of patronage and priests
With kindling fury in their breasts
Or tell what new taxation's coming
And wonder at the folks in London.

As bleak-faced All Saints' Day returns
They hold jovial, festive harvest-homes
When rural life of every station
Unite in communal recreation;
Love blinks, Wit slaps and social Mirth
Forgets there's care upon the earth.

That merry day the year begins,
They bar the door on frosty win's;
The nappy reeks wi' mantling ream,
An' sheds a heart-inspiring steam;
The luntin pipe, an' sneeshin mill,
Are handed round wi' right guid will;
The cantie auld folks crackin crouse,
The young anes ranting thro' the house –
My heart has been sae fain to see them,
That I for joy hae barkit wi' them.

Still it's owre true that ye hae said
Sic game is now owre aften play'd;
There's monie a creditable stock
O' decent, honest, fawsont folk,
Are riven out baith root and branch,
Some rascal's pridefu' greed to quench,
Wha thinks to knit himsel the faster
In favor wi' some gentle master,
Wha, aiblins thrang a parliamentin',
For Britain's guid his saul indentin' –

CAESAR

Haith, lad, ye little ken about it:
For Britain's guid! guid faith! I doubt it.
Say rather, gaun as Premiers lead him:
An' saying aye or no's they bid him:
At operas an' plays parading,
Mortgaging, gambling, masquerading:
Or maybe, in a frolic daft,
To Hague or Calais taks a waft,
To make a tour an' tak a whirl,
To learn bon ton, an' see the worl'.
There at Vienna or Versailles,
He rives his father's auld entails;
Or by Madrid he taks the rout,
To thrum guitars an' fecht wi' nowt;
Or down the Italian vista startles,
Whore-hunting amang groves o' myrtles;
Then bowses drumlie German-water,
To mak himsel look fair an' fatter,
An' purge the bitter ga's an' cankers
O' curst Venetian bores an' chancres.
For Britain's guid! For her destruction!
Wi' dissipation, feud an' faction.

That merry day the year begins
They bar the door on frosty winds
The ale steams with a mantle of froth
And sheds a heart-inspiring steam.
The lit pipe, and snuff mill
Are handed round with right good will
The lively old folk gossiping cheerfully
The young ones romping through the house.
My heart has been so glad to see them
That I for joy have barked with them.

Still it's too true what you have said
Such sport is now too often played;
There's many a creditable stock
Of decent, honest, respectable folk
Are torn out, both root and branch
Some rascal's prideful greed to quench
Who thinks to secure himself faster
In favour with some gentle master
Who perhaps is busy in parliament
Pledging his soul for Britain's good.

CAESAR

Faith, lad, you know little about it:
For Britain's good! Good faith! I doubt it.
Say, rather, going as Premiers lead him
And saying yes or no as they bid him
At operas and plays parading
Mortgaging, gambling, masquerading.
Or maybe in a daft frolic
To The Hague or Calais takes a trip
To make a tour and have a fling
To learn of Europe and see the world.
There, at Vienna or Versailles
He tears up his father's old entails
Or by Madrid he takes the road
To strum guitars and fight with bulls
Or rushes about the Italian countryside
Whore-hunting in the myrtle groves
Then drinks muddy German water
To make himself look fair and fatter
And clear the bitter sores and ulcers
Of cursed Venetian bores and chancres[2].
For Britain's good! for her destruction!
With dissipation, feud and faction.

[2] First symptoms of syphilis, literally holes and lesions.

LUATH

Hech man! dear sirs! is that the gate
They waste sae monie a braw estate!
Are we sae foughten an' harass'd
For gear tae gang that gate at last?
O would they stay aback frae courts,
An please themsels wi' countra sports,
It wad for ev'ry ane be better,
The laird, the tenant, an' the cotter!
For thae frank, rantin, ramblin billies,
Fient haet o' them's ill-hearted fellows:
Except for breakin o' their timmer,
Or speaking lightly o' their limmer,
Or shootin of a hare or moor-cock,
The never-a-bit they're ill to poor folk.
But will ye tell me, master Caesar:
Sure great folk's life's a life o' pleasure?
Nae cauld nor hunger e'er can steer them,
The vera thought o't need na fear them.

CAESAR

Lord, man, were ye but whyles whare I am,
The gentles, ye wad ne'er envy 'em!
It's true, they need na starve or sweat,
Thro' winter's cauld, or simmer's heat;
They've nae sair wark to craze their banes,
An' fill auld-age wi' grips an granes:
But human bodies are sic fools,
For a' their colleges an' schools,
That when nae real ills perplex them,
They mak enow themsels to vex them;
An' ay the less they hae to sturt them,
In like proportion, less will hurt them.
A countra fellow at the pleugh,
His acre's till'd, he's right enough;
A countra girl at her wheel,
Her dizzen's done, she's unco weel;
But gentlemen, an' ladies warst,
Wi' ev'n down want o' wark are curst:
They loiter, lounging, lank an' lazy;
Tho' deil-haet ails them, yet uneasy:
Their days insipid, dull an' tasteless;
Their nights unquiet, lang an' restless.
An' even their sports, their balls an' races,
Their galloping through public places,
There's sic parade, sic pomp an' art,
The joy can hardly reach the heart.

LUATH

Heavens, man! Dear sirs! Is that the way
They waste so many fine estates?
Are we so troubled and harassed
For wealth to be spent like that at last?
O would they stay away from courts,
And please themselves with country sports
It would be better for everyone
The laird, the tenant and the cottager!
For these frank, boisterous, drinking lads
Devil the one of them's evil-hearted;
Except for breaking their wooden bowls
Or speaking lightly of their lovers
Or shooting a hare or moor-cock,
They're never the least bit harsh to poor folk.
But, will you tell me, Master Caesar,
Surely great folks' lives are lives of pleasure?
No cold nor hunger ever can harass them
The very thought of it need not scare them.

CAESAR

Lord, man, were you but sometimes where I am
You would never envy the gentlefolk.
It's true they need not starve nor sweat
Through winter's cold or summer's heat;
They've no hard work to damage their bones
And fill old age with gripes and groans.
But human beings are such fools
For all their colleges and schools
That when no real ills perplex them
They make enough themselves to vex them
And always the less they have to upset them
In like proportion, less will hurt them.
A country fellow, at the plough
His acre tilled, he's doing all right;
A country girl at her(spinning) wheel
Her dozen's done, she's very well.
But gentlemen and ladies worst
With downright want of work are cursed:
They loiter, lounging, lanquid and lazy
Though there's nothing wrong with them, yet uneasy
Their days insipid, dull and tasteless
Their nights unquiet, long and restless
And even their sports, their balls and races
Their galloping through public places
There's such parade, such pomp and artifice
That joy can scarcely reach the heart.

The men cast out in party-matches,
Then sowther a' in deep debauches;
Ae night they're mad wi' drink an' whoring,
Niest day their life is past enduring.
The ladies arm-in-arm in clusters,
As great an' gracious a' as sisters;
But hear their absent thoughts o' ither.
They're a' run deils an' jads thegither,
Whyles, owre the wee bit cup an' platie,
They sip the scandal-potion pretty;
Or lee-lang nights, wi' crabbit leuks,
Pore owre the devil's pictur'd beuks;
Stake on a chance a farmer's stackyard,
An' cheat like onie unhang'd blackguard.
There's some exceptions, man an' woman;
But this is Gentry's life in common.

By this, the sun was out o' sight,
An' darker gloamin brought the night;
The bum-clock humm'd wi' lazy drone;
The kye stood rowtin' i' the loan;
When up they gat, an' shook their lugs,
Rejoic'd they were na men, but dogs;
An' each took aff his several way,
Resolv'd to meet some ither day.

The men fall out in party-matches
Then make up again in deep debauches
One night they're mad with drink and whoring
Next day their life is beyond enduring.
The ladies arm in arm in clusters
All as great and gracious as sisters
But hear their thoughts on another who's absent,
They're all out and out rogues and worthless.
Sometimes over the dainty cup and plate
They sip the scandal-potion prettily
Or live-long nights with bad-tempered looks
Pore over the devil's pictured books [playing cards]
Stake, on a chance, a farmer's stackyard
And cheat like any unhanged blackguard.
There's some exceptions, man and woman
But this is gentry's life in common.

By this time, the sun was out of sight
And darker twilight brought the night;
The beetle hummed with lazy drone
The cattle stood lowing in the driving-road
When up they got and shook their ears
Rejoiced they were not men but dogs
And each took off his own way,
Resolved to meet some other day.

Dedication to Gavin Hamilton (1786)

In April of this year, James Armour had refused to have Robert Burns for a son-in-law. Just before that, Burns had started to make arrangements to publish his poetry. His brother Gilbert's account claims that Robert's desire to publish was to obtain enough money to take him off to Jamaica. Although Gilbert says that the publishing was Gavin Hamilton's idea, the '*Epistle to William Simpson*' shows that the plan had been in Burns's own mind a year before.

Whatever the case, the Kilmarnock Edition was published on July 31st, 1786. The 612 copies ran out within a month and Burns had second thoughts about emigrating.

Gavin Hamilton, a lawyer, was Burn's landlord and his friend. The trials and tribulations he endured under 'Auld Licht' Presbyterianism are noted in the preface to '*Holy Willie's Prayer*'.

The Dedication

Burns appears to be sufficiently class-conscious of Gavin Hamilton's status to address him as 'Sir' throughout the dedication – or is this just the colloquial 'sir' which Scotsmen use to address equals? Even as he insists that he will not be flattering the lawyer, Burns pays him generous compliments.

Burns claims at first that he is not going to be praising Gavin Hamilton, because it would offend Gavin's modesty.

Expect na, Sir, in this narration,	Do not expect, Sir, in this narration
A fleechin', fleth'rin dedication,	A flattering, cajoling dedication
To roose you up, an' ca' you guid,	To praise you up and call you good
An' sprung o' great an' noble bluid,	And sprung of great and noble blood
Because ye're surnam'd like his Grace –	Because you have the same surname as his Grace
Perhaps related to the race;	Perhaps related to the race;
Then when I'm tir'd – and sae are ye,	Then when I'm tired – and so are you
Wi' monie a fulsome, sinfu' lie, –	With many a fulsome, sinful lie
Set up a face how I stop short,	How I stop short of putting on a face
For fear your modesty be hurt.	For fear your modesty be hurt.

Burns emphasises his own lower status but, as patron and poet, they have an understanding.

This may do – maun do, Sir, wi' them wha	This may do – must do, Sir, with them who
Maun please the great folk for a wamefou;	Must please the great folk to fill their stomachs.
For me! sae laigh I needna bow,	For me! so low I don't need to bow
For, Lord be thankit, I can plough;	For, the Lord be thanked, I can plough
And when I downa yoke a naig,	And when I cannot yoke a nag,
Then, Lord be thankit, I can beg;	Then, the Lord be thanked, I can beg;
Sae I shall say, an' that's nae flatt'rin',	So I shall say, and that's no flattering
It's just sic poet, an' sic patron.	It's just such a poet and such a patron.
The Poet, some guid angel help him,	The poet, some good angel help him
Or else, I fear some ill ane skelp him!	Or else, I fear some evil one will beat him

He may do weel for a' he's done yet,
But only – he's no just begun yet.
The Patron, (Sir, ye maun forgie me;
I winna lie, come what will o' me),
On ev'ry hand it will allow'd be,
He's just – nae better than he should be.

He may do well for all he's done yet
But only – he's not just begun yet.
The Patron (Sir, you must forgive me,
I will not lie, come what will of me)
On every hand, it will be conceded
He's just – no better than he should be.

A list of Hamilton's virtues which Burns says are not inspired by religion, but are part of his nature..

I readily and freely grant,
He downa see a poor man want;
What's no his ain, he winna tak it;
What ance he says, he winna break it;
Ought he can lend he'll no refus't,
'Till aft his guidness is abus'd;
And rascals whyles that do him wrang,
E'en that, he does na mind it lang,
As master, landlord, husband, father,
He does na fail his part in either.

I readily and freely grant,
He cannot see a poor man want
What's not his own, he will not take it
When he gives his word, he will not break it.
Anything he can lend, he'll not refuse it
Until often his goodness is abused
And rascals sometimes that do him wrong.
Even that, he does not remember for long
As master, landlord, husband, father,
He does not fail as any of these.

But then, nae thanks to him for a' that;
Nae godly symptom ye can ca' that;
It's naething but a milder feature
Of our poor sinfu', corrupt nature:
Ye'll get the best o' moral works,
'Mang black Gentoos and pagan Turks,
Or hunters wild on Ponotaxi,
Wha never heard of orthodoxy.
That he's the poor man's friend in need,
The gentleman in word and deed,
It's no thro' terror of damnation;
It's just a carnal inclination,
And och! that's nae regeneration.

But then, no thanks to him for all that
No godly symptom you can call that
It's nothing but a milder feature
Of our poor sinful, corrupt nature.
You'll find the best of moral works
Among black Hindus and pagan Turks
Or hunters wild on Ponotaxi
Who never heard of orthodoxy
That he's the poor man's friend in need
The gentleman in word and deed
It's not through terror of damnation
It's just a carnal inclination
And o! that's no regeneration.

He apostrophises Morality, but this is the morality of Calvinist hypocrisy. This is as vividly satirical as '*Holy Willie's Prayer*'.

Morality, thou deadly bane,
Thy tens o' thousands thou hast slain!
Vain is his hope, whose stay and trust is
In moral mercy, truth and justice!

Morality, thou deadly scourge
Thy tens o' thousands thou hast slain!
Vain is his hope, whose stay and trust is
In moral mercy, truth and justice!

No – stretch a point to catch a plack;
Abuse a brother to his back;
Steal thro' a winnock frae a whore,
But point the rake that taks the door;
Be to the poor like onie whunstane,
And haud their noses to the grunstane,

No – stretch a point to catch a small coin
Abuse a brother behind his back
Steal through a window from a whore
But point out the rake that takes the door.
Be to the poor like any whinstone
And hold their noses to the grindstone

Ply ev'ry art o' legal thieving;
No matter – stick to sound believing.

Learn three-mile pray'rs an' half-mile graces,
Wi' weel-spread looves, and lang wry faces;
Grunt up a solemn, lengthen'd groan,
And damn a' parties but your own;
I'll warrant then, ye're nae deceiver,
A steady, sturdy, staunch believer.

Ply every art of legal thieving;
No matter – stick to sound believing.

Learn three-mile prayers and half-mile graces
With well-spread palms and long wry faces;
Grunt up a solemn, lengthened groan
And damn everyone but yourself;
I'll warrant then, you're no deceiver
A steady, sturdy, staunch believer.

Burns now adopts the persona of the Calvinist minister and delivers a masterpiece of satirical pulpit rhetoric.

O ye wha leave the springs o' Calvin,
For gumlie dubs of your ain delvin'!
Ye sons of heresy and error,
Ye'll some day squeal in quaking terror!
When Vengeance draws the sword in wrath,
And in the fire throws the sheath;
When Ruin, with his sweeping besom,
Just frets 'till Heav'n commission gies him:
While o'er the harp pale Mis'ry moans,
And strikes the ever-deep'ning tones,
Still louder shrieks, and heavier groans!

O ye who leave the springs of Calvin
For muddy puddles of your own digging
You sons of heresy and error
You'll some day squeal in quaking terror!
When Vengeance draws the sword in wrath
And in the fire throws the sheath
When Ruin, with his sweeping broom
Just frets till Heaven commissions him
While over the harp pale Misery moans
And strikes the ever-deepening tones
Still louder shrieks, and heavier groans!

You can almost hear him clearing his throat as he calms down to make a sarcastic apology, pretending that religion gets him carried away. Back on track, he returns to the dedication.

Your pardon, Sir, for this digression:
I maist forgat my dedication;
But when divinity comes cross me.
My readers still are sure to lose me.
So, Sir, ye see 'twas nae daft vapour,
But I maturely thought it proper,
When a' my works I did review,
To dedicate them, Sir, to you:
Because (ye need na tak it ill)
I thought them something like yoursel'.

Your pardon, Sir, for this digression.
I almost forgot my dedication
But when divinity comes cross me
My readers still are sure to lose me.
So, Sir, you see, it was no daft vapour
But I maturely thought it proper
When all my works I did review
To dedicate them, Sir, to you
Because (you need not take it ill)
I thought them something like yourself.

Then patronise them wi your favor,
And your petitioner shall ever –
I had amaist said, ever pray,
But that's a word I need na say:
For prayin' I hae little skill o't;
I'm baith dead sweer, an' wretched ill o't;
But I'se repeat each poor man's pray'r,
That kens or hears about you, Sir –

Then patronise them with your favour
And your petitioner shall ever –
I had almost said, ever pray
But that's a word I need not say
For praying I have little skill of it;
I'm both very loath, and really bad at it
But I would repeat each poor man's prayer
That knows or hears about you, Sir –

"May ne'er misfortune's gowling bark,
Howl thro' the dwelling o' the Clerk!
May ne'er his gen'rous, honest heart,
For that same gen'rous spirit smart!
May Kennedy's far-honour'd name
Lang beet his hymeneal flame,
Till Hamiltons, at least a dizzen,
Are frae their nuptial labours risen:
Five bonnie lasses round their table,
And seven braw fellows, stout an' able,
To serve their king and country weel,
By word, or pen, or pointed steel!
May health and peace, with mutual rays,
Shine on the ev'ning o' his days;
'Till his wee curlie John's-ier-oe,
When ebbing life nae mair shall flow,
The last, sad, mournful rites bestow!"

'May never misfortune's howling bark
Howl through the dwelling of the Clerk!
May never his generous honest heart
For that same generous spirit smart!
May Kennedy's far-honour'd name
Long fan the flame of his marriage
Till at least a dozen Hamiltons
Have sprung from their sexual coupling:
Five bonnie lasses round their table
And seven handsome lads, sturdy and able
To serve their king and country well
By word, or pen, or pointed steel!
May health and peace, with mutual rays
Shine on the evening of his days
Till his little curly-headed great grandchild
When ebbing life no more shall flow
Bestows the last sad, mournful rites.

This section is entirely in English, suitable for Gavin's higher status. Do you feel the change to formal English causes the poem to lose its vitality?

He ends by telling Hamilton that, if ill fortune ever makes him 'as poor a dog' as he is, Burns would no longer be Hamilton's 'humble servant', but his 'friend and brother'.

I will not wind a lang conclusion,
With complimentary effusion:
But whilst your wishes and endeavours
Are blest with Fortune's smiles and favours,
I am, dear Sir, with zeal most fervent,
Your much indebted, humble servant.

I will not wind a long conclusion
With complimentary effusion:
But whilst your wishes and endeavours
Are blessed with Fortune's smiles and favours,
I am, dear Sir, with zeal most fervent,
Your much indebted, humble servant.

But if (which Pow'rs above prevent)
That iron-hearted carl, Want,
Attended, in his grim advances,
By sad mistakes, and black mischances,
While hopes, and joys, and pleasures fly him,
Make you as poor a dog as I am,
Your 'humble servant' then no more;
For who would humbly serve the poor?

But if (which Powers above prevent)
That iron-hearted peasant, Want,
Attended, in his grim advances,
By sad mistakes, and black mischances,
While hopes, and joys, and pleasures fly him,
Make you as poor a dog as I am,
Your 'humble servant' then no more;
For who would humbly serve the poor?

But, by a poor man's hopes in Heav'n!
While recollection's pow'r is giv'n,
If, in the vale of humble life,
The victim sad of Fortune's strife,
I, thro' the tender-gushing tear,
Should recognise my master dear;
If friendless, low, we meet together,
Then, sir, your hand – my FRIEND and BROTHER!

But, by a poor man's hopes in Heaven!
While recollection's power is given,
If, in the vale of humble life,
The victim sad of Fortune's strife,
I, through the tender-gushing tear,
Should recognise my master dear;
If friendless, low, we meet together,
Then, sir, your hand – my FRIEND and BROTHER!

Epistle to a Young Friend (1786)

This poem was written in May 1786. Only weeks before, the pregnant Jean Armour had been spirited off to her Paisley relatives and Burns was exchanging marriage vows with Mary Campbell, with whom he was planning to emigrate to Jamaica. It is more than a little ironic that, in verse 6, he advises the young friend on the debasing effect of illicit love.

The poem reeks with the moralising reminiscent of Polonius's speech to Laertes (Hamlet Act 1, Scene 3), but there is also some advice which sounds blatantly exploitive and self-seeking, e.g. verse 5.

From verse 7 onwards, the counsel is largely platitudinous and pious, but gloriously redeemed by the final four lines, where Burns discards the moralising persona and reverts to being himself, expressing the hope that the young friend will heed advice better than he himself ever did!

1.
I lang hae thought, my youthfu' friend,
A something to have sent you,
Tho' it should serve nae ither end
Than just a kind memento:
But how the subject-theme may gang,
Let time and chance determine:
Perhaps it may turn out a sang;
Perhaps, turn out a sermon.

2.
Ye'll try the world soon, my lad;
And, Andrew dear, believe me,
Ye'll find mankind an unco squad,
And muckle they may grieve ye:
For care and trouble set your thought,
Ev'n when your end's attained;
And a' your views may come to nought,
Where ev'ry nerve is strained.

3.
I'll no say, men are villains a':
The real, harden'd wicked,
Wha hae nae check but human law,
Are to a few restricked;
But, och! Mankind are unco weak
An' little to be trusted;
If Self the wavering balance shake,
It's rarely right adjusted!

4.
Yet they wha fa' in Fortune's strife,
Their fate we should na censure;

1.
I long have thought, my youthful friend
Of something to have sent you
Though it should serve no other end
Than just a kind memento:
But how the subject theme may go
Let time and chance determine
Perhaps it may turn out a song
Perhaps, turn out a sermon.

2.
You'll try the world soon, my lad
And, Andrew dear, believe me
You'll find mankind a strange lot
And much they may grieve you
For care and trouble set your thought
Even when your end is attained
And all your views may come to nothing
Where every nerve is strained.

3.
I'll not say, men are villains all:
The real, hardened wicked.
Who have no check but human law
Are few in number.
But, oh! Mankind are very weak
And little to be trusted;
If Self the wavering balance shakes
It is rarely accurately adjusted!

4.
Yet they who fall in Fortune's strife
Their fate we should not censure

For still, th' important end of life	For still, the important end of life
They equally may answer:	They equally may answer.
A man may hae an honest heart,	A man may have an honest heart
Tho' poortith hourly stare him;	Though poverty hourly stares at him
A man may tak a neebor's part,	A man may take a neighbour's part
Yet hae nae cash to spare him.	Yet have no cash to spare him.
5.	**5.**
Ay free, aff han', your story tell,	Always free, off hand, your story tell
When wi' a bosom cronie;	When with a bosom pal
But still keep something to yoursel	But still keep something to yourself
Ye scarcely tell to onie:	You scarcely tell to anybody
Conceal yoursel as weel's ye can	Conceal yourself as well as you can
Frae critical dissection:	From critical dissection
But keek thro' ev'ry other man	But examine every other man
Wi' sharpen'd, sly inspection.	With sharpened, sly inspection.
6.	**6.**
The sacred lowe o' weel-plac'd love,	The sacred flame of well placed love
Luxuriantly indulge it;	Luxuriantly indulge it
But never tempt th' illicit rove,	But never attempt the illicit rove
Tho' naething should divulge it:	Though nothing should divulge it.
I waive the quantum o' the sin,	I do not quantify the sin
The hazard of concealing;	The hazard of concealing
But, och! it hardens a' within,	But, oh! it hardens all within
And petrifies the feeling!	And petrifies the feeling!
7.	**7.**
To catch Dame Fortune's golden smile,	To catch Dame Fortune's golden smile
Assiduous wait upon her;	Assiduously wait upon her
And gather gear by ev'ry wile	And gather wealth by every wile
That's justify'd by honor:	That is justified by honour
Not for to hide it in a hedge,	Not to hide it in a hedge
Not for a train-attendant;	Not for a train-attendant
But for the glorious privilege	But for the glorious privilege
Of being independent.	Of being independent.
8.	**8.**
The fear o' Hell's a hangman's whip	The fear of Hell is a hangman's whip
To haud the wretch in order;	To hold the wretch in order
But where ye feel your honour grip,	But where you feel your honour grip
Let that ay be your border:	Let that always be your border.
Its slightest touches, instant pause –	Its slightest touch, instantly pause –
Debar a' side-pretences;	Debar all side pretences
And resolutely keep its laws,	And resolutely keep its laws
Uncaring consequences.	Uncaring of the consequences.

9.
The great Creator to revere
Must sure become the creature;
But still the preaching cant forbear,
And ev'n the rigid feature:
Yet ne'er with wits profane to range
Be complaisance extended;
An atheist-laugh's a poor exchange
For Deity offended!

10.
When ranting round in Pleasure's ring,
Religion may be blinded;
Or if she gie a random sting,
It may be little minded;
But when on Life we're tempest-driv'n –
A conscience but a canker –
A correspondence fix'd wi' Heav'n,
Is sure a noble anchor!

11.
Adieu, dear, amiable youth!
Your heart can ne'er be wanting!
May prudence, fortitude, and truth,
Erect your brow undaunting!
In ploughman phrase, 'God send you speed,'
Still daily to grow wiser;
And may ye better reck the rede,
Than ever did th' adviser!

9.
The great Creator to revere
Must surely become the creature
But still the preaching cant forbear
And even the rigid feature
Yet never with wits profane to range
By complacency extended[1];
An atheist's laugh's a poor exchange
For Deity offended!

10.
When frolicking in Pleasure's ring
Religion may be blinded
Or if she gives a random sting
It may be little minded
But when on Life we are tempest driven
A conscience but a canker[2]
A correspondence fixed with Heaven
Is sure a noble anchor!

11.
Adieu, dear, amiable youth!
Your heart can never be wanting!
May prudence, fortitude, and truth
Erect your brow undaunting!
In ploughman phrase, 'God send you speed,'
Still daily to grow wiser
And may you better heed the counsel
Than ever did the adviser!

[1] Never be so complacent that you go too far in the company of blasphemers or irreverent companions.
[2] Small sore.

The Auld Farmer's New-Year Morning Salutation to his Auld Mare, Maggie. On giving her the accustomed ripp of corn to hansel in the new-year. (1786)

As one might expect, an old farmer would talk to his mare in fulsome Scots; the mare has fluent vernacular. The poem resonates with affectionate nostalgia for the past that belongs to both man and beast.

1.

A Guid New-Year I wish thee, Maggie!
Hae, there's a ripp to thy auld baggie:
Tho' thou's howe-backit now, an' knaggie,
I've seen the day
Thou could hae gaen like onie staggie,
Out-owre the lay.

A good New Year I wish you, Maggie!
Hey, here's a handful for your old belly
Though you're hollow backed now and knobbly
I've seen the day
You could have gone like any young horse
Over the fields.

2.

Tho' now thou's dowie, stiff, an' crazy,
An' thy auld hide as white's a daisie,
I've seen thee dappl't, sleek an' glaizie,
A bonie gray:
He should been tight that daur't to raize thee,
Ance in a day.

Though now you're dull, stiff and infirm
And your old hide is as white as a daisy
I've seen you dappled, sleek and glossy
A lovely grey;
He should have been prepared that dared to spur you on
Once in a day.

3.

Thou ance was i' the foremost rank,
A filly buirdly, steeve, an' swank:
An' set weel down a shapely shank
As e'er tread yird;
An' could hae flown out-owre a stank,
Like onie bird.

You once were of the first rank
An elegant fillie, trim and lithe
And set well down as shapely a leg
As ever trod earth
And could have flown right over a pond
Like any bird.

4.

It's now some nine-an'-twenty year
Sin' thou was my guid-father's meere;
He gied me thee, o' tocher clear,
An' fifty mark;
Tho' it was sma', 'twas weel-won gear,
An' thou was stark.

It's now some twenty nine years
Since you were my father-in-law's mare
He gave you to me as a dowry
And fifty marks[1];
Though it was small, it was well-won property,
And you were strong.

5.

When first I gaed to woo my Jenny,
Ye then was trottin wi' your minnie:
Tho' ye was trickie, slee, an' funnie,
Ye ne'er was donsie;
But hamely, tawie, quiet, an' cannie,
An' unco sonsie.

When first I went to woo my Jenny
You then were trotting with your mother
Though you were tricky, sly and funny
You were never dull
But homely, docile, quiet and careful
And very good natured.

[1] A mark was worth two thirds of the old pound Scots.

6.

That day, ye pranc'd wi' muckle pride,	That day you pranced with great pride
When ye bure hame my bonie bride:	When you brought home my lovely bride
An' sweet an' gracefu' she did ride,	And sweet and graceful she did ride
Wi' maiden air!	With maiden air!
Kyle-Stewart I could bragged wide,	Kyle-Stewart[2] I could have challenged
For sic a pair.	To equal such a pair.

7.

Tho' now ye dow but hoyte and hobble,	Though now you can only limp and tremble
An' wintle like a saumont-coble,	And roll from side to side like a salmon cobble
That day, ye was a jinker noble,	That day you were a noble mover
For heels an' win'!	For heels and wind!
An' ran them till they a' did wauble,	And ran them till they all did totter
Far, far behin'!	Far, far behind.

8.

When thou an' I were young and skiegh,	When you and I were young and high-spirited
An' stable-meals at fairs were driegh,	And stable-meals at fairs were dull and tiresome
How thou wad prance, an' snore, an' skriegh,	How you would prance, and snore and screech
An' tak the road!	And take the road!
Town's-bodies ran, an' stood abiegh,	Townsfolk ran and stood aside
An' ca't thee mad.	And called you mad.

9.

When thou was corn't, an' I was mellow,	When you were corned[3], and I was mellow
We took the road ay like a swallow:	We took the road – yes – like a swallow
At brooses thou had ne'er a fellow,	At wedding races you never had an equal
For pith an' speed;	For vigour and speed
But ev'ry tail thou pay't them hollow,	But every tail you beat them hollow
Whare'er thou gaed.	Wherever you went.

10.

The sma, droop-rumpl't, hunter cattle	The small sloping-backed hunter cattle
Might aiblins waur't thee for a brattle;	Might perhaps outdo you in a short race
But sax Scotch miles thou try't their mettle,	But for six Scotch miles you tried their spirit
And gar't them whaizle:	And made them wheeze:
Nae whip nor spur, but just a wattle	No whip nor spur but just a switch
O' saugh or hazle.	Of willow or hazel.

11.

Thou was a noble fittie-lan',	You were as noble a plough horse
As e'er in tug or tow was drawn!	As ever in harness or rope was drawn!
Aft thee an' I, in aught hours' gaun,	Often you and I in eight hours going,
On guid March-weather,	In good March weather
Hae turn'd sax rood beside our han'	Have turned six roods[4] beside our other plough horse,
For days thegither.	For days together.

[2] The part of Kyle north of the River Ayr.

[3] Fed.

[4] A rood was a ¼ acre.

12.

Thou never braing't, an' fetch't, an' fliskit;	You never rushed away recklessly, and fought and fretted
But thy auld tail thou wad hae whiskit,	But your old tail you would have swept about
An' spread abreed thy weel-fill'd brisket,	And spread abroad your well-filled breast,
Wi' pith an' pow'r;	With vigour and power
Till sprittie knowes wad rair't, an' risket	Till tough knolls would crack and split
An' slypet owre.	And [the soil] slide over.

13.

When frosts lay lang, an' snaws were deep,	When frosts lay long and snows were deep
An' threaten'd labour back to keep,	And threatened to hold back the work
I gied thy cog a wee bit heap	I heaped up your wooden bowl
Aboon the timmer:	Above the wood [brim];
I ken'd my Maggie wad na sleep	I knew my Maggie would not sleep
For that, or simmer.	Without that, until summer.

14.

In cart or car thou never reestit;	In cart or sledge you never tilted
The steyest brae thou wad hae fac't it;	The steepest slope you would have faced it
Thou never lap, an' sten't, an' breastit,	You never leapt, reared or sprang forward
Then stood to blaw;	Then stood to blow
But just thy step a wee thing hastit,	But just quickened your step a little
Thou snoov't awa.	And you moved smoothly away.

15.

My pleugh is now thy bairntime a',	My plough team is now [made up of] all your children
Four gallant brutes as e'er did draw;	Four brutes as gallant as ever did draw
Forbye sax mae I've sell't awa,	Forbye six more, I've sold away
That thou hast nurst;	That you have nursed
They drew me thretteen pund an' twa,	They earned me thirteen pounds and two [shillings]
The vera warst.	The very worst [of them].

16.

Monie a sair darg we twa hae wrought,	Many a hard day's work we two have done
An' wi' the weary warl' fought!	And fought with the weary world
An' monie an anxious day I thought	And many an anxious day I thought
We wad be beat!	We would be beaten!
Yet here to crazy age we're brought,	But here to infirm age we're brought
Wi' something yet.	With something yet.

17.

An' think na, my auld trusty servan',	And think not, my old trusty servant
That now perhaps thou's less deservin,	That now perhaps you're less deserving
An' thy auld days may end in starvin;	And your old days may end in starving,
For my last fow,	For my last fork load
A heapet stimpart, I'll reserve ane	A heaped measure of corn I'll reserve
Laid by for you.	Laid by for you.

18.

We've worn to crazy years thegither;
We'll toyte about wi' ane anither;
Wi' tentie care I'll flit thy tether
To some hain'd rig,
Whare ye may nobly rax your leather
Wi' sma' fatigue.

We've worn to feeble old age together
We'll totter about with one another
With attentive care I'll move your tether
To some ridge of uncut grass
Where you may nobly stretch your hide
Without tiring yourself out.

The author's earnest cry and prayer to the Scotch Representatives in the House of Commons (1786)

The Wash Act (1784) lowered duties on spirits in England and the Scottish Lowlands. This naturally led to a huge increase in legal whisky production in Lowland Scotland, much of which was exported to England. The London gin distillers were not pleased. They put pressure on the government, as a result of which the government passed the Scotch Distillery Act (1786), increasing the tax on spirits exported to England. At the same time, they changed their method of taxation. This increase in duty made it much harder for Scottish distillers to sell their whisky in England.

This poem is supposed to be a letter of protest, addressed to the 45 Scottish representatives in the House of Commons, urging them to support the cause of the Scottish whisky industry. It is, of course, a mockery, an excuse for some ribald comedy with irony thrown in and pseudo-respect for the government.

Burns does not address the Honourable Members in polished English, but in rich, idiomatic colloquial Scots. The colourful metaphors of Verses 2 and 7, for example, create verbal cartoons. Nor is he hesitant about socking it to them! He tells them they were very smart at vote-gathering – but they have to fulfil their side of the bargain; urges them to speak out boldly without keeping one eye on safeguarding their promotion prospects or pensions, appeals to their patriotism and flatters their eloquence. However, if they fail, Scotland will cease to be a 'kind, auld cantie carlin', but will tuck up her tartan petticoat and take to the streets with dirk and pistol!

The postscript is a reminder to King George of the loyalty and courage of Scottish soldiers, even to the death – when they are fortified by a dram.

The final verse is rather enigmatic, with its apostrophising of Scotland as an old respected mother who sometimes takes a drink then pisses herself, sitting on the heather. Equally enigmatic is the word freedom in the much-quoted final lines. Is this freedom of the individual or is it freedom from King George and his English-dominated government, or is it both?

1.

Ye Irish lords, ye knights an' squires,	You Irish lords, you knights and squires,
Wha represent our brughs an' shires,	Who represent our burghs and shires
An' doucely manage our affairs	And soberly manage our affairs
In Parliament,	In Parliament,
To you a simple Bardie's prayers	To you a simple bard's prayers
Are humbly sent.	Are humbly sent.

2.

Alas! my roupit Muse is haerse!	Alas! my dry-throated Muse is hoarse
Your Honours' hearts wi' grief 'twad pierce,	It would pierce Your Honours' hearts with grief
To see her sittin on her arse	To see her sitting on her arse
Low i' the dust,	Low in the dust
And scriechin out prosaic verse,	And screeching out prosaic verse
An' like to brust!	And likely to burst!

3.

Tell them wha hae the chief direction,
Scotland an' me's in great affliction,
E'er sin' they laid that curst restriction
On aqua-vitae;
An' rouse them up to strong conviction,
An' move their pity.

Tell them who have the chief direction
Scotland and I are in great affliction,
Ever since they laid that cursed restriction
On whisky,
And rouse them up to strong conviction,
And move their pity.

4.

Stand forth, an' tell yon Premier youth
The honest, open, naked truth:
Tell him o' mine an' Scotland's drouth,
His servants humble:
The muckle deevil blaw you south,
If ye dissemble!

Stand forth and tell that Premier youth
The honest, open, naked truth:
Tell him of Scotland's and my thirst,
His humble servants.
May the great devil blow you south
If you dissemble.

5.

Does onie great man glunch an' gloom?
Speak out, an' never fash your thumb!
Let posts an' pensions sink or soom
Wi' them wha grant 'em:
If honestly they canna come,
Far better want 'em.

Does any great man scowl and grumble?
Speak out and don't worry about it!
Let posts and pensions sink or swim
With them who grant them:
If they can't come honestly,
Far better do without them.

6.

In gath'rin votes you were na slack;
Now stand as tightly by your tack:
Ne'er claw you lug, an' fidge your back,
An' hum an haw;
But raise your arm, an' tell your crack
Before them a'.

In gathering votes you were not slack:
Now keep your side of the bargain.
Never scratch your ear and shrug your shoulders
And prevaricate,
But raise your arm and say your piece
Before them all.

7.

Paint Scotland greetin owre her thrisstle;
Her mutchkin stowp as toom's a whissle;
An' damn'd excisemen in a bustle,
Seizin a stell,
Triumphant, crushin't like a mussel,
Or lampit shell!

Paint Scotland weeping over her thistle
Her pint tankard as empty as a whistle
And damned excisemen in a bustle,
Seizing a whisky still,
Triumphantly crushing it like a mussel
Or limpet shell!

8.

Then, on the tither hand, present her –
A blackguard smuggler right behint her,
An' cheek-for-chow, a chuffie vintner
Colleaguing join,
Pickin her pouch as bare as winter
Of a' kind coin.

Then, on the other hand, present her –
A blackguard smuggler right behind her,
And cheek for jowl, a fat-faced vintner
Join forces,
Picking her pocket as bare as winter
Of all kinds of coin.

9.

Is there, that bears the name o' Scot,
But feels his heart's bluid rising hot,
To see his poor auld mither's pot
Thus dung in staves,
An' plunder'd o' her hindmost groat,
By gallows knaves?

Is there, that bears the name of Scot,
That does not feel his heart's blood rising hot,
To see his poor old mother's pot
Thus smashed to pieces
And plundered of her last groat[1]
By gallows knaves?

10.

Alas! I'm but a nameless wight,
Trode i' the mire out o' sight!
But could I like Montgomerie fight,
Or gab like Boswell,
There's some sark-necks I wad draw tight,
An' tie some hose well.

Alas, I'm but a nameless creature,
Trod in the mire out of sight
But could I like Montgomerie[2] fight
Or talk like Boswell[3]
There are some shirt necks I would draw tight
And tie some hose well.

11.

God bless your Honours! can ye see't,
The kind, auld, cantie carlin greet,
An' no get warmly to your feet,
An' gar them hear it,
An' tell them wi' a patriot-heat,
Ye winna bear it?

God bless your Honours, can you see it,
The kind, old, cheerful old wife weep
And not get warmly to your feet,
And make them hear it
And tell them with patriotic fervour
You will not stand for it?

12.

Some o' you nicely ken the laws,
To round the period an' pause,
An' with rhetoric clause on clause
To mak harangues:
Then echo thro' Saint Stephen's wa's
Auld Scotland's wrangs.

Some of you have an accurate knowledge of the laws
To round the period and pause,
And with rhetoric clause on clause
To make harangues:
Then echo through Saint Stephen's walls[4]
Old Scotland's wrongs.

13.

Dempster, a true blue Scot I'se warrant;
Thee, aith-detesting, chaste Kilkerran;
An' that glib-gabbet Highland baron,
The Laird o' Graham;
An' ane, a chap that's damn'd auldfarran,
Dundas his name:

Dempster, a true blue Scot I'll warrant;
You, oath-detesting, chaste Kilkerran
And that glib-tongued Highland baron
The Laird of Graham,
And one, a chap that's damned astute,
Dundas his name.

14.

Erskine, a spunkie Norland billie;
True Campbells, Frederick and Ilay;
An' Livistone, the bauld Sir Willie;
An' monie ithers,
Whom auld Demosthenes or Tully
Might own for brithers.

Erskine, a spirited northern lad
True Campbells, Frederick and Ilay;
And Livingstone, the bold Sir Willie;
And many others,
Whom old Demosthenes[5] or Tully[6]
Might own for brothers.

[1] Small coin worth fourpence.
[2] M.P. for Ayrshire 1761-62.
[3] James Boswell.

[4] St. Stephen's Chapel in the Old Palace of Westminster.
[5] Greek orator & statesman.
[6] Marcus Tullius Cicero, Roman orator & statesman.

15.

Thee sodger Hugh, my watchman stented,
If Bardies e'er are represented;
I ken if that your sword were wanted,
Ye'd lend your hand;
But when there's ought to say anent it,
Ye're at a stand.

You, soldier Hugh[7], my vanguard watchman
If Bards ever are represented
I know that if your sword was wanted,
You'd lend your hand,
But when there's anything to say about it,
You're at a standstill.

16.

Arouse, my boys! exert your mettle,
To get auld Scotland back her kettle;
Or faith! I'll wad my new pleugh-pettle,
Ye'll see't or lang,
She'll teach you, wi' a reekin whittle,
Anither sang.

Rouse yourselves, my boys! Show your mettle,
To get old Scotland back her cooking pot[8]
Or faith! I'll pledge my new plough scraper
You'll see it before long
She'll teach you, with a smoking dirk
Another song.

17.

This while she's been in crankous mood,
Her lost Militia fir'd her bluid;
(Deil na they never mair do guid,
Play'd her that pliskie!)
An' now she's like to rin red-wud
About her whisky.

This while she's been in a bad temper
Her lost Militia fired her blood
(Not a bit of good will they ever do more
who played her that trick)
And now she's likely to go berserk
About her whisky.

18.

An' Lord! if ance they pit her till't
Her tartan petticoat she'll kilt,
An' durk an' pistol at her belt,
She'll tak the streets,
An' rin her whittle to the hilt,
I' the first she meets!

And Lord! if once they put her to it
Her tartan petticoat she'll gather up,
And dirk and pistol at her belt,
She'll take to the streets,
And run her knife up to the hilt,
In the first she meets!

19.

For God-sake, sirs! then speak her fair,
An' straik her cannie wi' the hair,
An' to the Muckle House repair,
Wi' instant speed,
An' strive, wi' a' your wit an' lear,
To get remead.

For God's sake, sirs! then speak well of her
And stroke her hair gently[9]
And to the Big House[10] repair,
With instant speed,
And strive, with all your wit and learning
To get redress.

20.

Yon ill-tongu'd tinkler, Charlie Fox,
May taunt you wi' his jeers an' mocks;
But gie him't het, my hearty cocks!
E'en cowe the cadie!
An' send him to his dicing box
An' sporting lady.

That foul-mouthed tinker, Charlie Fox[11]
May taunt you with his jeers and mockery
But give him it hot, my hearty cocks
Even intimidate the fellow!
And send him to his gambling den
And sporting lady.

---

[7] Hugh Montgomerie, 12th Earl of Eglinton.
[8] Whisky still.
[9] Don't provoke her.

[10] House of Commons.
[11] Prominent Whig M.P. and life-long opponent of William Pitt.

21.

Tell yon guid bluid of auld Boconnock's,
I'll be his debt twa mashlum bonnocks,
An' drink his health in auld Nanse Tinnock's
Nine times a-week.
If he some scheme, like tea an' winnocks
Wad kindly seek.

Tell that good blood of old Boconnock's[12]
I'll be in his debt two mixed-grain scones
And drink his health in old Nanse Tinnock's[13]
Nine times a week.
If he some scheme, like tea and windows
Would kindly seek.

22.

Could he some commutation broach,
I'll pledge my aith in guid braid Scotch,
He needna fear their foul reproach
Nor erudition,
Yon mixtie-maxtie, queer hotch-potch,
The Coalition.

If he could bring about some change
I'll pledge my oath in good broad Scots
He need not fear their foul reproach
Nor erudition,
That strange mixed up hotch-potch,
The Coalition.

23.

Auld Scotland has a raucle tongue;
She's just a devil wi' a rung;
An' if she promise auld or young
To tak their part,
Tho' by the neck she should be strung,
She'll no desert.

Old Scotland has a rough tongue
She's just a devil with a cudgel;
And if she promises old or young
To take their part,
Though by the neck she should be strung,
She won't desert them.

24.

And now, ye chosen Five-and-Forty,
May still your mither's heart support ye;
Then, tho' a minister grow dorty,
An' kick your place,
Ye'll snap your fingers, poor an' hearty,
Before his face.

And now, you chosen Five-and-Forty,
May your mother's heart still support you
Then, though a minister may grow peevish
And kick your place,
You'll snap your fingers, poor and hearty,
Before his face.

25.

God bless your Honours, a' your days
Wi' sowps o' kail and brats o' claes,
In spite o' a' the thievish kaes,
That haunt St. Jamie's!
Your humble Bardie sings an' prays,
While Rab his name is.

God bless your Honours, all your days,
With spoonfuls of cabbage and rags of clothes
In spite of all the thieving jackdaws
That haunt St James's!
Your humble bard sings and prays,
As long as Rab is his name.

Postscript.

26.

Let half-starv'd slaves in warmer skies
See future wines, rich-clust'ring, rise;
Their lot auld Scotland ne'er envies,
But, blythe and frisky,
She eyes her freeborn, martial boys
Tak aff their whisky.

Let half-starved slaves in warmer skies,
See future wines, rich-clustering, rise;
Their lot old Scotland never envies
But, cheerful and frisky,
She eyes her freeborn, martial boys,
Drink up their whisky.

[12] Boconnock in Cornwall was the estate of William Pitt's grandfather.
[13] An inn in Mauchline.

27.

What tho' their Phoebus kinder warms,	What though their sun more kindly warms,
While fragrance blooms and Beauty charms,	While fragrance blooms and Beauty charms,
When wretches range, in famish'd swarms,	When wretches range, in famished swarms,
The scented groves;	The scented groves,
Or, hounded forth, dishonour arms	Or, hounded forth, dishonour arms
In hungry droves!	In hungry droves!

28.

Their gun's a burden on their shouther;	Their gun's a burden on their shoulder
They downa bide the stink o' powther;	They cannot abide the stink of [gun] powder
Their bouldest thought's a hank'ring swither	Their boldest thought is a hesitant uncertainty
To stan' or rin,	Whether to stand or run
Till skelp – a shot – they're aff, a' throw'ther,	Till bang – a shot – they're off in total confusion
To save their skin.	To save their skin.

29.

But bring a Scotsman frae his hill,	But bring a Scotsman from his hill,
Clap in his cheek a Highland gill,	Give him to drink a Highland gill
Say, such is royal George's will,	Say, such is royal George's will,
An' there's the foe!	And there's the foe!
He has nae thought but how to kill	He has no thought but how to kill
Twa at a blow.	Two at one blow.

30.

Nae cauld, faint-hearted doubtings tease him;	No cold, faint-hearted doubts tease him
Death comes, wi' fearless eye he sees him;	Death comes, with fearless eye he sees him;
Wi' bluidy han' a welcome gies him;	With bloody hand a welcome gives him
An' when he fa's,	And when he falls
His latest draught o' breathin lea'es him	His last breath leaves him
In faint huzzas.	In faint cheers.

31.

Sages their solemn een may steek	Sages may shut their solemn eyes
An' raise a philosophic reek,	Or raise a philosophic smoke
An' physically causes seek,	And physically seek causes
In clime an' season;	In climate and season,
But tell me whisky's name in Greek:	But tell me whisky's name in Greek:
I'll tell the reason.	I'll tell the reason

32.

Scotland, my auld, respected mither!	Scotland, my old respected mother!
Tho' whiles ye moistify your leather,	Though sometimes you wet your leather[14]
Till whare ye sit on craps o' heather,	Till where you sit on crops of heather
Ye tine your dam,	You wet yourself
Freedom and whisky gang thegither,	Freedom and whisky go together
Tak aff your dram!	Drink up !

[14] Take a drink.

The Holy Fair (1785)

How can a fair, which is an occasion for festivity and pleasure-seeking, have any connection with dour relentless 18th century Scottish Calvinism?

This poem is describing a field preaching, when hundreds of people would turn up to hear the local ministers deliver their hell-fire sermons and take communion. But there was more to it than that. The occasion was also a festive socialising one. Indeed, Burns makes it clear that the thundering religious aspects of the occasion feed the flames not just of pleasure, but passion!

Throughout the poem, Burns is like a camera-man preparing a documentary. His lens continuously moves from the holy to the festive, sometimes providing the broader picture, sometimes panning in on small telling details. In his poetic commentary it is as if he is constantly questioning which is more powerful – the spiritual force or the human life force. He leaves us in no doubt about his answer!

The poem starts with the poet meeting his companion for the fair, a beautiful girl who skips and laughs. She is the personification of Fun. Alongside her, sour-faced and wearing black, are Superstition and Hypocrisy, also appropriate visitors to such a gathering, but not the poet's choice of companion!

The picture of the bustling crowds is full of colour and energy: young men and women in their Sunday best, the gentry shielded from the peasants, some Kilmarnock weavers. The camera pans in on a black crow of an elder collecting the pennies, a handful of whores blinking in the light. With marvellous irony, Burns sets up a series of antitheses to offset the spiritual against the secular (verse 10).

What does he see as the finest part of the proceedings? Having his lass sit beside him with his arm around her and the chance to fondle her breast!

Suddenly the camera swings back to focus on the religious (verse 12). The ministers hold the stage, only to be sent up by merciless reductive description and irony. Moodie's face would scare off the Devil himself. He is a hell-fire preacher, who gives it his all, squealing and looking like a pig. Burns's comment is sheer genius. He claims the sermon fires the heart like 'Cantharidian plaisters', which were used to draw out poison, but also had an aphrodisiac effect. The fear of hellfire and damnation stirs up all kinds of passion!

Smith is a Moderate, whose measured approach is not strong enough meat for the truly 'godly'. They leave, ironically, to take drink. Peebles, the next minister, is slammed for his meek attitude to religion, while the last one, Miller, although a Moderate, socks it to them because, cynically, he's on the look-out for a manse.

The camera returns to the crowd where drink has loosened tongues and debate is 'loud an lang'. The poet produces a heartfelt eulogy – on drink.

Black Russell, the final preacher, dishes out the fire and brimstone so successfully that the people think they can hear Hell's fire roaring – but no, it's just someone snoring. The balance has now shifted. People are sitting about blethering to one another, the young folk are planning when they will meet again, the camera pans in on the circulating cups and jugs of ale, the bread and cheese, the old man setting down his bunnet to say grace.

As the day draws to a close, what are the poet's thoughts? Mainly he is desperately sorry for any lad or lass who has not found a partner! As the camera catches lassies removing their shoes before the long walk home, the atmosphere is one of relaxation, hope and expectation. Many people have been converted, the poet muses, but their conversion is not religious. Stone hearts have been softened not by religion but by human contact and the lubrication of drink. Things begun that day may well be consummated, sexually and otherwise, another day. We are left in no doubt whether religion or humanity is the more powerful force.

This is a beautifully balanced and elegantly crafted poem. The figures of speech are concise, perfectly judged and inspirational.

1
Upon a simmer Sunday morn,
When Nature's face is fair,
I walked forth to view the corn
An' snuff the caller air.
The risin' sun owre Galston Muirs
Wi' glorious light was glintin;
The hares were hirplin down the furrs,
The lav'rocks they were chantin
Fu' sweet that day.

2
As lightsomely I glowr'd abroad,
To see a scene sae gay,
Three hizzies, early at the road,
Cam skelpin up the way.
Twa had manteeles o' dolefu' black,
But ane wi' lyart linin;
The third, that gaed a wee a-back,
Was in the fashion shining,
Fu' gay that day.

3
The twa appear'd like sisters twin,
In feature, form, an' claes;
Their visage wither'd, lang an' thin,
An' sour as ony slaes.
The third cam up, hap-step-an'-lowp
As light as ony lambie,
An' wi' a curchie low did stoop,
As soon as e'er she saw me,
Fu' kind that day.

4
Wi' bonnet aff, quoth I, "Sweet lass,
I think ye seem to ken me;
I'm sure I've seen that bonie face,

1
Upon a summer Sunday morn,
When Nature's face is fair,
I walked forth to view the corn
And sniff the fresh air.
The rising sun, over Galston Moors,
With glorious light was glinting;
The hares were hopping down the furrows,
The larks were chanting
Full sweet that day.

2
As lightheartedly I gazed around,
To see a scene so gay,
Three young women, early on the road,
Came prancing up the way,
Two had mantles of doleful black,
But one with grey lining;
The third, who walked a bit behind,
Was in the fashion shining
Full gay that day.

3
The two appeared like twin sisters,
In feature, form, and clothes;
Their faces withered, long and thin,
And sour as any sloes:
The third came up, hop step and jump,
As light as any lamb,
And with a curtsey low did bow,
As soon as ever she saw me,
Full kind that day.

4
With bonnet off, said I, "Sweet lass,
I think you seem to know me;
I am sure I have seen that lovely face,

But yet I canna name ye.”
Quo’ she, an’ laughin as she spak,
An’ taks me by the han’s,
“Ye, for my sake, hae gien the feck
Of a’ the Ten Comman’s
A screed some day.”

5

“My name is Fun – your cronie dear,
The nearest friend ye hae;
An’ this is Superstition here,
An’ that’s Hypocrisy.
I’m gaun to Mauchline Holy Fair,
To spend an hour in daffin:
Gin ye’ll go there, yon runkled pair,
We will get famous laughin
At them this day.”

6

Quoth I, “With a’ my heart, I’ll do’t;
I’ll get my Sunday’s sark on,
An’ meet you on the holy spot;
Faith, we’se hae fine remarkin!”
Then I gaed hame at crowdie-time,
An’ soon I made me ready;
For roads were clad frae side to side,
Wi’ monie a wearie body,
In droves that day.

7

Here, farmers gash, in ridin graith,
Gaed hoddin by their cotters,
There swankies young, in braw braidclaith,
Are springin owre the gutters.
The lasses, skelpin barefit, thrang,
In silks an’ scarlets glitter,
Wi’ sweet-milk cheese in mony a whang,
And farls, bak’d wi’ butter,
Fu’ crump that day.

8

When by the plate we set our nose,
Weel heaped up wi’ ha’pence,
A greedy glowr Black Bonnet throws,
An’ we maun draw our tippence.
Then in we go to see the show:
On ev’ry side they’re gath’rin,

But yet I cannot name you.”
Said she, and laughing as she spoke,
And takes me by the hands,
“You, for my sake, have torn the bulk
Of all the Ten Commandments
In tatters at some time.”

5

“My name is Fun – your dear pal,
The closest friend you have
And this is Superstition here,
And that’s Hypocrisy.
I’m going to Mauchline Holy Fair,
To spend an hour in larking:
If you’ll go there, that wrinkled pair,
We’ll get a great laugh
At them this day.”

6

Said I, “With all my heart, I’ll do it;
I’ll get my Sunday’s shirt on
And meet you on the holy spot;
Faith, we’ll have a fine time observing!”
Then I went home at breakfast time,
And soon I made myself ready
For roads were clad, from side to side
With many a weary body
In droves that day.

7

Here smug farmers, in riding gear,
Went jogging past their cottagers;
There strapping youngsters in lovely broad cloth,
Are springing over the ditches.
Groups of lasses, padding barefoot,
In silks and scarlets glitter,
With sweet-milk cheese, in many a large slice
And bannocks, baked with butter
Full crisp that day.

8

When by the plate we set our nose
Well heaped up with halfpences[1],
A greedy glare the church elder throws
And we must hand over our twopences.
Then in we go to see the show:
On every side they’re gathering

Some carryin dails, some chairs an' stools,
An' some are busy bleth'rin
Right loud that day.

9

Here stands a shed to fend the showers,
And screen our country gentry;
There Racer Jess, and twa-three whores,
Are blinkin' at the entry.
Here sits a raw o tittlin' jades
Wi heavin' breast an bare neck;
And there a batch o wabster lads,
Blackguarding frae Kilmarnock,
For fun this day.

10

Here some are thinkin on their sins,
An' some upo' their claes;
Ane curses feet that fyl'd his shins,
Anither sighs an' prays:
On this hand sits a chosen swatch,
Wi' screw'd-up grace-proud faces;
On that a set o' chaps at watch,
Thrang winkin on the lasses
To chairs that day.

11

O happy is that man and blest!
Nae wonder that it pride him!
Whase ain dear lass that he likes best,
Comes clinkin down beside him!
Wi' arm repos'd on the chair back,
He sweetly does compose him;
Which by degrees slips round her neck,
An's loof upon her bosom,
Unkenn'd that day.

12

Now a' the congregation o'er
Is silent expectation;
For Moodie speels the holy door,
Wi' tidings o' salvation.
Should Hornie, as in ancient days,
'Mang sons o' God present him,
The vera sight o' Moodie's face,
To's ain het hame had sent him
Wi' fright that day.

Some carrying planks, some chairs and stools
And some are busy gossiping
Right loud that day.

9

Here stands a shed to keep off showers
And screen our country gentry,
There Racer Jess, and two or three whores
Are leering at the entrance.
Here sits a row of whispering wild young women
With heaving breasts and bare neck
And there a batch of weaver lads
Boisterous from Kilmarnock
For fun this day.

10

Here some are thinking on their sins
And some upon their clothes;
One curses feet that soiled his shoes
Another sighs and prays.
On this hand sits a chosen sample[2],
With screwed-up, grace-proud faces;
On that a set of chaps, at watch,
Busy winking on the lasses
To chairs that day.

11

O happy is that man and blessed!
No wonder that it prides him!
Whose own dear lass, that he likes best,
Falls into the seat beside him!
With arm resting on the back of the chair,
He sweetly arranges himself;
Which by degrees, slips round her neck
And his palm upon her bosom
Secretly that day.

12

Now the entire congregation
Is in silent expectation
For [Rev] Moodie climbs the holy door
With tidings of damnation:
Should the Devil, as in ancient days,
Among sons of God present himself
The very sight of Moodie's face
To his own hot home would send him
With fright that day.

[2] The Elect: see page 48.

13

Hear how he clears the points o' Faith
Wi' rattlin an' wi' thumpin!
Now meekly calm, now wild in wrath,
He's stampin, an' he's jumpin!
His lengthen'd chin, his turn'd-up snout,
His eldritch squeal and gestures,
Oh, how they fire the heart devout,
Like cantharidian plaisters,
On sic a day!

14

But hark! the tent has chang'd its voice;
There's peace and rest nae langer;
For a' the real judges rise,
They canna sit for anger.
Smith opens out his cauld harangues,
On practice and on morals;
An' aff the godly pour in thrangs,
To gie the jars an' barrels
A lift that day.

15

What signifies his barren shine
Of moral pow'rs and reason?
His English style an' gesture fine
Are a' clean out o' season.
Like Socrates or Antonine,
Or some auld pagan heathen,
The moral man he does define,
But ne'er a word o' faith in
That's right that day.

16

In guid time comes an antidote
Against sic poison'd nostrum;
For Peebles, frae the water-fit,
Ascends the holy rostrum:
See, up he's got the word o' God,
An' meek an' mim has view'd it,
While Common Sense has ta'en the road
An's aff, an' up the Cowgate
Fast, fast that day.

17

Wee Miller niest the Guard relieves,
An' Orthodoxy raibles,

13

Hear how he clears the points of Faith
With rattling and thumping!
Now meekly calm, now wild in wrath,
He's stamping, and he's jumping!
His lengthened chin, his turned-up nose,
His unearthly squeal and gestures,
O how they fire the heart devout
Like Cantharidian plasters[3]
On such a day.

14

But hark! the tent has a new minister;
There is peace and rest no longer
For all the real judges rise,
They cannot sit for anger:
Smith opens out his cold harangues,
On practice and on morals;
And off the godly pour in throngs,
To give the jars and barrels [of ale]
A lift that day.

15

What signifies his barren shine
Of moral powers and reason?
His English style, and gesture fine
Are all clean out of season.
Like Socrates or Antonine
Or some old pagan heathen,
The moral man he does define,
But never a word of faith in
That's right that day.

16

In good time comes an antidote
Against such poisoned nostrum;
For [Rev] Peebles, from the water foot,
Ascends the holy rostrum:
See, he's picked up the word of God,
And meek and mild has viewed it,
While Common sense has taken the road,
And is off, and up the Cowgate
Fast, fast that day

17

Little [Rev] Miller next, the Guard relieves,
And orthodoxy recites by rote,

[3] Cantharidian (Spanish Fly) plasters were used as an aphrodisiac.

Tho' in his heart he weel believes
An' thinks it auld wives' fables:
But faith! the birkie wants a manse,
So cannilie he hums them;
Altho' his carnal wit an' sense
Like hafflins-wise o'ercomes him
At times that day.

Though in his heart he well believes,
And thinks it old wives' tales:
But faith! the fellow wants a manse
So carefully he mumbles
Although his carnal wit and sense
Nearly half overcomes him
At times that day.

18

Now butt an' ben the change-house fills
Wi' yill-caup commentators;
Here's cryin out for bakes an gills,
An' there the pint-stowp clatters;
While thick an' thrang, an' loud an' lang,
Wi' logic an' wi' Scripture,
They raise a din, that in the end
Is like to breed a rupture
O' wrath that day.

18

Now from front to back, the drinking den fills
With ale-cup commentators:
Here's (someone) cryin out for biscuits and drink
And there the pint tankard clatters;
While crowded and busy, and loud and long
With logic and with Scripture,
They raise a din, that in the end
Is like to breed a rupture
Of wrath that day.

19

Leeze me on drink! it gies us mair
Than either school or college;
It kindles wit, it waukens lear,
It pangs us fou o' knowledge:
Be't whisky-gill or penny-wheep,
Or ony stronger potion,
It never fails, on drinkin deep,
To kittle up our notion,
By night or day.

19

I love drink! It gives me more
Than either school or college
It wakens wit, it wakens learning
It crams us full of knowledge.
Be it whisky gill or thin ale
Or any stronger potion,
It never fails, on drinking deep,
To stimulate
By night or day.

20

The lads an' lasses, blythely bent
To mind baith saul an' body,
Sit round the table weel content,
An' steer about the toddy,
On this ane's dress an' that ane's leuk,
They're makin observations;
While some are cozie i' the neuk,
An' forming assignations
To meet some day.

20

The lads and lasses, cheerfully intent
To mind both soul and body,
Sit round the table well content
And bustle about the toddy,
On this one's dress and that one's appearance
They're making observations
While some are cosy in the corner
And forming assignations
To meet some day.

21

But now the Lord's ain trumpet touts,
Till a' the hills are rairin,
An' echoes back return the shouts –
Black Russell is na sparin:
His piercing words, like Highlan' swords,

21

But now the Lord's own trumpet toots
Till all the hills are roaring
And echoes back return the shouts
[Rev] Black Russell is giving it his utmost
His piercing words, like Highland swords,

Divide the joints an' marrow;
His talk o' Hell, whare devils dwell,
Our vera sauls does harrow
Wi' fright that day!

22
A vast, unbottom'd, boundless pit,
Fill'd fou o' lowin brunstane,
Whase ragin flame, an' scorching heat,
Wad melt the hardest whun-stane!
The half-asleep start up wi' fear,
An' think they hear it roarin;
When presently it does appear,
'Twas but some neibor snorin
Asleep that day.

23
'Twad be owre lang a tale to tell,
How mony stories past;
An' how they crouded to the yill,
When they were a' dismist:
How drink gaed round in cogs an' caups
Amang the furms an' benches;
An' cheese and bread frae women's laps
Was dealt about in lunches
An' dauds that day.

24
In comes a gausie, gash guidwife,
An' sits down by the fire,
Syne draws her kebbuck an' her knife;
The lasses they are shyer:
The auld guidmen, about the grace
Frae side to side they bother,
Till some ane by his bonnet lays,
And gi'es them't like a tether,
Fu' lang that day.

25
Waesucks! for him that gets nae lass,
Or lasses that hae naething!
Sma' need has he to say a grace,
Or melvie his braw clathing!
O wives, be mindfu' ance yoursel
How bonie lads ye wanted;
An' dinna, for a kebbuck-heel,
Let lasses be affronted
On sic a day!

Divide the joints and marrow;
His talk of Hell, where devils dwell,
Our very souls does harrow
With fright that day.

22
A vast, unbottomed, boundless pit,
Filled full of blazing brimstone
Whose raging flame and scorching heat
Would melt the hardest whinstone
The half-asleep start up with fear
And think they hear it roaring
When presently it does appear
'Twas but some neighbour snoring
Asleep that day.

23
It would be too long a tale to tell
How many stories passed
And how they crowded to the ale,
When they were all dismissed:
How drink went round in jugs and cups
Among the forms and benches
And cheese and bread from women's laps
Was dealt about in lunches
And big chunks that day.

24
In comes a fresh-faced, smart housewife
And sits down by the fire
Then takes out her cheese and her knife;
The lasses they are shyer.
The old men, about the grace
From side to side they confer,
Till some one takes off his bonnet and lays it down
And says a grace
At great length that day.

25
Alas! for him who gets no lass
Or lasses that have nothing!
He has little need to say a grace
Or get meal dust over his good clothes!
O wives, remember once yourself
How bonnie lads you wanted,
And do not, for a cheese-crust
Let lasses be affronted
On such a day!

26

Now Clinkumbell, wi' rattlin tow,
Begins to jow an' croon;
Some swagger hame the best they dow,
Some wait the afternoon.
At slaps the billies halt a blink,
Till lasses strip their shoon:
Wi' faith an' hope, an' love an' drink,
They're a' in famous tune
For crack that day.

27

How monie hearts this day converts
O' sinners and o' lasses
Their hearts o' stane, gin night, are gane
As saft as ony flesh is.
There's some are fou o' love divine,
There's some are fou o' brandy;
An' monie jobs that day begin,
May end in houghmagandie
Some ither day

26

Now the bellman, with rattling rope
Begins to toll the bell and sing in a low voice.
Some stagger home as best they can
Some wait (until) the afternoon.
At gaps in the walls, lads stop for a moment
Till lasses take off their shoes;
With faith and hope, and love and drink,
They're all in a great mood
For banter that day.

27

How many hearts this day converts
Of sinners and of lasses;
Their hearts of stone, by night-time, have gone
As soft as any flesh is
There's some are full of love divine
There's some are full of brandy
And many jobs that day begun
May end in fornication
Some other day

The Holy Fair.

A robe of seeming truth and trust
Hid crafty observation;
And secret hung, with poison'd crust,
The dirk of Defamation:
A mask that like the gorget show'd
dye-varying, on the pigeon;
And for a mantle large and broad,
He wrapt him in Religion. —

Hypocrisy a-la-Mode

Upon a simmer Sunday morn,
    When Nature's face is fair,
I walked forth to view the corn,
    An' snuff the callor air:
The rising sun owre Galston muirs,
    Wi' glorious light was glintan;
The hares were hirplan down the furrs,
    The lav'rocks they were chantan
                        Fu' sweet that day.

As lightsomely I glowr'd abroad,
    To see a scene sae gay,
Three hizzies, early at the road,
    Cam skelpan up the way.
Twa had manteeles o' dolefu' black,
    But ane wi' lyart lining;
The third, that gaed a wee aback,
    Was in the fashion shining
                        Fu' gay that day

The twa appear'd like sisters twin,
    In feature, form an' claes;
Their visage—wither'd, lang an' thin,
    An' sour as onie slaes:
The third cam up, hap-step-an'-loup,
    As light as onie lambie,
An' wi' a curchie low did stoop,
    As soon as e'er she saw me.
                        Fu' kind that day

Wi' bonnet aff, quoth I, "Sweet lass,
    "I think ye seem to ken me;
"I'm sure I've seen that bonie face,
    "But yet I canna name ye—"
Quo' she, an' laughan as she spak,
    An' taks me by the hands,
"Ye, for my sake, hae gien the feck
    "Of a' the ten commands
                        A screed some day

122

"My name is Fun— your crony dear,
  "The nearest friend ye hae;
"An' this is Superstition here,
  "An' that's Hypocrisy.
"I'm gaun to ********* holy fair,
  "To spend an hour in daffin:
"Gin ye'll go there, yon runkl'd pair,
  "We will get famous laughin
                                    At them this day."

6

Quoth I, "With a' my heart, I'll do't;
  "I'll get my Sunday's sark on,
"An' meet you on the holy spot;
  "Faith we'se hae fine remarkin!"
Then I gaed hame, at crowdie-time,
  An' soon I made me ready;
For roads were clad, frae side to side,
  Wi' monie a weary body,
                                    In droves that day

7

Here, farmers gash, in ridin graith,
  Gaed hoddan by their cotters;
There, swankies young, in braw braid-claith,
  Are springan owre the gutters.
The lasses, skelpan barefit, thrang,
  In silks an' scarlets glitter;
Wi' sweet-milk cheese, in mony a whang,
  An' farls, bak'd wi' butter,
                                    Fu' crump that day.

When by the plate we set our nose,
  Weel heaped up wi' ha'pence,
A greedy glowr Black-bonnet throws,
  An' we maun draw our tippence.
Then in we go to see the show,
  On ev'ry side they're gath'ran;
Some, carryan dails, some chairs an' stools,
  An' some are busy bleth'ran
                                    Right loud that day.

Here, stands a shed to fend the show'rs,
　An' screen our countra Gentry;
There, racer Jess, an' twathree wh—res,
　Are blinkan at the entry —
Here sits a raw o' titlan jads,
　Wi' heaving breasts an' bare neck;
An' there, a batch o' Wabster lads,
　Blackguarding frae K******k
　　　　　　　　　　　　For fun this day.

　　　　　10.
Here, some are thinkan on their sins,
　An' some upo' their claes;
Ane curses feet that fyl'd his shins,
　Anither sighs an' prays:
On this hand sits an' elect swatch,
　Wi' screw'd-up, grace-proud faces;
On that, a set o' chaps, at watch,
　Thrang winkan on the lasses
　　　　　　　　　　　　To chairs that day.

　　　　　11
O happy is that man, an' blest!
　Nae wonder that it pride him!
Whase ain dear lass, that he likes best,
　Comes clinkan down beside him!
Wi' arm repos'd on the chair back,
　He sweetly does compose him;
Which, by degrees, slips round her neck,
　An's loof upon her bosom
　　　　　　　　　　　　Unkend that day

　　　　　12
Now a' the congregation o'er,
　Is silent expectation;
For ——— speels the holy door,
　Wi' tidings o' salvation.
Should Hornie, as in ancient days,
　Mang sons o' G— present him,
The vera sight o' —————'s face,
　To's ain het hame had sent him
　　　　　　　　　　　　Wi' fright that day.

124

13.

Hear how he clears the points o' Faith
    Wi' rattlin an' thumpin!
Now meekly calm, now wild in wrath,
    He's stampan, an' he's jumpan!
His lengthen'd chin, his turn'd up snout,
    His eldritch squeel an' gestures,
O how they fire the heart devout,
    Like cantharidian plaisters
            On sic a day!

14.

But hark! the tent has chang'd it's voice;
    There's peace an' rest nae langer;
For a' the real judges rise,
    They canna sit for anger.
opens out his cauld harangues,
    On practice and on morals;
An' aff the godly pour in thrangs,
    To gie the jars an' barrels
            A lift that day.

15.

What signifies his barren shine,
    Of moral pow'rs an' reason;
His English style, an' gesture fine,
    Are a' clean out o' season.
Like Socrates or Antonine,
    Or some auld pagan heathen,
The moral man he does define,
    But ne'er a word o' faith in
            That's right that day.

16.

In guid time comes an antidote
    Against sic poosion'd nostrum;
For frae the water-fit,
    Ascends the holy rostrum:
See, up he's got the Word o' G——,
    An' meek an' mim has view'd it,
While Common-sense has taen the road,
    An' aff, an' up the Cowgate
            Fast, fast that day.

17.

Wee nieft, the guard relieves,
    An' Orthodoxy raibles,

Tho' in his heart he weel believes,
      An' thinks it auld wives' fables:
But faith! the bodie wants a Manse,
      So, cannilie he hums them;
Altho' his carnal Wit an' Sense
      Like hafflins-wise o'ercomes him
                              At times that day.
                    18.

Now, butt an' ben, the Change-house fills,
      Wi' yill-caup Commentators::
Here's crying out for bakes an' gills,
      An' there, the pint-stowp clatters;
While thick an' thrang, an' loud an' lang,
      Wi' Logic, an' wi' Scripture,
They raise a din, that, in the end,
      Is like to breed a rupture O' wrath that day.
                    19.

Leeze me on Drink! it gies us mair
      Than either School or Colledge;
It kindles Wit, it waukens Lear,
      It pangs us fou o' Knowledge.
Be't whisky-gill or penny-wheep,
      Or onie stronger potion,
It never fails, on drinkin deep,
      To kittle up our notion,
                    20.   By night or day.

The lads an' lasses, blythely bent
      To mind baith saul an' body,
Sit round the table, weel content,
      An' steer about the Toddy.
On this ane's dress, an' that ane's leuk,
      They're makin observations;
While some are cozie i' the neuk,
      An' forming assignations
                              To meet some day.
                    21.

But now the L——'s ain trumpet touts,
      Till a' the hills are rairan,
An' echos back return the shouts;
      Black ⅢⅢⅢ is na spairan:
His piercin words, like highlan swords,
      Divide the joints an' marrow;

His talk o' H—ll, whare devils dwell,
  Our vera "Sauls does harrow"*

22.   Wi' fright that day.

A vast, unbottom'd, boundless Pit,
  Fill'd fou o' lowan brunstane—
Whase raging flame, an' scorching heat,
  Wad melt the hardest whun-Stane!
The half-asleep start up wi' fear,
  An' think they hear it roaran,
When presently it does appear,
  'Twas but some neebor snoran,
                            Asleep that day

23.

'Twad be owre lang a tale to tell,
  How monie stories past—
An' how they crouded to the yill,
  When they were a' dismist:
How drink gaed round, in cogs an' caups,
  Amang the furms an' benches;
An' cheese an' bread, frae women's laps,
  Was dealt about in lunches,
                            An' dawds that day

24.

In comes a gaucie, gash Guidwife,
  An' sits down by the fire,—
Syn draws her kebbuck an' her knife;
  The lasses they are shyest.
The auld Guidmen, about the grace,
  Frae side to side they bother,—
Till some ane by his bonnet lays,
  An' gies them't, like a tether,
                            Fu' lang that day.

25.

Wae sucks! for him that gets nae lass,
  Or lasses that hae naething!
Sma' need has he to say a grace,
  Or melvie his braw claething!
O Wives, be mindfu', ance yoursel',
  How bonie lads ye wanted,
An' dinna, for a kebbuck-heel,
  Let lasses be affronted
                            On sic a day!

* Shakespeare's Hamlet.

26.

Now Clinkumbell, wi' rattl an tow,
    Begins to jow an' croon;
Some swagger hame, the best they dow,
    Some wait the afternoon.
At slaps the billies halt a blink,
    Till lasses strip their shoon;
Wi' faith an' hope, an' love, an' drink,
    They're a' in famous tune
                    For crack that day.

27.

How mony hearts this day converts,
    O' Sinners and o' Lasses!
Their hearts o' stane, gin night are gane,
    As saft as ony flesh is.
There's some are fou o' love divine;
    There's some are fou o' brandy;
An' mony jobs that day begin,
    May end in Houghmagandie
                      Some ither day.

The rantin dog, the daddie o't (1786)

Today, a rant usually means a noisy tirade. In Burns's time, the adjective 'ranting' meant 'boisterous, merry, uproarious'.

Burns writes in the persona of the young woman he has wronged. Her thoughts are the antithesis of 'ranting'; insecure, fearful of the future, intensely hopeful that Rob might be around. Although Burns shows touching empathy, the sexual urge reasserts itself!

Some people find this poem incredibly poignant: others find it difficult to reconcile Burns's irresponsible attitude to women with that empathy he so clearly feels about their plight. He had twelve children by four women, nine of them by his wife Jean Armour. Seven of his children were illegitimate, including the first four by Jean before they were married in 1788.

It is unknown whether Burns was thinking of Elizabeth Paton, whose daughter was born in May 1784, or Jean Armour, whose twins were born in September of the same year.

1.

O, wha my babie-clouts will buy?	O who will buy my baby's nappies?
O, wha will tent me when I cry?	O, who will pay attention to me when I cry?
Wha will kiss me where I lie? –	Who will kiss me where I lie?
The rantin dog, the daddie o't!	The wild dog, the daddy of it!

2.

O, wha will own he did the faut?	O, who will admit he did the harm?
O, wha will buy the groanin maut?	O, who will buy the celebratory ale?
O, wha will tell me how to ca't? –	O, who will tell me what name to give it?
The rantin dog, the daddie o't!	The wild dog, the daddy of it!

3.

When I mount the creepie-chair,	When I mount the confessional chair,
Wha will sit beside me there?	Who will sit beside me there?
Gie me Rob, I'll seek nae mair –	Give me Rob, I'll seek no farther –
The rantin dog, the daddie o't!	The wild dog, the daddy of it!

4.

Wha will crack to me my lane?	Who will chat with me when I'm alone?
Wha will mak me fidgin fain?	Who will excite me sexually?
Wha will kiss me o'er again? –	Who will kiss me over again?
The rantin dog, the daddie o't!	The wild dog, the daddy of it!

To a Louse (1786)

Yet again, Burns is making use of his wonderfully poised comic satire to address not just the offending louse but the divisive snobbery between rich and poor. This is better than a flea circus; the louse and the person addressing it both perform with style! To make matters worse, the incident takes place in church, where snobbery like this should have no place.

The descriptions of the louse's agile antics in verses 3 and 4 are hilariously enhanced by the onomatopoeic quality of the Scots language and the poet's mock horror at the creature's impertinence in daring to climb so high. The final verse sees Burns making his own accustomed leap from the concrete to the abstract and, in doing so, producing lines which have become some of the most quoted in the Scots language.

Ha! Whare ye gaun, ye crowlin ferlie?
Your impudence protects you sairly;
I canna say but ye strut rarely
Owre gauze and lace,
Tho' faith! I fear ye dine but sparely
On sic a place.

Ye ugly, creepin, blastit wonner,
Detested, shunn'd by saunt an' sinner,
How daur ye set your fit upon her –
Sae fine a lady!
Gae somewhere else and seek your dinner
On some poor body.

Swith! in some beggar's hauffet squattle:
There you may creep, and sprawl, and sprattle
Wi' ither kindred, jumping cattle;
In shoals and nations;
Whare horn nor bane ne'er daur unsettle
Your thick plantations.

Now haud you there! ye're out o' sight,
Below the fatt'rils, snug an' tight;
Na, faith ye yet! ye'll no be right,
Till ye've got on it –
The vera tapmost, tow'ring height
O' miss's bonnet.

My sooth! right bauld ye set your nose out
As plump an' grey as onie grozet:
O for some rank, mercurial rozet,
Or fell, red smeddum,
I'd gie ye sic a hearty dose o't,
Wad dress your droddum!

Hey! Where are you going, you crawling wonder?
Your impudence protects you greatly.
I have to say you strut admirably
Over gauze and lace
Though faith! I fear you'll get little to eat
On such a place.

You ugly, creeping blasted wonder
Detested, shunned by saint and sinner
How dare you set your foot upon her
So fine a lady!
Go somewhere else and seek your dinner
On some poor person.

Away! and squat in some beggar's cheek
There you may creep and crawl and scramble
With other kindred jumping cattle
In shoals and nations;
Where neither horn not bone[1] ever dare unsettle
Your thick plantations.

Now hold it there! you're out of sight
Below the trimmings, snug and tight,
No, you're still at it! you'll not be content
Till you've got on it –
The very topmost, towering height
Of miss's bonnet.

Truly! Right boldly you set your nose out
As plump and grey as any gooseberry
O for some strong resin with mercury
Or fierce red powder
I'd give you such a hearty dose of it
It would thrash your backside.

---

[1] A bone comb was used traditionally to seek out hair lice.

I wad na been surpris'd to spy
You on an auld wife's flainen toy;
Or aiblins some bit duddie boy,
On's wyliecoat;
But Miss's fine Lunardi! fye!
How daur ye do't.

O Jenny, dinna toss your head,
An' set your beauties a' abroad!
You little ken what cursed speed
The blastie's makin!
Thae winks an' finger-ends, I dread,
Are notice takin'!

O wad some Power the giftie gie us
To see oursels as ithers see us!
It wad frae monie a blunder free us,
An' foolish notion:
What airs in dress an' gait wad lea'e us,
An' ev'n devotion!

I would not have been surprised to spy
You on an old woman's flannel cap
Or perhaps some small ragged boy's
Flannel vest;
But Miss's fine Lunardi[2]! Shame on you!
How dare you do it.

O Jenny, don't toss your head
And scatter the beauties!
You little know what cursed speed
The pest is making!
Those winks and finger-ends, I dread,
Are taking note!

O would some Power grant us the gift
To see ourselves as others see us!
It would from many a blunder free us
And foolish notion:
What airs in dress and bearing would leave us
And even devotion!

[2] Lunardi was a pioneer of balloon flight. The Lunardi bonnet, very tall and balloon-shaped, was named after him.

To a Mountain Daisy (1786)

As this poem develops, Burns seems to get carried away with his own rhetoric. His sincerity seems to go out the window with his Scots as he writes in almost Biblical English to lament (one might say hypocritically, in view of his track record) the fate of the 'artless maid' and winds up indulging in some self-pity.

1.

Wee, modest, crimson-tippèd flow'r,	Small, modest, crimson-tipped flower
Thou's met me in an evil hour;	You have met me in an evil hour;
For I maun crush amang the stoure	For I must crush among the dirt
Thy slender stem:	Your slender stem:
To spare thee now is past my pow'r,	To spare you now is beyond my power,
Thou bonie gem.	You lovely gem.

2.

Alas! it's no thy neebor sweet,	Alas! it's not your neighbour sweet
The bonie lark, companion meet,	The lovely lark, a suitable companion
Bending thee 'mang the dewy weet,	Bending you among the dewy moisture
Wi' spreckl'd breast!	With its speckled breast!
When upward-springing, blythe, to greet	When springing upward, cheerful, to greet
The purpling east.	The purpling east.

3.

Cauld blew the bitter-biting north	Cold blew the bitter-biting north
Upon thy early, humble birth;	Upon thy early, humble birth
Yet cheerfully thou glinted forth	Yet cheerfully thou glinted forth
Amid the storm,	Amid the storm,
Scarce rear'd above the parent-earth	Scarcely reared above the parent-earth
Thy tender form.	Thy tender form.

4.

The flaunting flow'rs our gardens yield,	The flaunting flowers our gardens yield
High shelt'ring woods and wa's maun shield;	High sheltering woods and walls must shield
But thou, beneath the random bield	But thou, beneath the random shelter
O' clod or stane,	Of clod or stone
Adorns the histie stibble-field,	Adorn the bare stubble field
Unseen, alane.	Unseen, alone.

5.

There, in thy scanty mantle clad,	There, in thy scanty mantle clad,
Thy snawie bosom sun-ward spread,	Thy snowy bosom sunward spread
Thou lifts thy unassuming head	Thou lifts thy unassuming head
In humble guise;	In humble guise;
But now the share uptears thy bed,	But now the ploughshare tears up thy bed
And low thou lies!	And low thou lies!

6.

Such is the fate of artless maid,	Such is the fate of artless maid,
Sweet flow'ret of the rural shade!	Sweet floweret of the rural shade!
By loves simplicity betray'd,	By love's simplicity betrayed,
And guileless trust;	And guileless trust;
Till she, like thee, all soil'd, is laid	Till she, like thee, all soiled, is laid
Low i' the dust.	Low in the dust.

7.

Such is the fate of simple Bard,	Such is the fate of simple Bard,
On Life's rough ocean luckless starr'd!	On Life's rough ocean luckless starred!
Unskilful he to note the card	Unskillful he to note the card
Of prudent lore,	Of prudent lore,
Till billows rage, and gales blow hard,	Till billows rage, and gales blow hard,
And whelm him o'er'.	And whelm him over.

8.

Such fate to suffering Worth is giv'n,	Such fate to suffering Worth is given,
Who long with wants and woes has striv'n,	Who long with wants and woes has striven,
By human pride or cunning driv'n	By human pride or cunning driven
To mis'rys brink;	To misery's brink;
Till, wretch'd of ev'ry stay but Heav'n,	Till, wretched of every stay but Heaven,
He, ruin'd, sink!	He, ruined, sink!

9.

Ev'n thou who mourn'st the Daisy's fate,	Even thou who mourns the Daisy's fate,
That fate is thine – no distant date;	That fate is thine – no distant date;
Stern Ruin's plough-share drives elate,	Stern Ruin's plough-share drives elate,
Full on thy bloom,	Full on thy bloom,
Till crush'd beneath the furrow's weight	Till crushed beneath the furrow's weight
Shall be thy doom!	Shall be thy doom!

Rantin Rovin Robin (1787)

1787 was an eventful year for Burns. In April the first Edinburgh edition of his poems was published. He was also working on publishing a collection of songs. He became a father again in May. The mother of the child was May Cameron, for whom Burns showed only a little concern. He wrote to his lawyer friend, Robert Ainslie: *'send for the wench and give her ten or twelve shillings… and advise her out to some country (friends)… Call immediately, or at least as soon as it is dark, for God's sake lest the poor soul be starving.'* June saw him being fêted in Edinburgh, but he was not comfortable with the patronising attitude of many of the literati. He paid several more visits to the capital where, in November, he met Mrs Agnes McLehose, with whom he set up a correspondence. She became his Clarinda and he her Sylvander. The proceeds from the Edinburgh edition enabled him to make two tours of the Highlands, in June and August.

Rantin Rovin Robin

Robert Burns, by Robert Burns. This song is sung traditionally at Burns' suppers, to set the tone for an evening of unrestrained entertainment. It was probably written to celebrate his 28th birthday. As usual, he celebrates his sexuality without any attempt at coy innuendo.

There was a lad was born in Kyle,
But whatna day o' whatna style,
I doubt it's hardly worth the while
To be sae nice wi Robin.

Chorus
Robin was a rovin boy,
Rantin, rovin, rantin, rovin,
Robin was a rovin boy,
Rantin, rovin, Robin!

Our monarch's hindmost year but ane
Was five-and-twenty days begun,
'Twas then a blast o' Janwar' win'
Blew hansel in on Robin.
Robin was, &c.

The gossip keekit in his loof,
Quo' scho, "Wha lives will see the proof,
This waly boy will be nae coof:
I think we'll ca' him Robin."
Robin was, &c.

"He'll hae misfortunes great an' sma',
But aye a heart aboon them a',
He'll be a credit till us a':
We'll a' be proud o' Robin."
Robin was, &c.

There was a lad who was born in Kyle,
But on what day or in what manner,
I doubt it is hardly worth the while
To be so over particular with Robin.

Chorus
Robin was a roving boy,
Boisterous, roving, cheerful, roving,
Robin was a roving boy,
Rantin, roving, Robin!

Our monarch's last year but one[1]
Was five-and-twenty days begun,
It was then a blast of January wind
Blew a birth gift in on Robin.
Robin was, &c.

The gossip glanced in his palm,
Said she "Who lives will see the proof,
This sturdy boy will be no fool:
I think we'll call him Robin."
Robin was, &c.

"He'll have misfortunes great and small,
But always a heart above them all.
He'll be a credit to us all:
We'll all be proud of Robin!"
Robin was, &c.

[1] 1759.

"But sure as three times three mak nine,
I see by ilka score and line,
This chap will dearly like our kin',
So leeze me on thee, Robin!"
Robin was, &c.

"Guid faith," quo scho, "I doubt you gar
The bonie lasses lie aspar;
But twenty fauts ye may hae waur –
So blessins on thee, Robin!"
Robin was, &c.

"But sure as three times three makes nine,
I see by every score and line,
This chap will dearly like our kind,
So here's to you, Robin!"
Robin was, &c.

"Good faith," said she, "I doubt you'll make
The lovely girls lie outspread;
But twenty faults you may have worse
So blessings on you, Robin!"
Robin was, &c.

Address to a Haggis (1787)

When an animal was slaughtered, the offal (heart, liver, lungs etc.) deteriorated quickly, so it had to be prepared and cooked immediately. This was the origin of the haggis – made from chopped offal, oatmeal, onions, suet and spices, all of it stuffed in the sheep's stomach then boiled. There are many 'puddings' with a similar pedigree!

No one knows where haggis originated, but it has – largely thanks to Burns's poem – become Scotland's national 'delicacy'. It is served at a Burns Supper with mashed tatties and neeps (potatoes and turnip). Great respect is shown for it, as befits a dish which has all the life-enhancing qualities the poem describes.

Usually, it is carried to the top table. Guests stand as the piper precedes it, then it is set down with great respect. The piper drinks off his customary whisky and another dram is poured on the haggis which is then 'addressed', hopefully with the drama such a poem, with its outrageous hyperbole, deserves.

The poem is a celebration of nationalism, with the implication that, just as the haggis is superior to foreign food, Scotland is superior to any foreign country.

1.

Fair fa' your honest, sonsie face,	Blessing on your honest, plump face,
Great chieftain o' the puddin-race!	Great chieftain of the pudding race
Aboon them a' ye tak your place,	Above them all you take your place,
Painch, tripe, or thairm:	Belly, tripe or intestine.
Weel are ye wordy of a grace	You are well worthy of a grace
As lang's my arm.	As long as my arm.

2.

The groaning trencher there ye fill,	The groaning dish there you fill,
Your hurdies like a distant hill,	Your buttocks like a distant hill,
Your pin wad help to mend a mill	Your skewer would help to mend a mill
In time o' need,	In time of need,
While thro' your pores the dews distil	While through your pores the dews distil
Like amber bead.	Like amber bead.

3.

His knife see rustic Labour dight,	See the peasant wipe his knife
An' cut ye up wi' ready slight,	And cut you up with eager skill
Trenching your gushing entrails bright,	Carving your gushing bright entrails
Like onie ditch;	Like any ditch;
And then, O what a glorious sight,	And then O what a glorious sight,
Warm-reeking, rich!	Warm, steaming, rich!

4.

Then horn for horn, they stretch an' strive:	Then, spoon for spoon, they stretch and strive;
Deil tak the hindmost, on they drive,	Devil take the last, on they drive,
Till a' their weel-swall'd kytes belyve	Till all their well-swollen bellies soon

Are bent like drums;
Then auld Guidman, maist like to rive,
'Bethankit!' hums.

5.
Is there that ower his French *ragout*
Or *olio* that wad staw a sow
O *fricassée* wad mak her spew
Wi perfect scunner,
Looks doun wi sneerin scornfu view
On sic a dinner?

6
Poor devil! see him owre his trash,
As feckless as a wither'd rash,
His spindle shank a guid whip-lash,
His nieve a nit;
Tho' bluidy flood or field to dash,
O how unfit.

7.
But mark the Rustic, haggis-fed,
The trembling earth resounds his tread,
Clap in his walie nieve a blade,
He'll make it whistle;
An' legs, an' arms, an' heads will sned
Like taps o' thrissle.

8.
Ye pow'rs, wha mak mankind your care,
And dish them out their bill o' fare,
Auld Scotland wants nae skinking ware
That jaups in luggies;
But if ye wish her gratefu' prayer,
Gie her a Haggis!

Are bent like drums;
Then the old man of the house, though fit to burst,
Mutters '[Lord] Be thanked'.

Is there that over his French *ragout*
Or *olio* that would sicken a pig
Or *fricassée* that would make her vomit
With absolute disgust,
Looks down, with sneering, scornful view
On such a dinner?

Poor devil! see him over his trash[1],
As feeble as a withered rush,
His long leg a good whip-lash,
His fist a nut;
Through bloody flood or field to dash,
Oh, how unfit.

But observe the peasant, haggis-fed
The trembling earth resounds his tread,
Slap a knife in his sturdy fist,
He'll make it whistle
And legs and arms and heads he'll prune
Like the tops of thistles.

Ye powers, who make mankind your care,
And dish them out their daily food,
Old Scotland does not want any watery soup
That slops in bowls;
But if you want her grateful prayer,
Give her a haggis!

[1] Inferior food.

Apostrophe to Fergusson (1787)

Robert Fergusson's poetry, published the year before his tragic death in 1773, gave Robert Burns the impetus to continue writing poetry in Scots, and many of Burns's poems, e.g *The Holy Fair*, *The Twa Dugs* and *The Cottars' Saturday Night*, were inspired by Robert Fergusson's originals. Burns freely acknowledged his debt to him, as this short poem shows. However, it is a curious paradox that Burns wrote three tributes to Robert Fergusson – all in English.

When Burns discovered that Fergusson was buried in an unmarked grave in the Canongate Cemetery in Edinburgh, he applied to the officials for permission to erect a headstone in 1787 and commissioned the architect Robert Burn to erect it. Some of Fergusson's tragic story can be found in the introduction.

> Curse on ungrateful man, that can be pleas'd
> And yet can starve the author of the pleasure!
> O thou, my elder brother in misfortune,
> By far my elder brother in the Muse,
> With tears I pity thy unhappy fate!
> Why is the Bard unfitted for the world,
> Yet has so keen a relish of its pleasures?

The Birks o Aberfeldy (1787)

Burns visited the Moness Gorge and Falls near Aberfeldy, when he was on his way to Inverness on the second of his Highland tours in 1787. This lyrical evocation of landscape and love was the result.

Chorus
Bonny lassie, will ye go,
Will ye go, will ye go?
Bonny lassie, will ye go,
To the birks of Aberfeldy?

Chorus
Bonnie lass, will you go
Will you go, will you go?
Bonnie lass, will you go
To the birches of Aberfeldy?

1.
Now simmer blinks on flow'ry braes,
And o'er the crystal streamlet plays,
Come, let us spend the lightsome days
In the birks of Aberfeldy!

Now summer blinks on flowery hillsides,
And over them the crystal streamlet plays,
Come, let us spend the lighthearted days
In the birches of Aberfeldy!

2.
While o'er their heads the hazels hing,
The little birdies blythely sing,
Or lightly flit on wanton wing
In the birks of Aberfeldy!

While over their heads the hazels hang,
The little birdies blithely sing,
Or lightly flit on wanton wing
In the birches of Aberfeldy!

3.
The braes ascend like lofty wa's,
The foaming stream, deep-roaring, fa's
O'er hung with fragrant-spreading shaws,
The birks of Aberfeldy.

The hillsides rise like lofty walls
The foaming stream, deep-roaring, falls
Overhung with fragrant-spreading woods,
The birches of Aberfeldy.

4.
The hoary cliffs are crown'd wi' flowers,
White o'er the linns the burnie pours,
And, rising, weets wi' misty showers
The birks of Aberfeldy.

The hoary cliffs are crowned with flowers,
White over the falls the little stream pours
And, rising, wets with misty showers
The birches of Aberfeldy.

5.
Let Fortune's gifts at random flee,
They ne'er shall draw a wish frae me,
Supremely blest wi' love and thee
In the birks of Aberfeldy.

Let Fortune's gifts at random flee,
They never shall draw a wish from me
Supremely blest with love and thee
In the birches of Aberfeldy.

The Poet's Welcome to his Illegitimate Child (or Love-begotten daughter or Bastard wean) (1787)

There are several versions of this poem, with different order and numbers of verses. The poem was addressed to Burns's first illegitimate child, Elizabeth, daughter of Elizabeth Paton, born on May 22nd, 1775. In 1776 Elizabeth made a claim on Burns and accepted a settlement of £20, which Burns paid from the proceeds from the Kilmarnock Edition. The child came to live with the Burns family and stayed with Burns's mother until she died. Thereafter, she went to live with her own mother who, by that time, had married John Andrew, a farm servant.

After Elizabeth had become pregnant, Burns boasted shamelessly of the affair in his *Epistle to John Rankine.* (see page 79) This poem shows a complete change in attitude: from Don Juan to the tender father, who promises the bairn his love and support.

But there's more to it than that. It is interesting that the poem has different titles in different editions; the formally 'illegitimate' child, the colloquially 'bastard' wean and the tenderly 'love-begotten' daughter. All three perceptions of the child are present in the poem in the attitudes of the church, the gossips and the father himself.

Verses 3 and 4 remind us that this was Calvinist Scotland, where fornicators were summoned before the church congregation to confess and repent of their sins. Although Burns addresses the child throughout, his words are not for her – at least not for a few years! He is taking a swipe at his detractors, the 'Holy Willies' of the church, and freely acknowledging the child as his own – and as his responsibility, which he promises to discharge to the best of his ability. The second last verse sees him admitting that he has had trouble, cost and shame to overcome – but that, if the child's potential is fulfilled, his pride in fathering her makes up for it all.

Burns did provide for Elizabeth. When she was 21, she received £200 from her father's estate.

Thou's welcome, wean, mishanter fa' me,
If ought of thee, or of thy mammy,
Shall ever danton me, or awe me,
   My sweet wee lady,
Or if I blush when thou shalt ca' me
   Tit-ta or daddy.

You're welcome, child, misfortune befall me
If anything concerning you or your mummy
Shall ever be too much for me or overwhelm me,
   My sweet little lady,
Or if I blush when you shall call me
   Da-da or daddy.

What tho' they ca' me fornicator,
An' tease my name in kintra clatter,
The mair they talk I'm kenn'd the better,
   E'en let them clash!
An auld wife's tongue's a feckless matter
   To gie ane fash.

What though they call me fornicator
And bandy about my name in country gossip
The more they talk, the better I'm known
   So let them gossip!
An old woman's tongue is powerless
   To be troublesome to anyone.

Welcome, my bonie, sweet, wee dochter!
Tho' ye come here a wee unsought for,
And tho' your comin I hae fought for,
    Baith kirk and queir;
Yet, by my faith, ye're no unwrought for –
    That I shall swear.

Sweet fruit o' mony a merry dint,
My funny toil is no a' tint,
Sin' thou came to the warl asklent,
    Which fools may scoff at;
In my last plack thy part's be in't
    The better half o't.

Tho' I should be the waur bestead,
Thou's be as braw and bienly clad,
And thy young years as nicely bred
    Wi' education,
As onie brat o' wedlock's bed,
    In a' thy station.

Wee image of my bonny Betty,
I, fatherly, will kiss and daut thee,
As dear and near my heart I set thee
    Wi' as gude will
As a' the priests had seen me get thee
    That's out o' Hell.

Gude grant that thou may ay inherit
Thy mither's person, grace, an' merit,
An' thy poor worthless daddy's spirit,
    Without his failins!
'Twill please me mair to hear an' see it,
    Than stockit mailins.

An' if thou be what I wad hae thee,
An' tak the counsel I sall gie thee,
I'll never rue my trouble wi thee –
    The cost nor shame o't –
But be a loving father to thee,
    And brag the name o't.

Welcome, my lovely, sweet little daughter,
Though your arrival was not anticipated
And though I have fought, for your coming,
    A tug-of-war[1];
Yet, by my faith, you're not unsupported –
    That I shall swear.

Sweet fruit of many a merry opportunity,
My pleasurable labour is not all lost
Since you came into the world irregularly,
    Which fools may scoff at;
If I only had a few pence to my name,
    More than half would be yours.

Though I should be the worse provided
You'll be as pretty and finely dressed
And your young years as daintily cultivated
    With education,
As any youngster whose parents are married
    In all your station.

Small image of my lovely Betty
I, fatherly, will kiss and fondle you,
As dear and near my heart I set you
    With as good will
As if all the priests had seen me get you
    That are out of Hell.

God grant that you may always inherit
Your mother's nature, grace and merit,
And your poor worthless daddy's spirit,
    Without his failings!
It will please me more to hear and see it
    Than well-stocked farms.

And if you grow up as I would wish you to
And take the advice I shall give you,
I'll never regret my trouble with you –
    The cost nor shame of it –
But be a loving father to you,
    And boast of it.

[1] Literally 'both church and choir'.

Auld Lang Syne (1788)

This must be the world's best known song, the universal welcome to a new year – and yet few people can probably manage more than one verse though many do manage the intrusive 'for the sake of'! And few things set a Scot's teeth more on edge than hearing the phrase pronounced as 'auld lang **Z**yne'.

The song's simplicity is perhaps the key to its universal appeal. There's a challenge in the rhetorical questions of the first verse, making us feel an almost moral obligation to remember old friends and bygone days. In verses 3 and 4, Burns contrasts the intimacy of childhood with the distances of exile, so that nostalgia for the past becomes the common factor of humanity, enabling us to reach out and address anyone as a friend.

Chorus.
For auld lang syne, my jo,
For auld lang syne,
We'll tak a cup o' kindness yet,
For auld lang syne!

Chorus.
For old time's sake, my dear
For old time's sake
We'll take a cup of kindness yet,
For old time's sake!

1.
Should auld acquaintance be forgot,
And never brought to mind?
Should auld acquaintance be forgot,
And days o' auld lang syne?

Should old acquaintance be forgotten,
And never brought to mind?
Should old acquaintance be forgotten,
And days of long ago?

2.
And surely ye'll be your pint-stowp,
And surely I'll be mine,
And we'll tak a cup o' kindness yet,
For auld lang syne!

And surely you'll be your pint measure,
And surely I'll be mine,
And we'll take a cup of kindness yet,
For old time's sake!

3.
We twa hae run about the braes,
And pu'd the gowans fine;
But we've wander'd mony a weary fit,
Sin auld lang syne.

We two have run about the hillsides
And pulled the daisies fine
But we've wandered many a weary foot
Since days of long ago.

4.
We twa hae paidl'd i' the burn,
Frae mornin' sun till dine,
But seas between us braid hae roar'd
Sin auld lang syne.

We two have paddled in the stream
From sunrise until noon
But wide seas have roared between us
Since days of long ago.

5.
And there's a hand, my trusty fiere!
And gie's a hand o' thine!
And we'll tak a right guid willy waught,
For auld lang syne.

And there's my hand, my trusty friend!
And give me your hand
And we'll have a hearty goodwill drink
For old time's sake.

Of a' the airts the wind can blaw (1788)

On February 23rd 1788, Burns bought Jean Armour a mahogany bed and set up house with her. Ten days later, she gave birth to twin girls, both of whom died within the month.

This song celebrates his early love for Jean who appears to be part of every aspect of nature. Most of the song is quite ordinary in its vocabulary and imagery, and yet it is delightfully fresh. However, consider the world of affection and wonder in the poetic economy of 'I hear her charm the air'.

1.

Of a' the airts the wind can blaw
I dearly love the west,
For there the bonny lassie lives,
The lassie I lo'e best.
There wild woods grow, and rivers row
And monie a hill between,
But day and night my fancy's flight
Is ever wi' my Jean.

Of all the directions the wind can blow
I dearly love the west,
For there the bonny lassie lives,
The lassie I love best.
There wild woods grow, and rivers roll
And many a hill between,
But day and night my fancy's flight
Is ever with my Jean.

2.

I see her in the dewy flowers –
I see her sweet and fair.
I hear her in the tuneful birds –
I hear her charm the air.
There's not a bonny flower that springs
By fountain, shaw, or green,
There's not a bonny bird that sings,
But minds me o' my Jean.

I see her in the dewy flowers –
I see her sweet and fair.
I hear her in the tuneful birds –
I hear her charm the air.
There's not a lovely flower that springs
By fountain, wood, or green,
There's not a lovely bird that sings,
But reminds me of my Jean.

Sylvander to Clarinda (1788)

Burns met Mrs Agnes (Nancy) McElhose in December 1787. When she was an old lady in Edinburgh, she still spoke of her love and wept over his faded letters. They met in Edinburgh when Burns was being fêted by Edinburgh society.

Nancy (née Craig), the daughter of a well-off Glasgow doctor, was sent to Edinburgh when she was 16 to acquire genteel accomplishments. What she did acquire was a husband whom she married in 1776 when she was just 17. Four miserable years and three surviving children later, they separated and he went off to Jamaica leaving her dependent on the goodwill of friends and relatives. She was 28 when she met Robert Burns and they began a passionate correspondence immediately after.

It is obvious from the letters they exchanged that there was a smouldering passion between them which they tried unsuccessfully to rationalise into friendship. The two things that prevented the passion from igniting were Nancy's social position as a woman separated from her husband – and her Calvinism. She wrote this in one of her letters to Burns in January 1787:

> *The 'Hand of Friendship' I accept,*
> *May Honour be our guard!*
> *Virtue our intercourse direct,*
> *Her smiles our dear reward.*

Her anxiety about her vulnerable position in society is apparent in her cautioning Burns rather hypocritically, with: *'I hope you'll come afoot even though you take a chair home. A chair is so uncommon a thing in our neighbourhood, it is apt to raise speculation – but they are all asleep by ten.'*

They disagreed on religion, as Nancy was a dedicated Calvinist while Burns did not believe in 'the Elect'. He wrote to her, *'I firmly believe that every honest upright man, of whatever sect, will be accepted of the Diety'.*

From their letters, it is apparent that Nancy set restraints on their relationship which Burns, not surprisingly, was apt to overstep. The discussions they have about religion, literature and Edinburgh society barely mask the hunger for one another that is the sub-text of their correspondence. Nancy was certainly intelligent, witty and attractive, as this remark shows: *'If you'd caress the "mental intelligence" as you do the corporeal frame, indeed, Sylvander, you'd make me a philosopher'.*

It was Nancy who first called herself Clarinda, a name popular with the Romantic poets and associated with the rural paradise, Arcadia. Burns, who became Sylvander, approved.

When Burns, returned home after some months in the capital, he wrote to his Clarinda again, this time to vilify the heavily pregnant Jean Armour in a way more demeaning to him than to her: *'I, this morning, as I came home, called for a certain woman. I am disgusted with her – I cannot endure her! I, while my heart smote me for the profanity, tried to compare her with my Clarinda: 'twas setting the expiring glimmer of a farthing taper beside the cloudless glory of the meridian sun. Here was tasteless insipidity, vulgarity of soul and mercenary fawning; there, polished good sense, Heaven-born genius, and the most generous, the most delicate, the most tender passion. I have done with her, and she with me…I know the Indies must be my lot.'*

However, he did not go to the Indies. It must have astounded Nancy when she discovered he had set up home with Jean almost immediately after writing the above in February 1788. Whether he informed Nancy of this or she found out by chance, it is not known but Nancy was not happy! Burns wrote to her, a letter of self-vindication, where he suggests all might have been different had he 'seen the least glimmering of hope that these (i.e. Nancy's) charms could ever have been mine'. Jean gave birth to twin daughters in March: they both died within a month.

It absolutely beggars belief that, while all this was going on, Jenny Clow, Nancy's servant, had become pregnant by Burns and bore him a son in November 1788.

Nancy then went off to try to patch things up with her husband in Jamaica but, when this did not work out, she returned to Edinburgh.

Burns wrote nine songs for his Clarinda, one of which, Ae Fond Kiss, is one of the most passionately understated and enigmatic songs ever written.

Sylvander and Clarinda is included here to show Burns's capability for Augustan language but that is all it is. There is no natural Muse at work here and any sincere emotion has been flattened by the style.

1.
When dear Clarinda, matchless fair,
First struck Sylvander's raptur'd view,
He gaz'd, he listened to despair –
Alas! 'twas all he dared to do.

2.
Love from Clarinda's heavenly eyes
Transfix'd his bosom thro' and thro',
But still in Friendship's guarded guise –
For more the demon fear'd to do.

3.
That heart, already more than lost,
The imp beleaguer'd all *perdu*[1];
For frowning Honor kept his post –
To meet that frown he shrunk to do.

4.
His pangs the Bard refus'd to own,
Tho' half he wish'd Clarinda knew;
But Anguish wrung the unweeting groan –
Who blames what frantic Pain must do?

5.
That heart, where motley follies blend,
Was sternly still to Honor true:
To prove Clarinda's fondest friend
Was what a lover, sure, might do!

[1] Lost (French).

6.
The Muse his ready quill employ'd;
No nearer bliss he could pursue;
That bliss Clarinda cold deny'd –
'Send word by Charles how you do!'

7.
The chill behest disarm'd his Muse,
Till Passion all impatient grew:
He wrote, and hinted for excuse,
'Twas 'cause he'd nothing else to do.'

8.
But by those hopes I have above!
And by those faults I dearly rue!
The deed, the boldest mark of love,
For thee that deed I dare to do!

9.
O, could the Fates but name the price
Would bless me with your charms and you,
With frantic joy I'd pay it thrice,
If human art or power could do!

10.
Then, take, Clarinda, friendship's hand
(Friendship, at least, I may avow),
And lay no more your chill command –
I'll write, whatever I've to do.

Afton Water (1789)

In the summer of 1789 Burns met the antiquarian, Captain Francis Grose, who was touring Scotland for suitable material for his book, *'The Antiquities of Scotland.'* When Burns suggested that he should include Alloway Kirk in his collection. Grose agreed, on condition that Burns provided a 'witch story' to go with it. Burns supplied him with three – but that was not the end of it. In 1790, these stories were transformed into *'Tam o Shanter'*.

On 1st September, Burns started work as an excise officer at a salary of £50 per annum. To cover his district, he was riding up to 200 miles a week and trying to run the farm at Ellisland at the same time.

Afton Water

Apart from a handful of words, this well-loved song is entirely in English, but not the overblown English of the Edinburgh literati. It is generally believed that it was written in memory of Mary Campbell, Highland Mary, who died in 1786. This makes it all the more poignant as the lover asks the birds to hush and the very stream itself to flow gently so that Mary sleeps undisturbed. The simplicity of the words harmonises with the simplicity of the rural scene.

1.
Flow gently, sweet Afton, among thy green braes[1]!
Flow gently, I'll sing thee a song in thy praise!
My Mary's asleep by the murmuring stream –
Flow gently, sweet Afton, disturb not her dream!

2.
Thou stock dove whose echo resounds thro' the glen,
Ye wild whistling blackbirds in yon thorny den,
Thou green-crested lapwing, thy screaming forbear –
I charge you, disturb not my slumbering fair.

3.
How lofty, sweet Afton, thy neighbouring hills,
Far mark'd with the courses of clear, winding rills!
There daily I wander, as noon rises high,
My flocks and my Mary's sweet cot in my eye.

4.
How pleasant thy banks and green valleys below,
Where wild in the woodlands the primroses blow:
There oft, as mild ev'ning sweeps over the lea,
The sweet-scented birk[2] shades my Mary and me.

5.
Thy crystal stream, Afton, how lovely it glides,
And winds by the cot where my Mary resides!
How wanton thy waters her snowy feet lave,
As, gathering sweet flowerets, she stems thy clear wave!

6.
Flow gently, sweet Afton, among thy green braes!
Flow gently, sweet river, the theme of my lays!
My Mary's asleep by thy murmuring stream –
Flow gently, sweet Afton, disturb not her dream!

[1] Slopes.
[2] Birch.

Address to the toothache (1789)

In a letter to his publisher, Creech, in 1789, Burns wrote, *"I had intended to have troubled you with a long letter, but at present the delightful sensation of an omnipotent toothache so engrosses all my inner man, as to put it out of my power even to write nonsense."*

In the poem, Burns intensifies his feelings by personifying Toothache. He is not talking <u>about</u> the 'hell o' a' diseases', but addressing it personally, as if the toothache was actively attacking him and he needs to hit back.

Notice how the words 'stang' and 'twang' resonate in the first verse – just as toothache throbs. Similarly 'freezes' and 'squeezes' in verse 2 seem to intensify the pain. There are several examples of Burns using language here very cleverly to dramatic effect.

1.
My curse upon your venom'd stang,
That shoots my tortur'd gooms alang,
An' through my lug gies monie a twang
Wi' gnawing vengeance,
Tearing my nerves wi' bitter pang,
Like racking engines!

1.
My curse upon your venomed sting,
That shoots along my tortured gums,
And through my ear gives many a tingle
With gnawing vengeance,
Tearing my nerves with bitter pang,
Like racking engines!

2.
When fevers burn, or ague freezes,
Rheumatics gnaw, or colic squeezes,
Our neighbour's sympathy may ease us,
Wi' pitying moan;
But thee! – thou hell o' a' diseases,
Aye mocks our groan!

2.
When fevers burn, or ague freezes,
Rheumatics gnaw, or colic squeezes,
Our neighbour's sympathy may ease us
With pitying moan;
But thee! – thou hell of all diseases,
Always mocks our groan!

3.
Adown my beard the slavers trickle,
I kick the wee stools o'er the mickle,
While round the fire the giglets keckle,
To see me loup,
An' raving mad, I wish a heckle
Were in their doup!

3.
Down my beard the saliva trickles,
I kick the small stools over the milking pail
While round the fire the children cackle
To see me leap,
And raving mad, I wish them a beating
On their backsides!

4.
Of a' the num'rous human dools –
Ill-hairsts, daft bargains, cutty-stools,
Or worthy frien's laid i' the mools,
Sad sight to see!
The tricks o' knaves, or fash o' fools –
Thou bear'st the gree!

4.
Of all the numerous human miseries –
Poor harvests, daft bargains, confession stools,
Or worthy friends laid in the earth,
Sad sight to see!
The tricks of knaves, or annoyance of fools –
You take the biscuit!

5.

Whare'er that place be priests ca' Hell,
Whare a' the tones o' misery yell,
An' ranked plagues their numbers tell,
In dreadfu' raw,
Thou, Toothache, surely bear'st the bell
Amang them a'!

6

O thou grim, mischief-making chiel,
That gars the notes o' discord squeal,
Till humankind aft dance a reel
In gore a shoe-thick,
Gie a' the faes o' Scotland's weal
A towmond's toothache.

5.

Wherever that place be priests call Hell,
Where all the tones of misery yell,
And ranked plagues their numbers tell
In a dreadful line,
Thou, Toothache, surely bear the bell
Among them all!

6

O thou grim, mischief-making lad,
That makes the notes of discord squeal,
Till humankind often dance a reel
In gore a shoe-thick,
Give all the foes of Scotland's well-being,
A twelve month's toothache.

John Anderson my jo (1790)

This is a timeless, beautifully tender, understated song of love: love that endures. It is sentiment without sentimentality and written in simple, yet very moving, domestic language.

The original version was a bawdy folk song, which Burns 'cleaned up'. In the original, it was a masterpiece of earthy sexual innuendo. Indeed, the version of Jimmy MacBeath's, collected in 1965 by the musician Peter Shepheard, dispensed with innuendo!

1.
John Anderson my jo, John,
When we were first acquent,
Your locks were like the raven,
Your bonie brow was brent;
But now your brow is beld, John,
Your locks are like the snaw,
But blessings on your frosty pow,
John Anderson my jo!

2.
John Anderson my jo, John,
We clamb the hill thegither,
And monie a cantie day, John,
We've had wi' ane anither;
Now we maun totter down, John,
And hand in hand we'll go,
And sleep thegither at the foot,
John Anderson my jo!

1.
John Anderson my sweetheart, John,
When we were first acquainted,
Your locks were like the raven,
Your handsome brow was unlined;
But now your brow is bald, John,
Your locks are like the snow,
But blessings on your frosty head,
John Anderson my sweetheart!

2.
John Anderson my sweetheart, John,
We climbed the hill together,
And many a pleasant day, John,
We've had with one another;
Now we must totter down, John,
And hand in hand we'll go,
And sleep together at the foot,
John Anderson my sweetheart!

My Heart's in the Highlands (1790)

Highland Romanticism! At this time, tartan was banned and Gaelic forbidden by The Act of Proscription of 1746, which was an attempt to crush the clan system. It is difficult, perhaps to empathise with songs like this when the historical facts define the defeat of the culture.

Chorus
My heart's in the Highlands, my heart is not here,
My heart's in the Highlands a-chasing the deer,
A-chasing the wild deer and following the roe –
My heart's in the Highlands, wherever I go!

1.
Farewell to the Highlands, farewell to the North,
The birthplace of valour, the country of worth!
Wherever I wander, wherever I rove,
The hills of the Highlands for ever I love.

2.
Farewell to the mountains high cover'd with snow,
Farewell to the straths and green valleys below,
Farewell to the forests and wild-hanging woods,
Farewell to the torrents and loud-pouring floods!

My love she's but a lassie yet (1790)

At first sight, this song seems to be a disjointed effort and it was indeed compiled from various lines from other songs. However its three verses deal with very Burnsian preoccupations: love and the power of money, drink as a social lubricant, the church and sexual desire.

The singer is complaining that the girl he attempted to woo was really more interested in money than in love – but the chorus suggests that time may erode her vanity and she might have to settle for less. Whatever the case, some fellowship with drinking companions will always be a joyful experience, unlike the wooing of conceited ambitious young women! The final verse leads from drink to the church and the consequences for the straight-laced minister who perhaps had one too many and lost his Calvinist cool!

Chorus
My love, she's but a lassie yet,
My love, she's but a lassie yet!
We'll let her stand a year or twa,
She'll no be half sae saucy yet!

1.
I rue the day I sought her, O!
I rue the day I sought her, O!
Wha gets her need na say he's woo'd,
But he may say he has bought her, O.

2.
Come draw a drap o' the best o't yet,
Come draw a drap o' the best o't yet,
Gae seek for pleasure whare ye will,
But here I never missed it yet.

3.
We're a' dry wi' drinkin o't,
We're a' dry wi' drinkin o't!
The minister kiss't the fiddler's wife –
He could na preach for thinkin o't!

Chorus
My love, she's just a lassie yet,
My love, she's just a lassie yet!
We'll let her stand a year or two,
She'll not be half as saucy yet!

1.
I rue the day I sought her, O!
I rue the day I sought her, O!
Who gets her need not say he's wooed,
But he may say he has bought her, O.

2.
Come draw a drop of the best of it yet,
Come draw a drop of the best of it yet,
Go seek for pleasure where you will,
But here I never missed it yet.

3.
We're all dry with drinking of it,
We're all dry with drinking of it!
The minister kissed the fiddler's wife –
He could not preach for thinking of it!

Tam o Shanter (1790)

This is a rollicking fast-paced narrative poem, interrupted every now and then by an impersonal voice of wisdom that attempts to advise and philosophise. This gives the poem even more dramatic tension and the moralising voice can only be seen as irony, the dour voice of pleasure-denying Scottish Calvinism. The poem is in mock heroic mode, which means the attitude to the 'hero' is ironic.

The poem can also be seen, at another level, as one of suppressed guilt that manifests itself in distortions of reality, distortions that are also fuelled by the over-indulgence in alcohol. Far from being a warning against the evils of drink and sex, the poem is a celebration of these.

The scene is set as market day draws to a close and weary men go for a drink in the pub before going home. The drink dispels the thought of the long wearisome journey and the bad-tempered wife waiting for you at the end of it.

When chapmen billies leave the street,	When peddlers leave the street
And drouthy neibors, neibors meet;	And thirsty neighbours meet,
As market days are wearing late,	As market-days are wearing late
An' folk begin to tak the gate;	And people begin to leave the town
While we sit bousing at the nappy,	While we sit drinking the ale
And getting fou and unco happy,	And getting drunk and very happy,
We think na on the lang Scots miles,	We think not on the long Scots miles,
The mosses, waters, slaps, and styles,	The bogs, waters, hollows and stiles,
That lie between us and our hame,	That lie between us and our home
Where sits our sulky sullen dame,	Where sits our sulky, sullen wife
Gathering her brows like gathering storm,	Knitting her brows like a gathering storm,
Nursing her wrath to keep it warm.	Nursing her wrath to keep it warm.
This truth fand honest Tam o' Shanter,	This truth found honest Tam O Shanter,
As he frae Ayr ae night did canter:	As he from Ayr one night did canter
(Auld Ayr, wham ne'er a town surpasses	(Old Ayr, whom never a town surpasses
For honest men and bonie lasses.)	For honest men and bonnie lassies.)

The moralising voice reminds Tam of his wife's disapproval. Note how the moralist looks for empathy from the 'gentle dames'. It is almost like the 'gentle reader' of Jane Austen. This underlines the irony.

O Tam! had'st thou but been sae wise,	O Tam, had you but been so wise,
As ta'en thy ain wife Kate's advice!	And taken your own wife Kate's advice!
She tauld thee weel thou was a skellum,	She told you in no uncertain terms,
A blethering, blustering, drunken blellum;	You were a drunken, garrulous ne'er-do-well
That frae November till October,	That from November till October,
Ae market-day thou was nae sober;	Each market-day you were not sober;
That ilka melder, wi' the miller,	That each meal-grinding with the miller,
Thou sat as lang as thou had siller;	You sat as long as you had silver [money];
That every naig was ca'd a shoe on,	That every horse that was shod a shoe on,
The smith and thee gat roaring fou on;	The smith and you got roaring drunk on;

That at the Lord's house, even on Sunday,
Thou drank wi' Kirkton Jean till Monday.
She prophesied that late or soon,
Thou would be found deep drown'd in Doon,
Or catch'd wi' warlocks in the mirk,
By Alloway's auld haunted kirk.

Ah, gentle dames! it gars me greet,
To think how mony counsels sweet,
How mony lengthen'd, sage advices
The husband frae the wife despises!

That at the Lord's house, even on Sunday,
You drank with Kirkton Jean till Monday.
She prophesied, that, late or soon,
You would be found deep drowned in Doon[2]
Or caught with warlocks in the dark
By Alloway's old haunted church.

Ah! gentle ladies, it makes me weep,
To think how many counsels sweet,
How many lengthened, sage advices
The husband from the wife despises.

The narrative continues. Tam is experiencing every kind of pleasure that good company, lubricated by drink, can offer him. Care, a vivid Personification, gives up and commits suicide by drowning himself in whisky.

But to our tale:- Ae market-night,
Tam had got planted unco right,
Fast by an ingle, bleezing finely,
Wi' reaming swats, that drank divinely;
And at his elbow, Souter Johnny,
His ancient, trusty, drouthy crony;
Tam lo'ed him like a vera brither –
They had been fou for weeks thegither.
The night drave on wi' sangs and clatter;
And ay the ale was growing better:
The landlady and Tam grew gracious,
Wi' favours secret, sweet and precious;
The Souter tauld his queerest stories;
The landlord's laugh was ready chorus:
The storm without might rair and rustle,
Tam did na mind the storm a whistle.

Care, mad to see a man sae happy,
E'en drown'd himsel' amang the nappy!
As bees flee hame wi' lades o' treasure,
The minutes wing'd their way wi' pleasure:
Kings may be blest, but Tam was glorious.
O'er a' the ills o' life victorious!

But to our tale:- One market-night,
Tam had got very comfortably ensconced
Fast by a fireplace blazing finely,
With foaming new ale, that drank divinely
And at his elbow, Souter[3] Johnny,
His ancient, trusty, thirsty crony:
Tam loved him like a very brother,
They had been drunk for weeks together.
The night drove on with songs and noise
And always the ale was growing better.
The landlady and Tam grew gracious
With secret favours, sweet and precious.
The Souter told his queerest stories
The landlord's laugh was ready chorus.
The storm outside might roar and rustle,
Tam did not mind the storm a whistle.

Care, mad to see a man so happy,
Even drowned himself among the ale.
As bees fly home with lodes of treasure,
The minutes winged their way with pleasure:
Kings may be blest but Tam was glorious,
Over all the ills of life victorious!

Once again, the moralising voice intervenes. Notice here the movement into English to make a philosophical statement about the ephemeral nature of pleasure. Some people read this as irony, some as straightforward sentiment. A worthy narrator goes for irony!

But pleasures are like poppies spread,
You sieze the flower, its bloom is shed;
Or like the snow falls in the river,
A moment white – then melts for ever;
Or like the borealis race,

But pleasures are like poppies spread:
You seize the flower, its bloom is shed;
Or like the snow falls in the river,
A moment white – then melts for ever;
Or like the Borealis[4] race,

[2] River Doon.
[3] Cobbler.
[4] Northern Lights.

That flit ere you can point their place;
Or like the rainbow's lovely form
Evanishing amid the storm.

That flit before you can point their place;
Or like the rainbow's lovely form
Vanishing amid the storm.

Enter harsh reality! The warmth, light and camaraderie of the pub are replaced by cold, dark, violent storms that rip the night apart – and Tam is all alone, prey to fears of the supernatural, constantly looking behind him to see if anything might be creeping up on him, singing to pretend to himself he's not afraid.

Nae man can tether time or tide,
The hour approaches Tam maun ride;
That hour, o' night's black arch the key-stane,
That dreary hour he mounts his beast in:
And sic a night he taks the road in,
As ne'er poor sinner was abroad in.
The wind blew as 'twad blawn its last;
The rattling showers rose on the blast;
The speedy gleams the darkness swallow'd;
Loud, deep, and lang, the thunder bellow'd;
That night, a child might understand,
The Deil had business on his hand.

No man can tether time or tide,
The hour approaches Tam must ride:
That hour, of night's black arch the key-stone,
That dreary hour Tam mounts his beast in
And such a night he takes the road in
As never poor sinner was abroad in.
The wind blew as it would have blown its last
The rattling showers rose on the blast
The speedy gleams the darkness swallowed
Loud, deep, and long the thunder bellowed.
That night, a child might understand
The Devil had business on his hand.

Weel mounted on his gray mare, Meg,
A better never lifted leg,
Tam skelpit on thro' dub and mire,
Despisin' wind and rain and fire;
Whiles holding fast his gude blue bonnet,
Whiles crooning o'er some auld Scots sonnet,
Whiles glowring round wi' prudent cares,
Lest bogles catch him unawares:
Kirk-Alloway was drawing nigh,
Whare ghaists and houlets nightly cry.

Well mounted on his grey mare Meg,
A better never lifted leg,
Tam galloped on through puddle and mire,
Despising wind, and rain, and fire.
Now holding fast his good blue bonnet,
Now crooning over some old Scots sonnet,
Now glowering round with prudent cares,
Lest spectres catch him unawares.
Kirk-Alloway[5] was drawing nigh,
Where ghosts and owls nightly cry.

Frightening stories from the past add to the terror. The pace picks up as the storm gets worse.

By this time he was cross the ford,
Whare, in the snaw, the chapman smoor'd;
And past the birks and meikle stane,
Whare drunken Chairlie brak's neck-bane;
And thro' the whins, and by the cairn,
Whare hunters fand the murder'd bairn;
And near the thorn, aboon the well,
Whare Mungo's mither hang'd hersel'.
Before him Doon pours all his floods;
The doubling storm roars thro' the woods;
The lightnings flash from pole to pole,
Near and more near the thunders roll:
When, glimmering thro' the groaning trees,

By this time he was across the ford
Where in the snow the peddler was smothered
And past the birches and big stone
Where drunken Charlie broke his neck-bone;
And through the gorse, and by the cairn
Where hunters found the murdered child
And near the hawthorn, above the well
Where Mungo's mother hanged herself.
Before him the Doon pours all his floods
The doubling storm roars through the woods
The lightnings flash from pole to pole
Near and more near the thunders roll
When, glimmering through the groaning trees,

[5] Kirk-Alloway: Alloway Church in South Ayrshire.

Kirk-Alloway seem'd in a bleeze;	Kirk-Alloway seemed in a blaze,
Thro' ilka bore the beams were glancing,	Through every crack the beams were glancing,
And loud resounded mirth and dancing.	And loud resounded mirth and dancing.

And just as the story becomes really exciting … 'the voice' intrudes, this time to apostrophise John Barleycorn, in other words, whisky!

A quick return to the tale sees Tam, steaming drunk and fearless, nudging his mare, Maggie, forward to get a better look. Maggie is stone cold sober.

Inspiring bold John Barleycorn,	Inspiring, bold John Barleycorn[6]!
What dangers thou canst make us scorn!	What dangers you can make us scorn!
Wi' tippeny, we fear nae evil;	With weak ale, we fear no evil,
Wi' usquabae, we'll face the devil!	With whisky, we will face the Devil!
The swats sae ream'd in Tammie's noddle,	The new-brewed ale so frothed in Tammie's head,
Fair play, he car'd na deils a boddle.	Fair play, he did not give a toss for the Devil.
But Maggie stood, right sair astonish'd,	But Maggie stood, right sore astonished,
Till, by the heel and hand admonish'd,	Until, by the heel and hand admonished,
She ventured forward on the light;	She ventured forward on the light
And, wow! Tam saw an unco sight!	And, wow! Tam saw a wondrous sight!

This is the heart of the poem, the revelation of the other world of sinister witchcraft and the Devil himself. What Tam sees is chilling and ghastly; shrouded corpses holding candles in their hands, murderers' bones wearing the chains from the gallows, two tiny unchristened babies, a thief cut from a rope, five blood-rusted tomahawks and five murdering scimitars, a garter that had strangled a baby, a knife a son had used to slit his father's throat. The lawyers' tongues and priests' hearts are added in a spirit of contempt for these vocations (These four lines were removed from later editions.).

Warlocks and witches in a dance;	Wizards and witches in a dance
Nae cotillion brent-new frae France,	No cotillion, brand new from France,
But hornpipes, jigs, strathspeys, and reels,	But hornpipes, jigs, strathspeys, and reels
Put life and mettle in their heels.	Put life and mettle in their heels.
A winnock-bunker in the east,	In a window seat in the east
There sat auld Nick, in shape o' beast;	There sat the Devil, in shape of beast
A towzie tyke, black, grim, and large,	A shaggy mongrel, black, grim, and large,
To gie them music was his charge:	To give them music was his charge.
He screw'd the pipes and gart them skirl,	He screwed the bagpipes and made them screech,
Till roof and rafters a' did dirl.	Till roof and rafters all did ring.
Coffins stood round, like open presses,	Coffins stood around, like open cupboards
That shaw'd the dead in their last dresses;	That showed the dead in their last dresses
And by some devilish cantraip slight,	And, by some devilish magic trick,
Each in its cauld hand held a light.	Each in its cold hand held a light
By which heroic Tam was able	By which heroic Tam was able
To note upon the haly table,	To note upon the holy table,
A murderer's banes in gibbet-airns;	A murderer's bones, in gibbet-irons
Twa span-lang, wee, unchristen'd bairns;	Two unchristened babes the size of your hand
A thief, new-cutted frae a rape, –	A thief newly cut from a gallows rope, –
Wi' his last gasp his gab did gape;	With his last gasp his mouth did gape
Five tomahawks, wi blude red-rusted,	Five tomahawks with blood red-rusted
Five scymitars, wi' murder crusted;	Five scimitars with murder crusted
A garter, which a babe had strangled;	A garter which a babe had strangled

[6] Whisky.

A knife, a father's throat had mangled –	A knife a father's throat had mangled
Whom his ain son o' life bereft –	Whom his own son of life bereft
The gray hairs yet stack to the heft;	The grey hairs still stuck to the heft
Wi' mair o' horrible and awfu',	With more of horrible and awful,
Which even to name wad be unlawfu'.	Which even to name would be unlawful.
Three lawyers' tongues, turn'd inside out,	Three lawyers' tongues, turned inside out,
Wi' lies seam'd like a beggar's clout;	With lies seamed like a beggar's cloth;
Three priests' hearts, rotten, black as muck,	Three priests' hearts, rotten, black as muck,
Lay stinking, vile, in every neuk.	Lay stinking, vile, in every corner.

The mood changes again as the focus switches from the horrible things lying around to the wild animation of the scene. Faster and faster, the pace increases until the climax is reached – when the dancing women throw off their outer clothes and dance almost naked in their shifts (short shirts).

As Tammie glowr'd, amaz'd, and curious,	As Tammie glowered, amazed, and curious,
The mirth and fun grew fast and furious;	The mirth and fun grew fast and furious
The piper loud and louder blew,	The piper loud and louder blew
The dancers quick and quicker flew;	The dancers quick and quicker flew
They reel'd, they set, they cross'd, they cleekit,	They reeled, they set, they crossed, they linked arms
Till ilka carlin swat and reekit,	Till every witch sweated and steamed
And coost her duddies to the wark,	And threw her ragged clothes into the effort
And linket at it in her sark!	And tripped at it in her under-shirt!

The moralising voice is definitely tongue in cheek, but here Burns turns the tables on the observer by revealing his latent lust! He forgets himself in the middle of his harangue and is ready to take the breeches off his backside just for a peek!

Now Tam, O Tam! had thae been queans,	Now Tam, O Tam! had they been girls,
A' plump and strapping in their teens!	All plump and strapping in their teens!
Their sarks, instead o' creeshie flannen,	Their under-shirts, instead of greasy flannel,
Been snaw-white seventeen hunder linnen!	Been snow-white fine linen!
Thir breeks o' mine, my only pair,	These trousers of mine, my only pair,
That ance were plush, o' gude blue hair,	That once were smart, of good blue wool,
I wad hae gi'en them off my hurdies,	I would have given them off my buttocks
For ae blink o' the bonie burdies!	For one glimpse of these sexy birds!
But wither'd beldams, auld and droll,	But withered grannies, old and a bit daft,
Rigwoodie hags wad spean a foal,	Horsey-looking hags that could wean a foal
Louping and flinging on a crummock,	Leaping and flouncing about on a shepherd's crook,
I wonder did na turn thy stomach!	I wonder they did not turn your stomach!

Tam is not daft. He has spotted the one dancer worth watching.

But Tam kend what was what fu' brawlie:	But Tam knew what was what full well:
There was ae winsome wench and waulie,	There was one winsome and beautiful wench,
That night enlisted in the core,	That night enlisted in the company,
Lang after ken'd on Carrick shore;	Known long after on Carrick[7] shore
(For mony a beast to dead she shot,	(For many an animal she shot to death,
And perish'd mony a bonie boat,	And caused many a bonnie boat to perish,
And shook baith meikle corn and bear,	And shook the tall corn and barley,

[7] District of South Ayrshire.

And kept the country-side in fear.)	And kept the country-side in fear.)
Her cutty-sark, o' Paisley harn,	Her short shift, of Paisley linen,
That while a lassie she had worn,	Which, as a young girl she had worn,
In longitude tho' sorely scanty,	Though it was very short,
It was her best, and she was vauntie…	It was her best, and she was proud.
Ah! little ken'd thy reverend grannie,	Ah, little did your revered grandmother know
That sark she coft for her wee Nannie,	That the shift she bought for her little Nannie
Wi' twa pund Scots, ('twas a' her riches),	With two pounds Scots (it was all her riches)
Wad ever grac'd a dance of witches!	Would ever have graced a dance of witches!

It is hard to imagine a more vigorous description of euphoria than this one. Imagine the devil bouncing up and down with excitement and Tam just 'bewitched', enchanted by the wild fervour of the dance – and appreciating it aesthetically too.

The crescendo is reached when Tam loses it altogether and bawls out his enthusiastic approval. From this climax of noise and pleasure and movement, there is a sudden dramatic darkness and silence – but only for a moment as the witches rally themselves to go after Tam.

But here my Muse her wing maun cour;	But here my Muse must clip her wings,
Sic flights are far beyond her pow'r;	Such flights are far beyond her power
To sing how Nannie lap and flang	To sing how Nannie leaped and flounced
(A souple jade she was, and strang),	(A supple lass she was and strong)
And how Tam stood, like ane bewitch'd,	And how Tam stood like one bewitched
And thought his very een enrich'd;	And thought his very eyes enriched.
Even Satan glowr'd, and fidg'd fu' fain,	Even Satan glowered, and got very excited,
And hotch'd and blew wi' might and main;	He jumped up and down and blew furiously
Till first ae caper, syne anither,	Till first one caper, then another,
Tam tint his reason a' thegither,	Tam lost his reason all together
And roars out, "Weel done, Cutty-sark!"	And roars out: "Well done, short-shift!"
And in an instant all was dark:	And in an instant all was dark.
And scarcely had he Maggie rallied,	And scarcely had he Maggie rallied
When out the hellish legion sallied.	When out the hellish legion sallied.

As bees bizz out wi' angry fyke,	As bees buzz out with angry bustle
When plundering herds assail their byke;	When plundering herds assail their hive,
As open pussie's mortal foes,	As a young hare's mortal foes
When, pop! she starts before their nose;	When, pop! she starts before their nose,
As eager runs the market-crowd,	As eager runs the market crowd,
When "Catch the thief!" resounds aloud;	When 'Catch the thief!' resounds aloud
So Maggie runs, the witches follow,	So Maggie runs, the witches follow
Wi' mony an eldritch skriech and hollow.	With many an unearthly screech and cry.

At this point, it seems as if the moralising observer can no longer stay aloof. He seems to be caught up in the excitement of the final denouement and almost sounds like a race commentator!

Ah, Tam! ah, Tam! thou'll get thy fairin'!	Ah, Tam! Ah, Tam! you'll get your come-uppance!
In hell they'll roast thee like a herrin'!	In hell they'll roast you like a herring!
In vain thy Kate awaits thy comin'!	In vain your Kate awaits your coming!
Kate soon will be a woefu' woman!	Kate soon will be a woeful woman!
Now, do thy speedy utmost, Meg,	Now, do your speedy utmost, Meg,

And win the key-stane o' the brig; | And win the key-stone of the bridge.
There at them thou thy tail may toss, | There, you can toss your tail at them,
A running stream they dare na cross! | A running stream they dare not cross!
But ere the key-stane she could make, | But before she could make it to the key-stone
The fient a tail she had to shake; | She had no tail to shake
For Nannie, far before the rest, | For Nannie, far before the rest,
Hard upon noble Maggie prest, | Hard upon noble Maggie pressed
And flew at Tam wi' furious ettle; | And flew at Tam with furious intent.
But little wist she Maggie's mettle! | But she underestimated Maggie's spirit!
Ae spring brought off her master hale, | One spring brought off her master whole
But left behind her ain gray tail; | But left behind her own grey tail:
The carlin claught her by the rump, | The witch clutched her by the rump
And left poor Maggie scarce a stump. | And left poor Maggie scarce a stump.

The last words come from the moralising voice – NO, the real last words have to come from Tam, whose only possible response to the moralising would be the Scottish double positive, 'Aye, right.'

Now, wha this tale o' truth shall read, | Now, who this tale of truth shall read,
Ilk man and mother's son take heed; | Each man, and mother's son, take heed:
Whene'er to drink you are inclin'd, | Whenever to drink you are inclined
Or cutty-sarks run in your mind, | Or short shifts run in your mind,
Think! ye may buy joys o'er dear: | Think! you may buy the joys too dear:
Remember Tam o' Shanter's mare. | Remember Tam O Shanter's mare.

Ae fond kiss (1791)

In March 1791, Anne Park, barmaid of the Globe Inn, gave birth to Burns's daughter, Elizabeth. In the following month, Jean gave birth to William Nicol Burns. The Burns family moved to Dumfries in November and, two weeks later, Burns went to Edinburgh where he met Nancy McElhose, his Clarinda, for the last time.

This song was his parting gift, sent to her on December 27th. It is a distillation of love, anguish and remembered happiness.

1.
Ae fond kiss, and then we sever!
Ae farewell, and then forever!
Deep in heart-wrung tears I'll pledge thee,
Warring sighs and groans I'll wage thee.

2.
Who shall say that Fortune grieves him,
While the star of hope she leaves him?
Me, nae cheerfu' twinkle lights me,
Dark despair around benights me.

3.
I'll ne'er blame my partial fancy:
Naething could resist my Nancy!
But to see her was to love her,
Love but her, and love for ever.

4.
Had we never lov'd sae kindly,
Had we never lov'd sae blindly,
Never met – or never parted –
We had ne'er been broken-hearted.

5.
Fare-thee-weel, thou first and fairest!
Fare-thee-weel, thou best and dearest!
Thine be ilka joy and treasure,
Peace, Enjoyment, Love and Pleasure!

6.
Ae fond kiss, and then we sever!
Ae farewell, alas, for ever!
Deep in heart-wrung tears I'll pledge thee,
Warring sighs and groans I'll wage thee.

1.
One fond kiss, and then we sever!
One farewell, and then forever!
Deep in heart-wrung tears I'll pledge thee,
Warring sighs and groans I'll wage thee.

2.
Who shall say that Fortune grieves him,
While the star of hope she leaves him?
Me, no cheerful twinkle lights me,
Dark despair around benights me.

3.
I'll never blame my partial fancy:
Nothing could resist my Nancy!
But to see her was to love her,
Love but her, and love for ever.

4.
Had we never loved so kindly,
Had we never loved so blindly,
Never met – or never parted –
We had never been broken-hearted.

5.
Fare-thee-well, thou first and fairest!
Fare-thee-well, thou best and dearest!
Thine be every joy and treasure,
Peace, Enjoyment, Love and Pleasure!

6.
One fond kiss, and then we sever!
One farewell, alas, for ever!
Deep in heart-wrung tears I'll pledge thee,
Warring sighs and groans I'll wage thee.

The Banks o' Doon (1791)

The first two versions of this song were in ballad form, while this third one was compiled to the tune of *'The Caledonian Hunt's Delight'*, and destined for publication in the *Scots Musical Museum* 1792.

The song was inspired by the plight of Peggy Kennedy, a niece of Mrs Gavin Hamilton. Peggy was an heiress, who succeeded to a large estate in Carrick. In 1786 she had a 'romance' with William McDouall, Laird of Logan, although she was betrothed when she was just 17 to Captain Maxwell, the M.P. for Wigtownshire. She became pregnant and later gave birth to an illegitimate daughter. Some years later, in 1794, she raised an action against the reluctant McDouall to declare their relationship legal (i.e. marriage by cohabitation) and their daughter legitimate. Tragically, Peggy died in 1795, but her daughter was awarded £3,000 when the case was finally resolved in 1798.

The song counterpoints innocent pastoral imagery of blooming valleys, warbling birds, wild roses and honeysuckle with heartbreak, loss and deception. The final metaphor blends these two opposing elements in a statement that sums up the beauty and pain that characterise both nature and human love.

1.
Ye banks and braes o' bonnie Doon,
How can ye bloom sae fresh and fair?
How can ye chant, ye little birds,
And I sae weary fu' o' care!
Thou'll break my heart, thou warbling bird,
That wantons thro' the flowering thorn!
Thou minds me o' departed joys,
Departed never to return.

2.
Aft hae I rov'd by bonnie Doon
To see the rose and woodbine twine,
And ilka bird sang o' its luve,
And fondly sae did I o' mine.
Wi' lightsome heart I pu'd a rose,
Fu' sweet upon its thorny tree!
And my fause luver stole my rose –
But ah! he left the thorn wi' me.

1.
Ye banks and braes of lovely Doon[1],
How can you bloom so fresh and fair?
How can you chant, ye little birds,
And I so weary full of care!
You'll break my heart, you warbling bird,
That flutters with joy through the flowering thorn!
You remind me of departed joys,
Departed never to return.

2.
Often have I roved by bonnie Doon
To see the rose and honeysuckle twine,
And every bird sang of its love
And fondly so did I of mine.
Lightheartedly I pulled a rose
Full sweet upon its thorny tree!
And my false lover stole my rose –
But ah! he left the thorn with me.

[1] Valley sides of the lovely River Doon.

Duncan Gray (1792)

This is another coarse old song which Burns has transformed into a comic love song. In the original version, Duncan's 'wooing' is rather more physically demanding! Here, the hyperbole deserves a singer with dramatic talent.

1.
Duncan Gray cam here to woo
Ha, ha, the wooing o't!
On blithe Yule-Night when we were fou
Ha, ha, the wooing o't!
Maggie coost her head fu' high,
Look'd asklent and unco skeigh,
Gart poor Duncan stand abeigh.
Ha, ha, the wooing o't!

2.
Duncan fleech'd, and Duncan pray'd;
Ha, ha, the wooing o't!
Meg was deaf as Ailsa Craig,
Ha, ha, the wooing o't!
Duncan sigh'd baith out and in,
Grat his een baith bleer't an' blin',
Spak o' lowpin o'er a linn –
Ha, ha, the wooing o't!

3.
Time and Chance are but a tide
Ha, ha, the wooing o't!
Slighted love is sair to bide
Ha, ha, the wooing o't!
'Shall I like a fool,' quoth he,
'For a haughty hizzie die?
She may gae to – France for me!
Ha, ha, the wooing o't!

4.
How it comes, let doctors tell,
Ha, ha, the wooing o't!
Meg grew sick, as he grew hale,
Ha, ha, the wooing o't!
Something in her bosom wrings,
For relief a sigh she brings,
And O! her een they spak sic things! –
Ha, ha, the wooing o't!

1.
Duncan Gray came here to woo
Ha, ha, the wooing o't!
On merry Christmas Eve when we were drunk
Ha, ha, the wooing o't!
Maggie tossed her head in the air
Looked away and seemed really disdainful
Made poor Duncan stand off.
Ha, ha, the wooing o't!

2.
Duncan flattered, and Duncan prayed
Ha, ha, the wooing o't!
Meg was as deaf as Ailsa Craig[1]
Ha, ha, the wooing o't!
Duncan sigh'd both out and in,
Wept till his eyes were bleary and blind,
Spoke of leaping over a waterfall -
Ha, ha, the wooing o't!

3.
Time and Chance are but a tide
Ha, ha, the wooing o't!
Slighted love is difficult to endure
Ha, ha, the wooing o't!
'Shall I like a fool,' said he,
'Die for a haughty hussy?
She may go to – France for me!
Ha, ha, the wooing o't!

4.
How it comes, let doctors tell
Ha, ha, the wooing o't!
Meg grew sick, as he grew well,
Ha, ha, the wooing o't!
Something in her bosom wrings,
For relief a sigh she brings,
And O! her eyes they speak such things –
Ha, ha, the wooing o't!

[1] An island in the Firth of Clyde west of Girvan.

5.
Duncan was a lad o' grace
Ha, ha, the wooing o't!
Maggie was a piteous case,
Ha, ha, the wooing o't!
Duncan couldna be her death,
Swelling pity smoor'd his wrath;
Now they're crouse and canty baith –
Ha, ha, the wooing o't!

5.
Duncan was a lad of grace
Ha, ha, the wooing o't!
Maggie was a piteous case
Ha, ha, the wooing o't!
Duncan could not be her death,
Swelling pity smothered his wrath;
Now they're both happy and contented
Ha, ha, the wooing o't!

My ain kind dearie, O (1792)

It is interesting to compare this song with '*The Rigs o Barley*'. Although the theme is similar, this song seems to signify a more gentle love affair, while the other is a glorious release of passion.

While the consummation in the corn rigs was lit by a brilliant moon, this song's only light is from the eastern star and dark Romantic imagery is used to define the lover's devotion.

1.
When o'er the hill the eastern star
Tells bughtin time is near, my jo,
And owsen frae the furrow'd field
Return sae dowf and weary, O,
Down by the burn, where scented birks
Wi' dew are hangin clear, my jo,
I'll meet thee on the lea-rig,
My ain kind dearie, O!

1.
When over the hill the eastern star
Tells it's time to bring the sheep to the fold, my love,
And oxen from the furrowed field
Return so dull and weary, O,
Down by the stream where scented birches
With dew are hanging clear, my love,
I'll meet thee on the grassy rig[1]
My own kind dearie, O!

2.
At midnight hour in mirkest glen,
I'd rove, and ne'er be eerie, O,
If thro' that glen I gaed to thee,
My ain kind dearie, O!
Altho' the night were ne'er sae wild,
And I were ne'er sae weary, O,
I'll meet thee on the lea-rig,
My ain kind dearie, O!

2.
At midnight hour in darkest glen
I'd rove and never be frightened, O,
If through that glen I was going to you,
My own kind dearie, O!
Although the night were never so wild,
And I were never so weary, O,
I'll meet thee on the lea-rig,
My own kind dearie, O!

3.
The hunter lo'es the morning sun,
To rouse the mountain deer, my jo;
At noon the fisher takes the glen
Adown the burn to steer, my jo:
Gie me the hour o' gloamin grey –
It maks my heart sae cheery, O,
To meet thee on the lea-rig,
My ain kind dearie, O!

3.
The hunter loves the morning sun
To rouse the mountain deer, my love
At noon the fisher takes the glen
Adown the burn to steer, my love
Give me the grey twilight hour –
It makes my heart so cheery, O,
To meet thee on the lea-rig,
My own kind dearie, O!

[1] Strip of land.

Such a parcel of rogues in a nation (1792)

'What are all the advantages which my country reaps from the union that can counterbalance the annihilation of her independence and even her very name?'

Robert Burns in a letter to Mrs Dunlop, 10th April 1790

The stimulus for this fiercely patriotic song goes back nearly 100 years to the Union of the Parliaments of Scotland and England in 1707. Many people felt the Union was a sell-out and that the more sparsely populated Scotland would always be the weaker partner: they felt keenly the loss of Scotland's independence.

'For every Scot in favour there is 99 against'… Daniel Defoe
'The whole nation appears against the Union'… Sir George Lockhart of Carnwath
'The treaty is contrary to the wishes of at least three-fourths of the kingdom'… Sir John Clerk of Penicuik

The 'parcel of rogues' are the 31 Scottish Commissioners who sold out to England and were rewarded with money, land and opportunities for free trade.

1.
Fareweel to a' our Scottish fame,
Fareweel our ancient glory!
Fareweel ev'n to the Scottish name.
Sae famed in martial story!
Now Sark rins over Solway sands,
An' Tweed rins to the ocean,
To mark where England's province stands –
Such a parcel of rogues in a nation!

2.
What force or guile could not subdue
Thro' many warlike ages
Is wrought now by a coward few
For hireling traitor's wages.
The English steel we could disdain,
Secure in valour's station;
But English gold has been our bane –
Such a parcel of rogues in a nation!

3.
O, would, or I had seen the day
That Treason thus could sell us,
My auld grey head had lien in clay,
Wi' Bruce and loyal Wallace!
But pith and power, till my last hour,
I'll mak this declaration:-
'We're bought and sold for English gold' –
Such a parcel of rogues in a nation!

1.
Farewell to all our Scottish fame
Farewell our ancient glory!
Farewell even to the Scottish name
So famed in martial story!
Now Sark runs over Solway sands[1],
And the River Tweed runs to the ocean
To mark where England's province stands –
Such a parcel of rogues in a nation!

2.
What force or guile could not subdue
Through many warlike ages
Is wrought now by a coward few
For hireling traitor's wages.
The English steel we could disdain,
Secure in valour's station;
But English gold has been our bane –
Such a parcel of rogues in a nation!

3.
O, would that I had seen the day
That Treason thus could sell us,
My old grey head had lain in clay
With Bruce and loyal Wallace!
But pith and power, till my last hour
I'll make this declaration:-
'We're bought and sold for English gold' –
Such a parcel of rogues in a nation!

[1] The River Sark flows into the Solway Firth.

Sic a wife as Willie had (1792)

Just north of the village of Tweedsmuir on the A701, there is a sign post which says, 'SITE OF LINKUMDODDIE'. Burns was said to have written the poem in the kitchen of the nearby Crook Inn where he stayed several times when he was travelling from Dumfries to Edinburgh. The lady who inspired this tribute was the wife of a farmer near Ellisland. Apparently, she had strong opinions which she had no hesitation in sharing. She claimed, for example, that tea would be 'the ruin of the nation', sugar was a 'sore evil' and china 'brunt (burned) clay', fit only for 'haudin the broo o' stinkin weeds', i.e. tea.

No one who has read this poem could accuse Burns of being politically correct!

1.

Willie Wastle dwalt on Tweed,
The spot they ca'd it Linkumdoddie.
Willie was a wabster guid
Could stown a clue wi' onie bodie.
He had a wife was dour and din,
O, Tinkler Maidgie was her mither!
Sic a wife as Willie had,
I wad na gie a button for her.

2.

She has an e'e – she has but ane,
The cat has twa the very colour,
Five rusty teeth, forbye a stump,
A clapper-tongue wad deave a miller;
A whiskin beard about her mou,
Her nose and chin they threaten ither:
Sic a wife as Willie had,
I wad na gie a button for her.

3.

She's bow-hough'd, she's hem-shinn'd,
Ae limpin leg a hand-breed shorter;
She's twisted right, she's twisted left,
To balance fair in ilka quarter;
She has a hump upon her breast,
The twin o' that upon her shouther:
Sic a wife as Willie had,
I wad na gie a button for her.

4.

Auld baudrons by the ingle sits,
And wi' her loof her face a-washin;
But Willie's wife is nae sae trig,
She dights her grunzie wi' a hushion;
Her walie nieves like midden-creels,
Her face wad fyle the Logan Water:
Sic a wife as Willie had,
I wad na gie a button for her.

1.

Willie Wastle dwelt on Tweed,
The spot they called it Linkumdoddie.
Willie was a good weaver
Who could pack a ball of wool with anybody.
He had a wife who was sullen and dark looking,
Oh, Tinker Maidgie was her mother.
Such a wife as Willie had,
I wouldn't give a button for her.

2.

She has an eye – she has but one,
The cat has two the very colour,
Five rusty teeth, besides a stump,
A rattling tongue that would deafen a miller,
A whisking beard about her mouth,
Her nose and chin threaten each other.
Such a wife as Willie had,
I wouldn't give a button for her.

3.

She's bandy-legged, her shins like haims[1]
One limping leg a hand's breadth shorter
She's twisted right, she's twisted left,
To balance fairly in every quarter.
She has a hump upon her breast,
The twin of that upon her shoulder.
Such a wife as Willie had,
I wouldn't give a button for her.

4.

The old cat sits by the fireside,
Washing her face with her palm;
But Willie's wife is not so particular,
She wipes her snout with an old stocking.
Her ample fists are like dung baskets,
Her face would pollute the Logan Water.
Such a wife as Willie had,
I wouldn't give a button for her.

---

[1] Haims: curved pieces of wood or metal covering the collar of a draught horse.

The Deil's aw wi the Exciseman (1792)

In February 1792, Burns was promoted to the Dumfries Port Division. His salary increased by £20 to £70 a year, and he was entitled also to some perks, viz large quantities of rum and brandy.

It is said that this song was composed when Burns was on duty with a group of fellow excisemen. They were keeping an eye on a ship in the Solway which they suspected of smuggling. When the excisemen realised the brig was staffed with a large crew, some of them went off for reinforcements. The song was born out of the tedium of hanging about on the Solway salt marshes for several hours.

It is on record that the ship, 'The Rosamond' was seized, despite resistance from the crew. When the ship, with what remained of its cargo, was later auctioned in Dumfries, it is said (although there is no proof of this) that Burns purchased four carronades (small cannons) which he sent to France to help the Revolution. The cannons were allegedly seized by the Customs officers at Dover and Burns reprimanded for what was considered inappropriate behaviour for an exciseman.

Obviously, excisemen were no more popular then than the Inland Revenue is today!

Chorus
The Deil's awa, the Deil's awa,
The Deil's awa wi' th' Exciseman!
He's danc'd awa, he's danc'd awa,
He's danc'd awa wi' th' Exciseman!

1.
The Deil cam fiddlin thro' the town,
And danc'd awa wi' th' Exciseman,
And ilka wife cries:– "Auld Mahoun,
I wish ye luck o' the prize, man!"

2.
"We'll mak our maut, and we'll brew our drink,
We'll laugh, sing, and rejoice, man,
And monie braw thanks to the meikle black Deil,
That danc'd awa wi' th' Exciseman."

3.
"There's threesome reels, there's foursome reels,
There's hornpipes and strathspeys, man,
But the ae best dance ere cam to the land
Was *The Deil's Awa wi' th' Exciseman*!"

Chorus
The Devil's away, The Devil's away
The Devil's away with the Exciseman
He's danced away, he's danced away
He's danced away with the Exciseman!

1.
The Devil came fiddling through the town
And danced away with the Exciseman
And every woman cries, "Old Mahoun[1],
I wish you luck of the prize, man!"

2.
"We'll make our malt, and we'll brew our drink
We'll laugh, sing, and rejoice, man,
And many grateful thanks to the big black Devil
That danced away with the Exciseman."

3.
"There's threesome reels, there's foursome reels,
There's hornpipes and strathspeys, man,
But the one best dance [that] ever came to the land
Was *The Devil's Away with the Exciseman*!"

[1] The Devil.

My Love is like a Red, Red Rose (1793)

Alongside *Auld Lang Syne*, this is probably Burns's best known and best loved song. This is partly because it is almost entirely in English and partly because of its honest simplicity.

The similes he uses are almost corny – and yet it works, because the images are timeless, like a distillation of every love song ever written.

1.
O, my luve's like a red, red rose,
That's newly sprung in June.
O, my luve's like the melodie,
That's sweetly play'd in tune.

2.
As fair art thou, my bonie lass,
So deep in luve am I,
And I will luve thee still, my dear,
Till a' the seas gang dry.

3.
Till a' the seas gang dry, my dear,
And the rocks melt wi' the sun!
O I will luve thee still, my dear,
While the sands o' life shall run.

4.
And fare thee weel, my only luve!
And fare thee weel a while!
And I will come again, my luve,
Tho' it were ten thousand mile!

1.
O, my love is like a red, red rose,
That's newly sprung in June.
O, my love is like the melody,
That's sweetly played in tune.

2.
As fair art thou, my bonnie lass,
So deep in love am I,
And I will love thee still, my dear,
Till all the seas go dry.

3.
Till all the seas go dry, my dear,
And the rocks melt with the sun!
O I will love thee still, my dear,
While the sands of life shall run.

4.
And fare thee well, my only love!
And fare thee well a while!
And I will come again, my love,
Though it were ten thousand mile!

The silver tassie (1793)

According to Burns himself, the first four lines of this song are 'old' or traditional: the rest, his. In very few words, Burns conjures up an atmosphere of wild weather and heroic adventure.

All the emotional conflict of parting is in this song. The descriptions of war are seductive: trumpets sounding, banners flying, spears glittering. The soldier must be anxious to be participating in such a glorious martial display – and yet, he wants to delay his departure, but only because he does not want to leave his 'bonnie Mary'.

1.
Go, fetch to me a pint o' wine,
And fill it in a silver tassie;
That I may drink before I go,
A service to my bonnie lassie;
The boat rocks at the pier o' Leith,
Fu' loud the wind blaws frae the Ferry,
The ship rides by the Berwick-Law,
And I maun leave my bonie Mary.

2.
The trumpets sound, the banners fly,
The glittering spears are ranked ready,
The shouts o' war are heard afar,
The battle closes deep and bloody.
It's not the roar o' sea or shore,
Wad mak me langer wish to tarry;
Nor shouts o' war that's heard afar –
It's leaving thee, my bonie Mary!

1.
Go, fetch to me a pint of wine,
And fill it in a silver goblet
That I may drink before I go
A service to my bonnie lass;
The boat rocks at the pier o' Leith,
Full loud the wind blows from the Ferry
The ship rides by the Berwick-Law[1],
And I must leave my bonnie Mary.

2.
The trumpets sound, the banners fly,
The glittering spears are ranked ready,
The shouts of war are heard afar,
The battle closes deep and bloody.
It's not the roar of sea or shore
Would make me longer wish to tarry
Nor shouts of war that's heard afar –
It's leaving thee, my bonnie Mary!

[1] A conical hill that overlooks North Berwick on the Firth of Forth.

Bruce's Address to his army at Bannockburn
(Scots wha hae) (1793)

Burns visited Bannockburn on his second trip to the Highlands in August 1787. In the Battle of Bannockburn, in 1314, the Scots, led by Robert the Bruce, defeated Edward II's English army in the struggle for independence. Burns's song is the imagined address that Bruce made to the Scottish army before the battle. Stark choices are offered: a bloody death or victory, cowardly slavery or freedom, their sons in chains or their own sacrifice – doing or dying.

Although this is the most stirring of Scottish patriotic songs, it is astonishing how few Scots words are to be found in it. This is almost full-blown English rhetoric that is used to express Scotland's nationalism and urge freedom from England.

In 1793, he wrote to his friend, George Thomson, a collector and publisher of music:

'You know that my pretensions to musical taste, are merely a few of Nature's instincts, untaught and untutored by Art. For this reason, many musical compositions, particularly where much of the merit lies in Counterpoint, however they may transport and ravish the ears of you Connoisseurs, affect my simple lug no otherwise than merely as melodious Din. On the other hand, by way of amends I am delighted with many little melodies which the learned Musician despises as silly and insipid. I do not know whether the old air, 'Hey tutti tatie', may rank among its number; but well I know that with Fraser's Hautboy, it has often filled my eyes with tears. There is a tradition, which I have met with in many places of Scotland, that it was Robert Bruce's March at the battle of Bannockburn. This thought, in my yesternight's evening walk warmed me to a pitch of enthusiasm on the theme of Liberty and Independence which I threw into a kind of Scots Ode, fitted to the Air, that one might suppose to be the gallant ROYAL SCOT'S address to his heroic followers on that eventful morning.'

He added a postscript, telling Thomson that he had shown the air to Pietro Urbani, a rival publisher, who had begged him *'to make soft verses for it.'* Thankfully, Burns's relationship with Urbani ended very soon after!

For some people, this would be the choice of a national anthem for Scotland; others, like Urbani, feel its sentiments are a little too robust. For the latter, it is worth pointing out one of the original verses of the 'British' national anthem:

> Lord grant that Marshal Wade
> May by thy mighty aid
> Victory bring.
> May he sedition hush,
> And like a torrent rush,
> Rebellious Scots to crush.
> God save the Queen!

Scots, wha hae wi' Wallace bled,
Scots, wham Bruce has aften led,
Welcome to your gory bed
Or to victorie!
Now's the day, and now's the hour:
See the front o' battle lour,
See approach proud Edward's power –
Chains and slaverie!

Wha will be a traitor knave?
Wha will fill a coward's grave?
Wha sae base as be a slave? –
Let him turn, and flee!
Wha for Scotland's King and Law
Freedom's sword will strongly draw,
Freeman stand or freeman fa',
Let him follow me!

By oppression's woes and pains,
By your sons in servile chains,
We will drain our dearest veins,
But they shall be free!
Lay the proud usurpers low!
Tyrants fall in every foe!
Liberty's in every blow! –
Let us do or die!

Scots, who have with Wallace bled,
Scots, whom Bruce has often led,
Welcome to your gory bed
Or to victory!
Now's the day, and now's the hour:
See the front of battle loom,
See approach proud Edward's power –
Chains and slavery!

Who will be a traitor knave?
Who will fill a coward's grave?
Who so base as be a slave? –
Let him turn, and flee!
Who for Scotland's King and Law
Freedom's sword will strongly draw,
Freeman stand or freeman fall,
Let him follow me!

By oppression's woes and pains,
By your sons in servile chains,
We will drain our dearest veins
But they shall be free!
Lay the proud usurpers low!
Tyrants fall in every foe!
Liberty's in every blow! –
Let us do or die!

Ca' The Yowes To The Knowes (1796)

This is the second version of the song, as Burns claimed to be dissatisfied with the original. It is a gentle pastoral poem, haunting in its summer evening synthesis of bird song, sheep folds, moonlight, lapping waters, ruins and, of course, the meeting of lovers.

Chorus
Ca' the yowes to the knowes,
Ca' them where the heather grows,
Ca' them where the burnie rowes,
My bonie dearie.

Hark, the mavis e'ening sang
Sounding Clouden's woods amang
Then a-faulding let us gang.
My bonie dearie.

Chorus

We'll gae down by Clouden side,
Thro the hazels, spreading wide
O'er the waves that sweetly glide
To the moon sae clearly.

Chorus

Yonder Clouden's silent towers
Where, at moonshine's midnight hours,
O'er the dewy bending flowers
Fairies dance sae cheery.

Chorus

Ghaist nor bogle shalt thou fear –
Thou'rt to Love and Heav'n sae dear
Nocht of ill may come thee near,
My bonie dearie.

Chorus

Chorus
Call the ewes to the hills,
Call them where the heather grows,
Call them where the streamlet runs,
My bonnie dearie.

Hark, the thrush's evening song
Sounding Clouden's[1] woods among
Then let us go to put the sheep in the folds
My bonnie dearie.

Chorus

We'll go down by Clouden side,
Through the hazels, spreading wide
Over the waves that sweetly glide
To the moon so clearly.

Chorus

Yonder Clouden's silent towers
Where, at moonshine's midnight hours,
Over the dewy bending flowers
Fairies dance so cheerfully.

Chorus

Ghost nor phantom shalt thou fear –
Thou art to Love and Heaven so dear
No ill will come thee near,
My bonnie dearie.

Chorus

[1] Cluden Water is a small tributary to the River Nith in Dumfriesshire.

The Tree of Liberty (1794)

This is a celebratory declaration of support for the French Revolution and its triple maxim of 'Liberty, Equality, Fraternity'. Ten years before, Burns had also written the *Ballad on the American War*, in support of the American War of Independence. As no original manuscript for *The Tree of Liberty* has ever been found, there are some critics who argue that Burns did not write it: others believe firmly that he did!

In 1789, the French had turned against their royal family and set up their own government. Many Scots, including Burns, sympathised with and supported the French. The 'Auld Alliance' with France was stronger than the 'forced marriage' with England of 1707. George III was extremely unpopular and there was widespread poverty and unemployment as the landowners cleared people from the land to carry out the agricultural 'Improvements' of the Lowland and Highland Clearances.

The government feared that the success of the French Revolution would lead to similar events in Britain. Eventually, Britain declared war on France in 1793 and issued warnings that persons who sympathised with the French would be sentenced without trial. Had this poem been published at the time, Burns would no doubt have been sentenced to hanging, slavery in Botany Bay or a long term of imprisonment – but the poem was not published until 1838.

Burns begins by describing the tree of liberty, its roots, growth and fruit in revolutionary France. Verse 8 shifts to Britain, which boasts of its English oak and Scots pine. However, between London and the Tweed, i.e. England, no tree of liberty can be found. Is Burns suggesting that England is the only nation where liberty can not flourish? Without it, life is just endless misery for the workers who toil to 'feed the titled knave' – and with Scotland tied politically to England by the 1707 Union of the Parliaments, Burns expresses the hope, in the last verse, that 'auld England' will plant the tree and 'give us liberty'. Verse 10 cleverly introduces the three revolutionary ideals of liberty, equality and fraternity, reinforced by a Biblical reference from Isaiah which defines the peace that these ideals would bring to the world:

They will beat their swords into plowshares and their spears into pruning hook: nation shall not lift up sword against nation, nor shall they learn war anymore.

Isaiah ch 2, v 4

1.

Heard ye o' the Tree o' France,
I watna what's the name o't;
Around it a' the patriots dance,
Weel Europe kens the fame o't.
It stands where ance the Bastile stood,
A prison built by kings, man,
When Superstition's hellish brood
Kept France in leading-strings, man.

1.

Have you heard of the Tree of France?
I don't know what its name is
Around it all the patriots dance,
Europe well knows how famous it is.
It stands where once the Bastile stood,
A prison built by kings, man,
When Superstition's hellish brood
Kept France in leading-strings, man.

2.

Upo' this tree there grows sic fruit,
Its virtues a' can tell, man:
It raises man aboon the brute,
It mak's him ken himsel', man.
Gif ance the peasant taste a bit,
He's greater than a lord, man,
And wi' the beggar shares a mite
O' a' he can afford, man.

3.

This fruit is worth a' Afric's wealth,
To comfort us 'twas sent, man:
To gie the sweetest blush o' health,
And mak us a' content, man.
It clears the een, it cheers the heart,
Mak's high and low guid friends, man;
And he wha acts the traitor's part,
It to perdition sends, man.

4.

My blessings ay attend the chiel
Wha pitied Gallia's slaves, man,
And staw a branch, spite o' the Deil,
Frae 'yont the western waves, man.
Fair Virtue water'd it wi' care,
And now she sees wi' pride, man,
How weel it buds and blossoms there,
Its branches spreading wide, man.

5.

But vicious folk ay hate to see
The works o' Virtue thrive, man.
The courtly vermin's bann'd the tree,
And grat to see it thrive, man;
King Louis thought to cut it down,
When it was unco sma', man;
For this the watchman crack'd his crown,
Cut aff his head and a', man.

6.

A wicked crew syne, on a time,
Did tak' a solemn aith, man,
It ne'er should flourish to its prime,
I wat they pledg'd their faith, man.
Awa they gaed wi' mock parade,
Like beagles hunting game, man,

2.

Upon this tree there grows such fruit,
Its virtues all can tell, man:
It raises man above the brute,
It makes him know himself, man.
If once the peasant tastes a bit,
He's greater than a lord, man,
And with the beggar shares a mite
Of all he can afford, man.

3.

This fruit is worth all Africa's wealth
To comfort us it was sent, man:
To give the sweetest blush of health,
And make us all content, man.
It clears the eyes, it cheers the heart,
Makes high and low good friends, man;
And he who acts the traitor's part,
It to perdition sends, man.

4.

My blessings always attend the man
Who pitied France's slaves, man
And stole a branch, despite the Devil
From beyond the western waves, man.
Fair Virtue watered it with care,
And now she sees with pride, man,
How well it buds and blossoms there,
Its branches spreading wide, man.

5.

But vicious folk always hate to see
The works of Virtue thrive, man.
The courtly vermin's banned the tree,
And wept to see it thrive, man;
King Louis thought to cut it down,
When it was very small, man;
For this the watchman cracked his crown,
Cut off his head and all, man.

6.

A wicked crew then, on a time,
Did take a solemn oath, man
It never should flourish to its prime,
I know they pledg'd their faith, man.
Away they went with mock parade
Like beagles hunting game, man,

But soon grew weary o' the trade,
And wish'd they'd been at hame, man.

7.

Fair Freedom, standing by the tree,
Her sons did loudly ca', man:
She sang a sang o' Liberty,
Which pleas'd them ane and a', man.
By her inspir'd, the new-born race
Soon drew the avenging steel, man:
The hirelings ran – her foes gied chase,
And bang'd the despot weel, man.

8.

Let Britain boast her hardy oak,
Her poplar, and her pine, man.
Auld Britain ance could crack her joke,
And o'er her neighbours shine, man.
But seek the forest round and round,
And soon 'twill be agreed, man,
That sic a tree can not be found,
'Twixt London and the Tweed, man.

9.

Without this tree, alake, this life
Is but a vale o' woes, man,
A scene o' sorrow mix'd wi' strife,
Nae real joys we know, man.
We labour soon, we labour late,
To feed the titled knave, man;
And a' the comfort we're to get
Is that ayont the grave, man.

10.

Wi' plenty o' sic trees, I trow,
The warld would live in peace, man;
The sword would help to mak' a plough,
The din o' war wad cease, man.
Like brethren in a common cause,
We'd on each other smile, man;
And equal rights and equal laws
Wad gladden every isle, man.

11.

Wae worth the loon wha wadna eat
Sic halesome, dainty cheer, man;
I'd gie the shoon frae aff my feet,

But soon grew weary of the trade
And wished they'd been at home, man.

7.

Fair Freedom, standing by the tree,
Her sons did loudly call, man.
She sang a song of Liberty,
Which pleased them one and all, man.
By her inspired, the new-born race
Soon drew the avenging steel, man.
The hirelings ran – her foes gave chase,
And banged the despot well, man.

8.

Let Britain boast her hardy oak,
Her poplar, and her pine, man.
Old Britain once could crack her joke
And over her neighbours shine, man.
But seek the forest round and round,
And soon it will be agreed, man,
That such a tree can not be found
Between London and the Tweed, man.

9.

Without this tree, alas, this life
Is but a vale of woes, man,
A scene of sorrow mixed with strife
No real joys we know, man.
We labour soon, we labour late,
To feed the titled knave, man,
And all the comfort we're to get
Is that beyond the grave, man.

10.

With plenty of such trees, I believe
The world would live in peace, man.
The sword would help to make a plough,
The din of war would cease, man.
Like brethren in a common cause,
We'd on each other smile, man;
And equal rights and equal laws
Would gladden every isle, man.

11.

A curse upon the fellow who would not eat
Such wholesome, dainty cheer, man
I'd give the shoes from off my feet

To taste the fruit o't here, man.
Syne let us pray, Auld England may
Sure plant this far-famed tree, man;
And blythe we'll sing, and herald the day
That gives us liberty, man.

To taste the fruit of it here, man.
Then let us pray, Old England may
Sure plant this far-famed tree, man;
And blythe we'll sing, and herald the day
That gives us liberty, man.

Does Haughty Gaul invasion threat? (1795)

Burns is now **British**, waving a threatening Union Jack at the French! With the threat of Napoleon preparing to invade Britain, the British Parliament passed an act in 1794, calling upon 'gentlemen of weight and property' to set up local defence plans and establish military companies. In response to this, Burns, by virtue of his government post as an excise officer, was one of the founding members of The Dumfries Volunteers in 1795.

This song was published in many newspapers in the area to encourage recruitment and even became popular in England. However, even while Burns is prepared to sing '*God save the King*', his overriding loyalty is to the people.

1.
Does haughty Gaul invasion threat?
Then let the loons beware, Sir!
There's wooden walls upon our seas
And volunteers on shore, Sir!
The Nith shall run to Corsincon,
And Criffel sink in Solway,
Ere we permit a foreign foe
On British ground to rally!

2.
O, let us not, like snarling tykes,
In wrangling be divided,
Till, slap! come in a unco loun,
And wi' a rung decide it!
Be Britain still to Britain true,
Amang oursels united!
For never but by British hands
Maun British wrangs be righted!

3.
The kettle o' the Kirk and State,
Perhaps a clout may fail in't;
But Deil a foreign tinkler loon
Shall ever ca' a nail in't!
Our father's blude the kettle bought,
And wha wad dare to spoil it,
By Heav'ns! the sacrilegious dog
Shall fuel be to boil it!

4.
The wretch that would a tyrant own,
And the wretch, his true-sworn brother,
Who would set the mob above the throne,

1.
Does haughty Gaul threaten invasion?
Then let the fools beware, Sir!
There's wooden walls upon our seas
And volunteers on shore, Sir!
The Nith shall run to Corsincon[1],
And Criffel[2] sink in Solway,
Ere we permit a foreign foe
On British ground to rally!

2.
O, let us not, like snarling dogs,
In wrangling be divided
Till wham! comes in an uncouth ruffian
And with a cudgel decides it!
Be Britain still to Britain true,
Among ourselves united!
For never but by British hands
Must British wrongs be righted!

3.
The kettle of the Church and State,
Perhaps a patch may fail in it;
But no foreign tinker riff-raff
Shall ever hammer a nail in it!
Our father's blood the kettle bought,
And who would dare to spoil it
By Heavens! the sacrilegious dog
Shall fuel be to boil it!

4.
The wretch that would a tyrant own,
And the wretch, his true-sworn brother,
Who would set the mob above the throne,

---

[1] Hill in New Cumnock, Ayrshire; i.e. the Nith will flow backwards and uphill.
[2] A mountain about five miles north of the Solway Firth.

May they be damned together!
Who will not sing God save the King
Shall hang as high as the steeple;
But while we sing God save the King
We'll ne'er forget the People!

May they be damned together!
Who will not sing God save the King
Shall hang as high as the steeple;
But while we sing God save the King
We'll never forget the People!

Is there for honest poverty?
(A man's a man for a' that) (1795)

Now we have Burns the International Socialist. Although the yearning for social equality appears in so much of Burns's work, this song is the best known. Although it is intensely Scottish, it embraces the whole world.

Rank is merely the worthless die used to denote how much the gold coin is worth: mankind is the gold. Nor do fine silks or decorations make a man; but honesty makes him a king – and an honest man cannot be 'created' in the way a king can dub a knight.

1.
Is there for honest poverty
That hings his head, an' a' that?
The coward slave, we pass him by –
We dare be poor for a' that!
For a' that, an' a' that,
Our toils obscure, an' a' that,
The rank is but the guinea's stamp,
The man's the gowd for a' that.

2.
What though on hamely fare we dine,
Wear hoddin grey, an' a' that?
Gie fools their silks, and knaves their wine –
A man's a man for a' that.
For a' that, an' a' that,
Their tinsel show, an' a' that,
The honest man, tho e'er sae poor,
Is king o' men for a' that.

3.
Ye see yon birkie ca'd 'a lord,'
Wha struts, an' stares, an' a' that?
Tho' hundreds worship at his word,
He's but a cuif for a' that.
For a' that, an' a' that,
His ribband, star, an' a' that,
The man o' independent mind,
He looks an' laughs at a' that.

4.
A prince can mak a belted knight,
A marquis, duke, an' a' that!
But an honest man's aboon his might –
Guid faith, he mauna fa' that!

1.
Is there for honest poverty
Who hangs his head and all that?
The coward slave, we pass him by
We dare be poor for all that!
For all that, and all that,
Our toils obscure, and all that,
The rank is but the guinea's stamp,
The man's the gold for all that.

2.
What though on homely fare we dine,
Wear course woollen cloth and all that?
Give fools their silks, and knaves their wine
A man's a man for all that.
For all that, and all that,
Their tinsel show, and all that,
The honest man, though ever so poor,
Is king of men for all that.

3.
You see that conceited fellow called a lord?
Who struts and stares and all that
Though hundreds worship at his word,
He's but a fool for all that!
For all that, and all that,
His ornamental ribbon, star, and all that
The man of independent mind,
He looks and laughs at all that.

4.
A prince can make a belted knight,
A marquis, duke, and all that!
But an honest man's beyond his power –
Good faith, he can't lay claim to that!

For a' that, an' a' that,
Their dignities, an' a' that,
The pith o' sense an' pride o' worth
Are higher rank than a' that.

5.
Then let us pray that come it may
(As come it will for a' that)
That Sense and Worth o'er a' the earth
Shall bear the gree an' a' that!
For a' that, an' a' that,
It's comin yet for a' that,
That man to man the world o'er
Shall brithers be for a' that.

For all that, and all that,
Their dignities, and all that
The pith of sense and pride of worth
Are higher rank than all that.

5.
Then let us pray that come it may
(As come it will for all that)
That Sense and Worth over all the earth
Shall have pre-eminence and all that
For all that, and all that,
It's coming yet for all that
That man to man the world over
Shall brothers be for all that.

The Selkirk Grace (1795)

The Selkirk Grace is a version of the older Covenanter's Grace. After Burns delivered it when he visited the Earl of Selkirk in 1794 at St Mary's Isle, the Selkirk estate in Kirkcudbright, it came to be known as 'The Selkirk Grace'.

Some hae meat and canna eat,	Some have meat and cannot eat
And some wad eat that want it;	And some would eat that do not have it,
But we hae meat and we can eat,	But we have meat and we can eat
And sae the Lord be thankit.	And so the Lord be thanked.

O wert thou in the Cauld blast (1796)

This must surely be one of the most poignant songs ever written, a mixture of overwhelming gratitude and heart-scalding emotion. It was written for Jessie Lewars who nursed Burns in his final illness and you can almost sense his physical weakness, as he attempts to project an image of strength and protectiveness. The very personal emotions and imagery are the prelude to the Romantic poetry of the 19th century.

From April 1796 until his death on 21st July, Burns was rarely able to leave his room. As Jean Armour was heavily pregnant, Jessie's gentle help was invaluable.

Jessie, a close friend of the Burns family, was the sister of John Lewars, a fellow exciseman.

1.	1.
O, wert thou in the cauld blast	O, wert thou in the cold blast
On yonder lea, on yonder lea,	On yonder lea, on yonder lea,
My plaidie to the angry airt,	My plaid to the angry direction [of the wind]
I'd shelter thee, I'd shelter thee.	I'd shelter thee, I'd shelter thee.
Or did Misfortune's bitter storms	Or did Misfortune's bitter storms
Around thee blaw, around thee blaw,	Around thee blow, around thee blow
Thy bield should be my bosom,	Your shelter would be my bosom
To share it a', to share it a'.	To share it all, to share it all.
2.	2.
Or were I in the wildest waste,	Or were I in the wildest waste,
Sae black and bare, sae black and bare,	So black and bare, so black and bare,
The desert were a Paradise,	The desert would be a Paradise,
If thou wert there, if thou wert there.	If thou wert there, if thou wert there.
Or were I monarch of the globe,	Or were I monarch of the globe,
Wi' thee to reign, wi' thee to reign,	With thee to reign, with thee to reign,
The brightest jewel in my crown	The brightest jewel in my crown
Wad be my queen, wad be my queen.	Would be my queen, would be my queen.

Index

Index of First Lines

Index of First Lines (contd.)

Address to the Deil (1786)

The Devil makes frequent appearances in Scottish literature: he pops up every now and then in many of Burns's poems. In this poem, Burns, as usual, uses comic reduction to cut him down to size. He calls him names with diminutives, like 'Clootie' and 'Hangie', even as he describes his power. Note too how he addresses him, sometimes familiarly and sometimes, as in stanza 3, with pseudo-religious tone. And would you describe Satan's doings as evil or mischief.

This original manuscript is reproduced courtesy of Irvine Burns Club.

Great is thy pow'r, an' great thy fame;
Far kend, an' noted is thy name;
An' tho' yon lowan heugh's thy hame,
                    Thou travels far;
An' faith thou's neither lag nor lame,
                    Nor blate nor scaur.

Whyles, ranging like a roaring lion,
For prey, a' holes an' corners tryin;
Whyles, on the strong-wing'd Tempest flyin,
                    Tirlan the kirks;
Whyles, in the human bosom pryin,
                    Unseen thou lurks.

I've heard my rev'rend Graunie say,
In lanely glens ye like to stray;
Or where auld, ruin'd castles, gray,
                    Nod to the moon,
Ye fright the nightly wand'rer's way,
                    Wi' eldritch croon.

When twilight did my Graunie summon,
To say her pray'rs, douse, honest woman,
Aft 'yont the dyke she's heard you bumman,
                    Wi' eerie drone;
Or, rustling, thro' the boortries coman,
                    Wi' heavy groan.

Ae dreary, windy, winter night,
The stars shot down wi' sklentan light,
Wi' you, mysel, I gat a fright,
                    Ayont the lough;
Ye, like a rash-buss, stood in sight,
                    Wi' waving sugh.

The cudgel in my nieve did shake,
Each bristl'd hair stood like a stake,
When wi' an eldritch, stoor quaick, quaick,
                    Amang the springs,
Awa ye squatter'd like a drake,
                    On whistling wings.

Let Warlocks grim, an' wither'd Hags,
Tell how wi' you, on ragweed nags,

O thro' them the moors an' dozzy crags,
                        Wi' wicked speed;
An' in kirk-yards renew their leagues,
                        Owre howckit dead.

Thence, countra wives, wi' toil an' pain,
May plunge an' plunge the kirn in vain;
For Och! the yellow treasure's taen,
                        By witching skill;
An' dawtet, twal-pint hawkie's gane
                        As yell's the Bill.

Thence, mystic knots mak great abuse,
On Young-guidmen, fond, keen an' crouse;
When the best wark-lum i' the house,
                        By cantraip wit,
Is instant made no worth a louse,
                        Just at the bit.

O When thowes dissolve the snawy hoord,
An' float the jinglan icy boord,
Then, Water-kelpies haunt the foord,
                        By your direction;
An' nighted Travellers are allur'd
                        To their destruction.

An' aft your moss-traversing Spunkies
Decoy the wight that late an' drunk is:
The bleezan, curst, mischievous monkies
                        Delude his eyes,
Till in some miry slough he sunk is,
                        Ne'er mair to rise.

When mason's mystic word an' grip,
In storms an' tempests raise you up,
Some cock, or cat, your rage maun stop,
                        Or, strange to tell!
O The youngest Brother ye wad whip
                        Aff straught to H—ll.

Lang syne in eden's bonie yard,
When youthfu' lovers first were pair'd,
An' all the Soul of Love they shar'd,
                        The raptur'd hour,
Sweet on the fragrant, flowry sward
                        In shady bow'r.

O Then you, ye auld, snick-drawing dog!
Ye cam to Paradise incog,

An' play'd on man a cursed brogue,   (Black be your fa'!)

An' gied the infant warld a shog,   'Maist ruin'd a'.

D'ye mind that day, when in a bizz,

Wi' reeket duds, an' reestet gizz,

Ye did present your smoutie phiz,   'Mang better folk,

An' skulented on the man of Uz?   Your spitefu' joke?

An' how ye gat him i' your thrall,

An' brak him out o' house an' hal',

While scabs an' botches did him gall,   Wi' bitter claw,

An' lows'd his ill-tongu'd, wicked Scawl   Was warst ava?

But a' your doings to rehearse,

Your wily snares an' fechtin fierce,

Sin' that day michael did you pierce,   Down to this time,

Wad ding a Lallan tongue, or Erse,   In Prose or Rhyme.

An' now, auld Cloots, I ken ye're thinkan,

A certain Bardie's rantin, drinkin,

Some luckless hour will send him linkan,   To your black pit;

But faith! he'll turn a corner jinkan,   An' cheat you yet.

But fare you weel, auld Nickie-ben!

O wad ye tak a thought an' men'!

Ye aiblins might — I dinna ken —   Still hae a stake —

I'm wae to think up' yon den,   Ev'n for your sake!

* Vide Milton, Book 6.th